In Search of This & That

A proto-archaeological moment from Colonial Williamsburg's prize-winning film Doorway To The Past *written and directed by the author.*

In Search of This & That

TALES FROM AN ARCHAEOLOGIST'S QUEST

Selected essays from the Colonial Williamsburg journal

By Ivor Noël Hume

The Colonial Williamsburg Foundation
Williamsburg, Virginia

Library of Congress Cataloging-in-Publication Data

Noël Hume, Ivor.
    In search of this and that / by Ivor Noël Hume.
      p. cm.
    Originally appeared in *Colonial Williamsburg,*
the journal of the Colonial Williamsburg Foundation.
Some essays updated or rev.
  ISBN 0-87935-164-0
    1. Tidewater (Va. : Region)—Antiquities. 2. Excavations
(Archaeology)—Virginia—Tidewater (Region)
3. Tidewater (Va. : Region)—History. 4. Archaeology
and history—Virginia—Tidewater (Region). 5. British—Virginia—
Tidewater (Region)—Antiquities. 6. Virginia—Antiquities.
7. British—Virginia—Antiquities. I. Colonial Williamsburg
Foundation. II. Title.
F232.T54N63   1996
975.5'101—dc20   96-21124
                                            CIP

Cover photograph courtesy of William K. Geiger

Printed in Hong Kong

Contents

Were it not for the encouragement of *Colonial Williamsburg* reader Gertrude Daversa, there would be no book.

Foreword

Ivor Noël Hume is more than an archaeologist.

He is historian, researcher and, more importantly, a sleuth. And we are talking about "sleuthing" in the finest detective story fashion. What he has done in the past and the amount of time and effort devoted to his investigative process is amazing, with the results being not only historic, but also sensational. They are of what good stories are made, as these essays will testify.

The stories were prepared for and first appeared in the marvelous quarterly journal *Colonial Williamsburg*. This may not be the first time you have seen them, but it is the first time they have been put together in a comprehensive form that sets us out on an intriguing archaeological adventure.

Through these writings one can easily see the eclectic Noël Hume, whose archaeological knowledge is as broad and as far-ranging as the colonial era he so enjoys investigating.

Not everyone has a naturally inquisitive nature, and it takes some amount of curiosity for anyone to pursue the profession of archaeology. There are many good archaeologists, but it takes a Noël Hume to take his craft to a higher level of professionalism. This is where we find the "professional" archaeological sleuth.

For example, during an early phase of an excavation near Williamsburg, Noël found a little gold point which he surmised was from an article of clothing. Not satisfied with just checking published works on costumes of the 17th century, he immediately set out to put this small inch and a quarter discovery into context. The search was not easy; it took time, effort, and talent, of which he has all three. The result was the location of an identical gold point on the garter in the portrait of Sir Henry Payton, in the collection of Sir Hereward Wake, at Courteenhall in Northampton-shire, England. The portrait was dated 1623, exactly the period for the tiny artifact discovered at Wolstenholme Towne, an early Virginia outpost begun in the second decade of the 17th century.

If he needed to put himself on the archaeological map, Noël succeeded with Wolstenholme Towne at what is now Carter's Grove, the great Burwell plantation on the shore of the James River. His lengthy and exhaustive study at Martin's Hundred, one of the first settlements after Jamestown, richly contributed to our expanding knowledge of Virginia's 17th-century life and the early settlement years of this nation.

Ivor Noël Hume is an Englishman come Virginian in the best form. He was born in 1927 in the Chelsea borough of London and received his schooling and early archaeological experience in Great Britain. He later traveled to the Colonies spending the last 40 years in Virginia, polishing his archaeological craft, setting new challenges for himself and creating a reputation that is now legendary.

There is a theatrical flair in much of his work, quite unusual for an archaeologist. You can see it in the lavishly illustrated slide presentations he often made at the annual Williamsburg Antiques Forum, in his writings, and in his life. That flare has not occurred by happenstance. In his youth, Noël set his sights on the stage; he longed to be a playwright. After a short stint in the British army late in World War II he spent four lean years (1945–1949) first as assistant stage manager for a London theater company and later stage director for several provincial theaters.

He then literally walked into archaeology. With time on his hands, he spent mornings learning to be a dramatist in London's Old Bailey, which he called the "best free show in town," and afternoons strolling the banks of the Thames at low tide. On those promenades Noël went in search of antiquities that he had been told were to be found there.

He would take his finds to Adrian Oswald, the curator of London's Guildhall Museum, who helped him identify them. In the summer of 1949 Oswald offered him a job with the museum. Noël, however, felt one of his plays was on the verge of being produced and was reluctant to accept. But being down on his luck and financially strapped, he accepted Oswald's offer, but only as a temporary situation until his theatrical success came.

A few days later Oswald became ill and never returned to the museum. Noël stayed on, to head the Guildhall's salvage archaeology efforts. Without any formal education in archaeology, he knew he had to specialize to gain any attention. Old wine bottles became Noël's focus specialty and he drove himself to read and understand everything he could about the evolution of wine bottles, and of countless other artifacts from the 17th century.

The Guildhall Museum had been closed during the war and its space taken by the city library. In those postwar days, it waited for the city fathers to recognize its worth. Brandishing his flair for the theatrical, Noël would contact a reporter friend at the BBC (British Broadcasting Corporation) whenever he made a new discovery. Thus, attention to the museum began to mount and publications like the London *Times* began to regularly report on its archaeological efforts.

In 1950 the National Park Service's distinguished archaeologist J. C. Harrington went to London searching for a 17th-century glass expert and Noël 's name was mentioned. The contact was made, and six years later Noël came to Colonial Williamsburg as a consultant. Invited to return to head an expanded archaeological unit, he moved to Virginia permanently in 1957 with his wife, Audrey, who since 1950 had been his assistant, colleague, and motivator—a role she continued to play until her death in 1993.

Noël's career at Colonial Williamsburg was lengthy, creative, and frequently exciting. He always made his discoveries known to news media, especially those persons who appeared to him to be interested in archaeology. In my days as a bureau chief/reporter with the Richmond *Times-Dispatch* newspaper, I got to know him and one afternoon was invited to dig with him in order to get a better understanding of and sharpen my awareness for the kind of work that was being done and to personally have a chance to relish the thrill of a find.

For Colonial Williamsburg he headed archaeological excavations at the Anthony Hay cabinet shop, Wetherburn's Tavern, the site of the Public Hospital of 1773, and a dozen others in the Historic Area, and eventually Wolstenholme Towne, where he and his crew uncovered much of the settlement, including a palisaded fort.

After his retirement in 1988, Noël continued consulting and headed a dig on Roanoke Island, North Carolina, in search of the long-lost fort of Sir Walter Ralegh's pre-Jamestown settlement, the one of "Lost Colony" fame. He also has pursued several other favorite projects, such as what did the original Jamestown settlement look like and where was its first fort.

Noël's writings have often ignited the passions and imaginations of people who previously had no interest whatsoever in archaeology. Some of his important works include *1775: Another Part of the Field, Here Lies Virginia,* the celebrated *Martin's Hundred,* and his most recent, *The Virginia Adventure: Roanoke to James Towne, an Archaeological and Historical Odyssey.*

In this collection of essays from *Colonial Williamsburg,* Noël Hume the sleuth is easily recognized in several of these tales. In his Roanoke Island dig, the quest for the Ralegh fort site turned into the finding of a metallurgist's furnace and associated scientific gear. "Salt-Glazed stoneware" described in an earlier dig proved to be fragments of rough-surfaced metallurgical crucibles and "Spanish majolica" proved to be English or Dutch ointment pots used by apothecaries, Noël explained.

"For Necessary Change" shows how the finding of various coins during excavations can help date a site, such as an Elizabethan silver half-groat (London 1590–1592) found at Jamestown. Noël also examines the backgrounds of other colonial coins that have been found elsewhere in Virginia and relates them to the historical events that took place there.

At the home site in Williamsburg of Martha Washington's famous father-in-law—John Custis—Noël found more than just the residue of bricks and mortar. Digs on the lot known as "Custis Square" revealed a well, which yielded "the finest hoard of historically important artifacts yet discovered in Williamsburg." Noël Hume, the detective, believes many of the items may have been tossed into the well by Martha Dandridge Custis herself when she cleaned out the house in 1757 after the death of her husband, Daniel Parke Custis.

In an earlier book, *All the Best Rubbish,* Noël wrote: "Both in archaeology and in antique collecting we are constantly groping into the unknown and more often than not we quickly find ourselves with nowhere to go." Now settle back, get ready for some exciting stories, and enjoy some good old-fashioned archaeological "sleuthing." The game is afoot.

—Wilford Kale

Kale wrote about Ivor Noël Hume's archaeological detective work for more than 20 years while working for the Richmond *Times-Dispatch.* He is now senior policy analyst for the Virginia Marine Resources Commission.

Preface

Archaeologists will argue over just about anything, but few debates are as persistent—and as pointless—as deciding whether archaeology is an art or a science. However, there can be no denying that its successes are more often the product of luck than of brilliance. I recall doing rescue work at the church of St. Olave's Hart Street—Samuel Pepys's church in London—and waiting impatiently while construction workers dug in the refuse cistern that I was eager to investigate. When the last laborer climbed out and quit for lunch, he said "If you find any gold, mate, it's mine."

I laughed and jumped down into the pit. "You mean, like this?" I asked, holding up a gold guinea of George I that had lain glittering at my feet. That doesn't happen very often. In fact I have only found two gold coins in 45 years as a professional archaeologist. At the same time, however, there have been surprises every step of the way.

You never know what you are going to find until you dig, and only then does one's next research project take shape. These chapters, which first appeared as articles in *Colonial Williamsburg*, demonstrate far better than can any summarizing words, how the archaeology leads the researcher and not the other way round.

Digging at the site of Williamsburg's colonial Public Hospital for the Insane which one hoped would reveal clues to the lives of inmates housed there when the building was first occupied, instead told us only about the hospital's last days and moments before it burned in 1885. Consequently, we spent the best part of a year reconstructing iron bedsteads, repairing the bottles and pap boats from the pharmacy, and trying to read scorched and charred newspapers that were there at the time of the fire.

At the other end of the historical time line, attempts to learn more about the Park Service's reconstructed earthwork on Roanoke Island in modern North Carolina, resulted in questioning its authenticity and finding the site of the first English colonial scientific research center in the New World. For months thereafter we focused on broken crucibles and tiny scraps of copper, slowly learning what mineral assaying was all about.

Sometimes the research would be fired by a single excavated object. What is it? How was it made? Who used it? These were questions often asked of the many weapon parts found in excavations at Carter's Grove and which dated from the plantation's Martin's Hundred era in the 1620s. That thinking prompted my late wife, Audrey, to spot an early pistol on a horologist's stall in England, which in turn led us to finding out about British military efforts in Tangier in the late 17th century.

Then there were the mermaids! Efforts to confirm Josiah Wedgwood's statement that he sent his best wares to the Caribbean and only the second rate to the continental colonies led us into several vacations exploring abandoned fort and home sites in Jamaica, St. Lucia, Antigua, and elsewhere. Those prompted a London dealer to invest in a transatlantic phone call offering a powder horn engraved by a soldier stationed in Jamaica around 1820. Bought unseen, the horn proved to have been decorated by an amateur naturalist whose sighting had included a mermaid! The strange and unexpected research byways prompted by that engraving eventually became the subject of "The Mermaid Mystique."

A seemingly empty deed box that Audrey wanted to throw away would turn out to contain more "treasure" than we ever found in the ground. The discovery of an 18th-century mousetrap at Littlecote House set us to wondering how such traps really worked—transforming theory into the reality of flat mice.

Whether it was digging beside the majestic ruins of Virginia's Rosewell, searching the Thames foreshore at low tide, or photographing graffiti carved by vandalistic tourists (and early archaeologists) on the temples of Egypt and on Williamsburg's Courthouse of 1770, the underlying questions were always the same: When? How? and Why? Sometimes we would be asking questions of ourselves; questions like: Why in the world are we doing this? and Do we dig and study at great, and often public expense only to amuse ourselves? I have never found a lastingly, or universally satisfying answer to either question, but you will find them presented and puzzled over amid these pages. But of this I have no doubt. I have had a wonderful time in my quests for grails both large and small, and would gladly have done for nothing (if I could have afforded to) what I have been paid to do for these 40 and more years. I dare hope that you will share some of that enjoyment as you dig among the stories that are now before you.

—*Ivor Noël Hume*
June 1996

Acknowledgments

Over time an author owes much to many, often more than he can remember. Lest that here be the case, I apologize in advance for any inadvertent omissions. High among the not forgotten is Brian Fagan, who introduced me to the DeMille ruins; Graham Hood, who helped interpret the Custis paintings; Colonial Williamsburg silversmith James Curtis, who made the plaque that lies buried in Egypt; Judge Robert T. Armistead, who knew who sat where in the Courthouse of 1770; Thomas W. Wood, Nicholas Luccketti, Baxter Hardinge, and the Evesham Historical Society, who allowed their coins and tokens to be photographed; and Eric P. Newman, who knows all there is to know about "hogge" money; the National Geographic Society, which paid for our coffin research; Julian Litten of the Victoria and Albert Museum, who led the charge; the late Earl De La Warr, who opened his family vault at Withyham; the Reverend John Flory of Lydiard Tregoz and the Reverend M. Berry at Steane Park, who let us dig holes in their churches; and architect François Jones, who found what we could not; Raymond and Frances Orf, who graciously let strangers into their home at Bremo Recess; Anita Schorsh, to whom George Wither was no stranger; Dennis Severs and the Jarvises of Spitalfields; Ira Block, the best traveling companion and photographer any man could want; Robin Hildyard and all those curators both here and in England, who knew where mermaids dwelt; Richard Schlecht, whose inspired pencil made Roanoke real; the ever-helpful Elizabeth Kostelny at the APVA; the Cliffe Bonfire Society of Lewes, U. K., and Patricia and Al Fanger of Houston, Texas, who made the connection; Louis Caywood and John Cotter, whose memories of Green Spring were longer and better than mine; photographer William K. Geiger, who can make a ruin look great in any weather; Colonel Cecil Wray Page, Jr., whose knowledge of Gloucester County is unrivaled; and George Whiting and his wonderful Rosewell Irregulars, who find the joy in archaeology that disdainful professionals pretend not to understand.

Photographer Dave Doody brought sparkle to the dullest subjects, while the creativity of editor Wayne Barrett and his assistants, first Sondra Rose and then Brenda DePaula, gave the articles and now the book their distinctive style. To all my abiding thanks; but none more so than to my friends Wilford Kale and John Hamant, who gave this book its beginning and end, and my wife, Carol, who convinced me that the middle bits weren't too bad.

"Happiness," insisted archaeological curator Audrey Noël Hume, "is finding all the pieces."

Writings on the Archaeological Wall
From Babylon to Virginia and the Ten Commandments

NABONIDUS is not a name regularly bandied about at the breakfast table—which is hardly surprising. He died in B.C. 539. But he earned his place in history as the last king of Babylon and reputedly the first archaeologist. So obsessed was Nabonidus with digging up and reconstructing lost Babylonian buildings that he failed to recognize the Persian menace at his door.

Father of the Biblically better remembered Belshazzar, Nabonidus's greatest archaeological achievement was his uncovering the remains of the great temple of Shimash at Sippar, where his workmen unearthed a foundation stone that identified the building as having been erected 3,200 years earlier. Thus, by using the inscribed stone to date the temple he employed written history to provide the information and so became a historical rather than a prehistorical archaeologist.

The difference may not loom large in the lay mind, but among archaeologists the division is of almost gulflike proportions. As the name suggests, prehistorians focus on places and cultures for which no written records exist to prove them wrong, whereas historical archaeologists are those who add an artifact-related dimension to time's written legacy—and whose mistakes can very easily be found out.

With that established: back to Nabonidus. Unlike today's historical archaeologists, his interest (and that of generations of archaeologists since) focused not on the homes or workplaces of the long gone and nameless, but on the palaces and monuments of the remembered great and powerful.

Similarly, here in Williamsburg when in 1929 the first archaeological work began, it was directed not toward reconstructing privies or slave quarters but to rebuilding the Capitol and the Governor's Palace. It is true that the Raleigh Tavern was among the first buildings reconstructed, though not because it was a tavern, but because it provided a meeting room for famous patriots. The reasoning was simple enough: The public wanted to see the places where people they'd heard of did things they knew about.

Ninety-nine point nine percent of our predecessors did nothing memorable and so survive, if at all, only as names in a ledger's fading ink or carved on weathered stone in half forgotten graveyards. Unlike written history that can so easily brush past virtually everybody by lumping us together as civilizations, peoples, empires, or cultures, historical archaeology is person specific. Here is half a bowl that so-and-so dropped, or there the thimble that his mother or maybe his sister mislaid. But to make either bowl or thimble worthy of our—that is, the public's—attention, it is imperative that so-and-so had a name that rings a bell, even if only in a tangential way.

A cracked Chinese porcelain plate found at Monticello and used by Thomas Jefferson's slaves becomes fascinating by association—regardless of the fact that as an example of the porcelain painter's art it has little to commend it. To an archaeologist or a social historian, the realization that at Monticello even slaves ate off imported porcelain is of great interest. But for the

Sir Austen Henry Layard, *Ninevah and Its Remains*, I, 1849

A big one for the British Museum (opposite): Archaeological collecting in Mesopotamia in the 1840s. Left: Traces of another ancient city in the desert; the same site (below) photographed in 1923 while still inhabited by slaves and other Californians. Opposite: Six years later archaeology began in Williamsburg—where pick and shovel work at the Capitol could be hard on those with a Monday morning hangover.

Ivor Noël Hume

Peter Brosnan

museum-going public, take away the Jefferson connection, and interest goes with it.

For this reason, along with several others, post-prehistorical archaeology has centered on the memorable and the magnificent. For 150 years or more, beginning in the early 19th century, archaeologists have been sent around the world by museums and wealthy collectors to bring back the best—and to leave the rest behind. That shattered pots and rusted iron might have had more to say about the place where they were found than did the sculptures and golden bowls went either unrecognized or ignored. Museum curators trained as art historians had neither the desire nor the space to store ancient garbage that no visitors would admire.

Even in Williamsburg where American historical archaeology was practiced long before the discipline had a name, enough was eventually defined as enough. Although from the start the saving of excavated artifacts was selective and limited to those that were either architecturally related or eye-catching enough to be interesting, processing them became a major problem. Brought back from the sites in wooden crates, the old bottles and rusted hoes not only took up space, they were also becoming numbingly repetitious—at least in the eyes of those for whom a bottle bottom was just that. Consequently, in the early 1950s an edict went out from the architects' office that henceforth only three crates of artifacts should be saved from any one site, and in 1957 it was seriously suggested that the still-crated backlog should be quietly dumped into Lake Matoaka or into the York River. Needless to say, as I was the newly arrived beneficiary of that advice, I ignored it.

Previously, Williamsburg's archaeological program had been directed by the architects and supervised by a draftsman skilled in interpreting building remains. Consequently it made sense to pay more attention to bricks, hinges, locks, window glass, and suchlike architectural remains than to potsherds or meat bones. Nevertheless, the then-curator of Williamsburg's antique collections felt compelled to warn his staff to stay away from the archaeological laboratory and all its junk!

By the 1960s, attitudes toward the past were changing, not only in Williamsburg but worldwide. Museums, which for decades had been praised for sponsoring archaeological expeditions to bring back exhibitable treasures, found themselves condemned for promoting the rape of other peoples' past. Long-held curatorial emphasis on the great and gorgeous began to give way to a fawning affection for the commonplace. In archaeology the old tenet defined as "keeping tops and bottoms" (meaning that you only kept the big bits of anything and discarded all the little ones that went between) was replaced by an insistence on retaining everything. At Colonial Williamsburg, beginning in 1957, our policy was to keep everything buried on any site prior to 1928—the year the Restoration began.

Although Colonial Williamsburg's vision continued to focus on the 18th century, we archaeologists were treating a well shaft filled with Prohibition-era bottles and Mason jars with the same care as any trove of colonial pottery. At first thought mildly demented by the architects, this policy paid off as Colonial Williamsburg's research interest extended into the town's later history. Consequently, in 1972, when we began excavations on the site of the Public Hospital, no one argued against saving everything that had survived from the fire of 1885.

Across the nation, archaeologists, many trained as prehistorians, were discovering the intellectual "gold" to be culled from sites as diverse and as recent as the garbage dumps of San Francisco and the backyards of a free black settlement in New York City. No longer were they debating how best to ship huge stone lions down the Tigris from Nineveh; now they were concerned with keeping the paint on rusting cola bottle caps. In the space of a century, archaeology had traveled from the sublime to the

Colonial Williamsburg

meticulous, and thereby sowed the seeds of its eventual undoing.

The concept that everything was worth keeping meant that it also had to be washed, sorted, conserved, cataloged, numbered, and stored—somewhere by somebody and at burgeoning expense. In the field, too, costs were rising. The days when, in Williamsburg, five or six sites could simultaneously be quickly and cheaply excavated by gangs of low-waged local laborers supervised by a single architectural draftsman were long since gone. Between 1928 and 1933 they had uncovered 45 major building foundations along with 107 buildings and 36 well shafts. In stark contrast, during the 25 years from 1957 to 1982, a team of professional archaeologists, photographers, draftsmen, conservators, and curatorial personnel working full time dug on 17 sites, documenting seven major buildings and excavating 21 outbuildings and 12 wells.

Just as computers have enabled anyone to address questions never before thought worthy of asking (and in many cases still aren't), so refined archaeological techniques have made it possible to recover all manner of previously ignored information. With the right experts and proper equipment we can learn what people had eaten before visiting the privy, and where they solved their problem if they found it occupied. We can recover microscopic pollen from the earth that tells us what plants were growing there; and, if the privy had a glass window, we may be able to determine how long ago it was broken by counting the layers of its surface decay. Other experts can use spectrographic analysis to determine where our potsherds were made, while yet others can identify the source of a seashell or lump of coal, or learn the age of a chip of charcoal. But at a price.

When, in Williamsburg, archaeology's mission was limited to finding building remains to help architects in their restorations and reconstructions, there was no need to spend time trying to date a teacup. Later, when curators realized that archaeology's

"junk" could be a reliable guide to assist in accurately furnishing the buildings, dating the cup became important and necessary. There remained, however, no pressing need in either architectural or curatorial eyes to determine the source of a piece of coal or whether an oyster shell was young or old when tonged from the bay.

Laymen might think that being always short of time and money, archaeologists can be forgiven for settling for coal being coal and shells being shells. Among their peers, however, failure to pull out all the stops and bring in all the costly consultants can today lead to charges of unprofessionalism and to the loss of accreditation—putting the Mark of Cain on those who make a living from short-term archaeological contracting.

Along with many another improved field technique, the salvaging of badly decayed artifacts such as bone and iron has developed to the point that we are able to save remains reduced to little more than dirty marks in the ground. But saving them and getting them to the laboratory is one thing. Making sure that they permanently survive once they get there is quite another.

Colonial Williamsburg's archaeological laboratory is one of the world's oldest, dating back to the early 1930s. Then equipped with little more than a tank of lye and a tub of hot wax, its commonsense conservators were able to preserve iron objects so efficiently that half a century later they have deteriorated not at all. The trick, however, was that the objects treated were only those that were in relatively good condition. Others considered "too far gone" had been thrown away.

In the 1957–1982 era virtually everything reached the lab and, with few exceptions, every piece of rusted iron from hinges to helmets was treated and preserved, often as many as 20 or 30 objects at a time—and by journeymen conservators having no formal scientific training. In those days conservation laboratories were only to be found in major museums and staffed by special-

Colonial Williamsburg

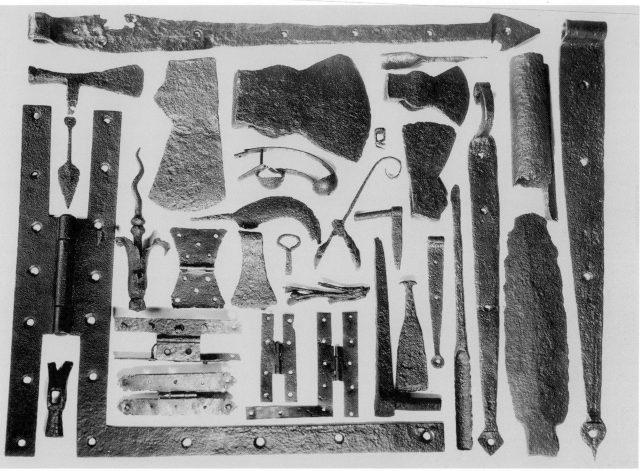

Colonial Williamsburg

The author and conservator Neil Frank (opposite) study a 17th-century mill from the site of Mathews Manor (left) near Denbigh, Virginia. In the 1930s archaeological conservation was quick, cheap, and primitive—but remarkably enduring, as the survival of the iron artifacts (above) attests. By the 1960s techniques had become more sophisticated—and much more costly.

Ivor Noël Hume

ists who would have felt professionally affronted if asked to clean the rust from 20 identical horseshoes.

Just as the qualifications for historical archaeologists improved (or at least escalated) in the 1980s, so archaeological conservation became a profession in its own right. No longer was there a place for the handyman conservator in any organization that claimed to meet museum standards. Needless to say, along with the new professionalism came professional equipment, professional paperwork, professional salaries—and far fewer objects conserved.

The 1970s notion that from coast to coast every homesite and trash dump merited archaeological attention, and that whenever federal or state funds were involved archaeological contracts would be forthcoming, provided work for numerous private companies and their graduate employees. Known to cynics as the "gypsies," a generation of well-qualified diggers became archaeology's equivalent of the migrant farm worker.

Land developers anxious to avoid the wrath of conservationists stood ready to fund archaeological surveys—providing they did not take too long or cost too much. On discovering that they did both, and that archaeology tended to generate publicity which on the one hand attracted unwelcome visitors and on the other focused as much on controversies as on discoveries, many a developer learned to seek ways of avoiding any archaeological involvement.

At the same time that developers' costs were rising, archaeologists' budgets were escalating to maintain the professional levels spelled out by state historic preservation agencies, but which often exceeded the actual needs of the sites. Thus when regulations required that work be done, it often cost more than was necessary,

and when there was no regulatory compulsion and the work depended on private funding, it might not be done at all.

Colonial Williamsburg is blessed with a strongly staffed archaeological department, and providing a home for what it finds has not yet become an insurmountable problem. But many archaeological endeavors are less fortunate. Whereas in Britain most counties and cities have a tax-supported museum and an archaeological curator, Virginia has no such repositories for the safekeeping and exhibiting of neighborhood discoveries. To make matters worse, few archaeological projects have conservation laboratories standing ready to give immediate attention to what is found. Instead, the directors are forced to rely on contract conservators to do at greater expense what could be done as efficiently and more economically by their own people.

Compounding the problem yet further is the fact that once conserved, artifacts that were in bad condition when recovered need to be housed in a climate controlled environment and their condition monitored from then until doomsday.

Recognizing that critics may ask "Why dig stuff up if you can't show it or look after it?" some professional archaeologists contend that what happens to the artifacts after they are done with them is no concern of theirs. Others duck the preservation problem by focusing their efforts on what in the jargon of the profession is called "non-invasive archaeology." This means doing whatever one can—short of digging a hole and finding something. Walking the ground, employing electronic scanners and suchlike devices to create computer-generated profiles of unidentified buried anomalies, taking aerial photographs, and quizzing the locals, are all part of the process.

As long ago as January 1965, the renowned archaeologist

Ivor Noël Hume

Over time Williamsburg's archaeological policies changed. Here (right) glass "treasures" from a Prohibition-era well at the James Anderson House site get the full research treatment. In earlier days so recent a shaft would not have been excavated; artifact collecting was more selective and somewhat less reverential (above).

Colonial Williamsburg

and poet Jacquetta Hawkes addressed precisely the same problem in Britain that bedevils us today in America: mounting costs, the bulldozer's relentless rumble, the inability of archaeologists to stay ahead of the destruction, and the philosophical differences that split the archaeological profession between scientists and humanists. Mrs. Hawkes rightly pointed out that both camps have their place and each needs the other. "In general," she wrote, "in spite of the difficulties and tensions that do occur, the Two Cultures are quite successfully reconciled within the archaeological realm. This," she added, "is well shown in excavation which lies—and surely always will—at the heart of the subject."

The merit of Jacquetta Hawkes's statement has never been better demonstrated than in the Virginia Company Foundation's recent excavation on the first English settlement site on Roanoke Island. Staffed by highly trained archaeologists, most of whom began their careers at Colonial Williamsburg, the team discovered part of a workshop floor that has been dubbed America's first science center. Pressed into it were seeds, nuts, coal, antimony, flint, glassware, crucible fragments containing copper oxide, and a miscellany of as yet unidentified substances—all calling for the expertise of botanists, mineralogists, geologists, metallurgists, and chemists to help determine what their Elizabethan counterparts had been up to in that tiny enclave on the edge of an unknown continent. Ironically, this was a site that had been subjected to "non-invasive" sub-surface electronic readings—readings that had failed to detect the science center's data-rich floor. As Jacquetta Hawkes told us so long ago, excavation does indeed remain at the heart of the subject. No amount of high-tech know-how can substitute for a down-in-the-dirt excavator with trowel in hand.

The dawning realization that there will never be the money or the labs and museums to make saving each site a viable proposition behooves each state and county to take realistic stock of its archaeological heritage and to establish a list of priorities. The need is to identify those that are of primary significance and must be preserved at all costs, those that are likely to be soon destroyed if something isn't done, and others that are deemed expendable and which need only to be watched and recorded as the developers take their toll. The trick, however, is first to determine what is a site of primary significance—and to whom.

There is, for example, a big difference between places that can be deemed "historic sites"—meaning important in history at the state or national level—and those that are merely historical sites, meaning surviving from the historical centuries. The 17th-century church tower at Jamestown, for example, is an undeniable historic site of importance to the nation. But what about the remains of Cecil B. DeMille's Egyptian set for his 1923 production of *The Ten Commandments* buried under the Guadalupe dunes near California's Vandenberg Air Force Base? Even archaeologists are divided about that one. Some contend that to excavate it and salvage pieces of the huge pharaonic gateway to house in a museum would be a travesty of serious archaeology. Others, myself among them, argue that a site recalling a great moment in the early history of the movie industry is every bit as important to the people of California as is, say, the ruin of John Page's Rosewell plantation to Virginians.

The choices are never easy, but choices must be made—always supposing that we have the opportunity to do so. In the absence of an agreed map of archaeological priorities, the decisions all too often are forced upon us by developers who pick

Dave Doody

Porcelain for Mr. Jefferson's people: Archaeologist William Kelso holds one of several Chinese export plates found at the Monticello slave avenue (above). At left, social studies teachers attending Colonial Williamsburg's first archaeological field school in 1972 began to take the measure of the colonial hospital that burned in 1885.

Ivor Noël Hume

Colonial Williamsburg

the acres and then keep their fingers crossed, hoping that archaeologists don't show up to get in the way.

In the Williamsburg area, probably because most builders are local residents and so have a feeling for the area's historical character, they have worked wonderfully well with archaeologists. Beginning with L. B. Weber at Denbigh in 1963 who built his development around its history and Anheuser Busch at Kingsmill in the 1970s, the cooperation has been exceptional. It continues today at Governor's Land at Two Rivers where the developers first underwrote an archaeological survey of their 1440 acres and then, after the discovery of aboriginal and early colonial sites, they agreed to adjust their golf course fairways to preserve them. Exceptional, of course, implies exceptions to the rule, and like every coin this one has its down side.

Every day in Tidewater Virginia when a cable or waterline trench is dug, a house lot is cleared, the land for a school, church, or shopping mall is stripped, the danger of archaeological sites both historical and prehistorical being lost is real and tragic. It is true that in some instances a preliminary archaeological survey is required. But experience has demonstrated (and archaeologists, when they are being frank, admit it) such tests are often likely to be inconclusive. Digging little holes across the site and finding nothing does not mean that there is nothing important lying buried between the holes. Not until the bulldozers move in and the tree stumps come out is the truth revealed—by which time the archaeologists are long gone.

But there is a solution—though it is one that many professional archaeologists may find repugnant. It means following in the fiscally threadbare footsteps of museums everywhere, namely training the old and the young to work alongside the paid professionals, not for money but for the sheer joy of learning and contributing. It also requires that localities hire at least one professional archaeologist who is empowered (like a building inspector) to monitor work on private and public earth-disturbing projects and who, aided by trained volunteers, can step in when suddenly revealed archaeological remains merit such intervention.

It is true that some professionals are convinced that volunteers are inherently unreliable, slow to learn, and reluctant to do all that is asked of them. However, my own experience has been otherwise, and I submit that in terms of historical archaeology's future, the writing is on the wall. Belshazzar couldn't read it. But what it said was MENE, MENE, TEKEL, UPHARSIN, which being interpreted meant "Thou has had thine chance and thou hast blown it!" The days of the richly funded, pros-only archaeological project are over. It is time to do the best we can with *what* and *who* we have—remembering always that the past belongs not to archaeologists but to everyone who cares to enjoy it, take pride in it, and learn from it. With more people involved who care about the nation's buried past, it follows that greater efforts must and will be made to ensure that its legacy survives.

Colonial Williamsburg

In the first decades of Williamsburg's restoration, finding foundations like those of the Raleigh Tavern was the name of the archaeological game (opposite, top). Sometimes they were easily uncovered and photographed (left), and measured (opposite, left); but at others they gave architectural archaeologist Jimmy Knight (opposite, far left) a cause to scratch his head.

A Night Remembered
Tainted by the smoke of scandal

CHIEF OF THE FIRE DEPARTMENT
COME AT ONCE AND BRING
ENGINE. EASTERN LUNATIC
ASYLUM ON FIRE. WILL BE DESTROYED
IF HELP IS NOT COMING SOON.
JAMES D. MONCURE
SUPERINTENDENT

Richard Stinely

THAT MESSAGE chattered over the telegraph wires to Richmond shortly after 11 o'clock on the night of June 7, 1885. About two hours and 40 minutes later, Richmond's volunteer firemen finished loading Steamer No. 3 onto a railroad flatcar and, as the *Richmond Dispatch* put it, "the relief train shot out from the Chesapeake and Ohio depot" heading for Williamsburg.

Dr. Moncure had been the asylum's superintendent for little more than a year, but when he sat in his office writing letters on that Sunday evening in June, he had reason to be pleased with his accomplishments. Although his arrival had resulted in a virtual clean sweep of the medical and administrative staff, and only the long-time matron, Miss M. A. Wootton, remained to provide continuity of experience, the more than 400 patients were responding well to Dr. Moncure's staff changes—at least to those at the lower level.

He was the first to admit that staffing an institution of this kind was difficult, particularly, as he put it, "in a community where work is looked upon as degrading." Certainly it was a pity that news of the "debauching" of a female patient had leaked out, and that rumors were rife in town that his clerk, supervisor, and assistant physician were frequently drunk while on duty in the asylum.

It was true, too, that some of the buildings were in no better shape. But on the credit side, renovations were going ahead briskly. New male and female wards were only four and two years old, respectively, and a much needed amusement hall had just been completed. So, too, had the asylum's most dramatic innovation: electric lighting.

Dr. Moncure's predecessor had complained in 1883 that "the Asylum is practically without any means of being lighted," that the gas generator had been condemned as worn-out 10 years earlier, and that gas lighting, even when working, was a fire hazard in an institution of this kind. It was with considerable satisfaction, therefore, that in his 1884 annual report Dr. Moncure assured his board of directors that the low-bidding Consolidated Electric Light Company "would be ready to light up the Asylum" within the time allowed by the contract. They were not disappointed.

An imaginative reporter noted that on the night of the fire "the electric lights in the Asylum sent out their bright gleams from many of the windows of the building, throwing a sort of ghostly glimmer upon the dense foliage of the trees near by and making a pretty picture of the grounds." In reality, not one but 10 major buildings made up the Eastern Lunatic Asylum complex, most of them forming three sides of a square flanking the colonial Public Hospital for the Insane, which had received its first patients 112 years earlier.

The historic 18th-century building, like many a latter-day dowager, had had its face lifted several times and was trussed together to control a dangerous bulge in its walls. Raised to a third story in 1841, this building bore scars of change hidden behind a thick waterproofing of stucco that, by 1884, was cracking and falling away. A hundred feet long and about 38 feet wide, the building originally provided 24 rooms for patients as well as an apartment for the keeper and a meeting room for the hospital's directors.

Exactly how the old building's space was allocated at the time of the fire is unclear, but it certainly contained some patients, room for the night watch, and the apartments of matron Wootton and her servants. The keeper, by then the superintendent, had his living quarters in the large 1850 structure variously known as the Doric Building, the White Building, or the White House. It was there that Dr. Moncure finished writing his letters shortly before 9:45 on that ill-fated June evening.

"While I was closing my correspondence for the morning mail," he wrote, "I noticed that the Electric light suddenly flared up giving an unusually bright flash, which indicated to me that a short circuit had occurred some where." Dr. Moncure was not unduly concerned, however. It had happened several times before. Three-quarters of an hour later he heard a scream from the direction of the old hospital building. Although, as he later explained, "this was not an uncommon occurrence in an Insane Asylum," the cry did not sound like that of a patient. Moments later came shouts of "Fire!"

The night was clear and the moon in its third quarter; but as Dr. Moncure hurried across the quadrangle in the direction of the cries, he could see only a hint of smoke against the night sky and "an unusual and unaccountable light beneath the roof" of the female ward, the asylum's second oldest building, in use since 1821. Hurrying to the second floor, the superintendent feared the worst but was relieved to find only "what appeared to be a ball of glowing embers about six inches in diameter and about two inches from the ceiling. There was no appearance of flame," he added, "only a globular mass heated to redness" from which two electrical wires protruded. A bucket of water would soon put that out, Dr. Moncure concluded. But on reaching the center of the building, he quickly changed his mind. An opening had been cut through the ceiling to let in light from the cupola, and through it

A photograph taken shortly before the fire shows the front of the 1773 hospital raised to a third story and the portico added. Afterwards, the statue of Lord Botetourt, originally at the Capitol, was removed to the College of William and Mary.

he could see "a sheet of fire" rising into the roof and running laterally through lathe and plaster ventilating shafts—shafts that he knew linked all the old buildings from the women's wing at the east, on through the colonial hospital, and into the men's wards to the west.

The hole cut through to the cupola was but one of many of the jackleg efforts of Dr. Moncure's predecessor to provide light and ventilation to wards built at a time when such niceties were of small account. As the result of these improvements, walls had been dangerously weakened. "Nothing but plastering separated the flames from the patients," wrote Moncure, "and whenever the roof should cave in the floors would crush down upon the patients in the two lower wards." Immediate and total evacuation of the asylum was the only recourse, and the crowds of Williamsburg citizens gathering in the quadrangle did what they could to help escort the patients and fight the rapidly spreading fire.

This was by no means the first time that the asylum's fire-fighting ability had been put to the test. Nine years earlier a newly erected multipurpose building housing kitchens, bakery, dining room, chapel, and amusement hall had been destroyed. A committee of inquiry subsequently concluded that there had been "culpable, not to say criminal neglect in the condition of the apparatus and management of the fire department."

In spite of much stable-door slamming, Dr. Moncure found himself little better off. Although tanks on two roof-top towers were full, their contents flowed down through two-inch pipes to feed l-3/4-inch cocks in the bathrooms. Once these were opened to help protect other threatened buildings, insufficient pressure

remained to throw water more than 10 feet from the fire-hose nozzle. In one respect, however, there had been an improvement: In the fire of 1876 the nozzle had been mislaid!

In human terms, however, Dr. Moncure and his staff worked a miracle. Close to 450 patients were safely evacuated. Only two women were concluded to have died in the fire (their remains were never found) and, regardless of the fact that many wandered away into the night, only one came to any harm. Her nude body was found the next day floating in College Creek. Unlike the aftermath of the 1876 fire, no charges of negligence were leveled at the asylum's administration; no blame attached itself to Dr. Moncure. Nevertheless, the smoke of scandal of a different kind hung in the air, and one senses that the superintendent was aware of it when, in his report, he made a curious observation:

"To the credit of the City," he declared, "I wish to record the fact that throughout the fire I did not see one drunken man, until after all effort to extinguish the fire, when I saw two young men who had taken too much to drink & one of them had worked nobly while it was of any use to work." He told, too, how "with few exceptions the voice of humanity superseded the bitter feelings of the partisan" and, how in the townspeople's eagerness to help, "a common sympathy drowned the feelings of hatred." Was Dr. Moncure reacting to real or imagined resentment toward Yankees on the staff of a southern asylum, and was he trying to finesse the drunkenness charges that would be directed at his employees later in the year? One twist he could not anticipate. He would never have guessed that nearly a century later, archaeologists digging through the rubble of the fire would stumble on

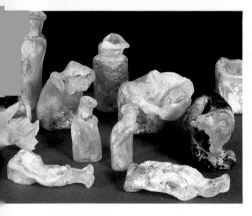

The heat of the fire reduced bottles in the hospital's dispensary to "silly putty" shapes (above). Probably stored on a shelf consumed in the blaze, they, and dozens more, lay close to a wall, cushioned in a bed of soft, gray ash.

evidence to support the accusers.

In the days and weeks following the fire, the cracked and blackened walls were knocked down and their bricks salvaged for reuse, an economy the asylum's directors hoped would greatly decrease the cost of rebuilding. Their need to do so became paramount when they discovered that two months before the disaster (allegedly without the board's knowledge) the Mutual Assurance Company of Virginia had reduced the asylum's insurance coverage from $30,000 to $20,000—against a loss "competent authority" put at $150,000.

Whether the insurance company had reacted to Dr. Moncure's predecessor hazarding attempts to increase ventilation or whether it had doubts about the safety of the new lighting is unclear. The latter certainly could have been a factor, for the newspaper account told how "the wires were run through the building in wooden tubes." At the subsequent inquiry a Professor Houston, described as "a distinguished electrician," testified that the wiring had been properly installed and that he could find no evidence that the lighting had caused the fire—hardly surprising, since he did not visit the scene until the walls had been knocked down and the evidence buried. The fact was not lost on Dr. Moncure who, regardless of the professor's "learned opinion," persisted in his conviction that the wiring had been the culprit. At the same time, in spite of a $150,000 loss to the contrary, he endorsed electricity as the way of the future, though urging that next time the wires be sheathed in lead.

Replacing the demolished building and, more importantly, raising the funds to do it was a slow process; and it took years before all the evacuated patients were adequately rehoused. The old asylum layout was not duplicated, however; and while some of the buildings occupied the same sites, others did not. Thus, for example, although a new infirmary paralleled the pivotal location of the colonial hospital, it was erected behind rather than on the site—an unintentional kindness to future archaeologists.

Foundations for the original Public Hospital for the Insane had been laid in 1770; 202 years later they were again exposed as Colonial Williamsburg took the first step toward reconstructing the last of the city's major 18th-century public buildings—an archaeological investigation destined to be the largest since the rebuilding of the Governor's Palace in 1930. The story of how the Palace ruins had yielded information crucial to the building's reconstruction and interpretation was well remembered, and because both Palace and hospital burned, hopes were high that the 1972 excavations would be as rewarding.

Like the Palace, the hospital's walls had been razed, the rubble-filled cellars covered over, and the site left more or less undisturbed to await the archaeologists—archaeologists whose techniques had improved considerably in the 42 years since their predecessors had dug into the Palace. The mission, however, remained the same: to retrieve any and all information that could help Colonial Williamsburg reconstruct the life and appearance of the 18th-century building. Unfortunately, there remained one critical difference. The Palace burned in 1781, ensuring that everything found in its ruins contributed to research. But the hospital did not; instead it became a time capsule for 1885—a date out of the mainstream of Colonial Williamsburg's interests.

Archaeological house cleaning! It took a vacuum cleaner to remove the last of the ashes without disturbing the hundreds of bottles revealed on the dispensary's storeroom floor. Shattered beer bottles in the middle of the room, contrasted with the crates and boxes of stored medicine bottles, posed questions that history alone could answer.

Ivor Noël Hume

Rarely do archaeologists find a sign to tell them where they are. This one (top) had fallen into the basement storage area shown on page 15. The age-old remedy of bleeding was still practiced in the hospital in 1885. The blood-letting tools called scarificators—one cleaned and the other preserved as found (bottom)—were discovered in the rubble under the dispensary. Made by George Thiemann & Co., illustrations from its 1879 catalog (center) identify their purpose.

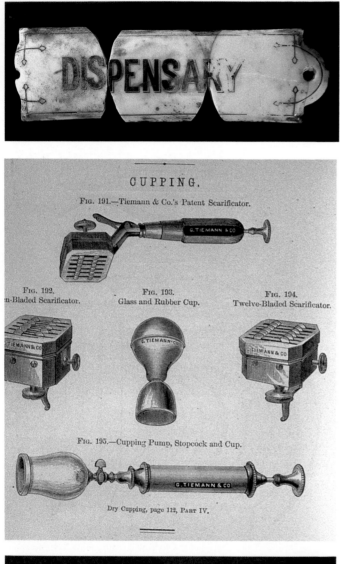

Ivor Noël Hume

We quickly discovered, however, that for archaeologists whose attention had hitherto focused squarely in the 18th century, the 19th century provided puzzles no less absorbing. Although a cement-walled steam tunnel serving the post-fire asylum had cut through the middle of the colonial foundation, the central cellars and basement cells (the latter added in 1799) remained undisturbed since the burning building's contents collapsed into them. How much of the rubble tumbled during the fire and how much was knocked down afterwards remains uncertain. Clearly identifiable, however, was a sizable part of the 1841 third-story wall that had fallen into the main cellar, covering a remarkable array of artifacts ranging from twisted iron beds and cast-iron radiators to Miss Wootton's tea service and porcelain mantelpiece ornaments.

Although we knew the matron's apartments were located in the building's central block in 1857, we had no documentary proof that they were still there in 1885—until we removed the fallen wall. Amid the crushed fragments of a pseudo-Japanese porcelain tea service lay a thin copper stencil of the kind used to mark household linen, its letters reading M. A. WOOTTON. Alongside lay two earthenware flowerpots and their trays, once home perhaps to the matron's geraniums.

Opening out of the main cellar beside a large fireplace was a room that yielded so many pins and buttons that the excavators decided that they were in a sewing room. This deduction received unexpected support from the discovery of a sewing machine. Subsequent cleaning in the laboratory revealed it to be a product of the Singer Manufacturing Company, a revelation that surprised no one.

Not all of the room's treasures related to sewing; on the contrary, the haul was surprisingly diverse. Large quantities of broken crockery were recovered; so were several stoneware bottles bearing the name N. ANTOINE & FILS, French manufacturers of what they described as "encre japonaise," and exactly paralleled by another found far away—in Quebec's Place Royale. Along with quantities of cutlery, a copper candlestick, two perforated iron shovels (probably "cinder shovels" listed in an 1860 inventory), many pieces of brass and copper pipe, and several ornamental gas cocks, were 19 brass keys of such curious design that we at first thought that they, too, were taps for controlling gas lamps. Once we cleaned them, we discovered that they fitted equally unusual locks used on cellar doors, locks with neither doorknobs nor conventional keyholes.

The first of the two subterranean cells added in 1799 at first offered us nothing but brick rubble. Later, however, beside what we took to be the base of Miss Wootton's apartment chimney, we came on a most unexpected trove: a large fossilized whale vertebra, probably as much as ten million years old and dating from the Miocene era. Evidently a curiosity picked up from the shore of the James or York rivers, where such relics are often discovered, it now found itself in strange company. Alongside it lay broken beer bottles, and below them the remains of a carpet bag, parts of an umbrella, 12 coat hooks, and a pair of ice skates. The hooks suggested that all the objects had been stored in a clothes closet and had fallen together into the basement when the flooring gave way. If that interpretation was correct, it left us with the need to explain the presence of beer bottles in Miss Wootton's closet.

Nothing more was found in the cell until its dirt floor was taken up, revealing part of a tiny Staffordshire pottery dog with a female figure seated on it. I was reminded that this square dungeon room had been built "under the first floor of the hospital for the reception of patients who may be in a state of raving phrensy," and wondered at the contradiction suggested by so delicate and gentle a toy. The surprise of finding it in so grim a place was broadened by the realization that the male pair to it was already in our archaeological collections. It had been found in 1930 during excavations at the Palace!

The companion cell to the north proved to be our "Tut's Tomb," for it contained not only artifacts that had fallen from the room above, but also its contents at the time of the fire. Though built to house dangerous patients and originally entered at the basement level under an arch barely big enough to crawl through, it had later been converted into a storeroom under what we cleverly deduced to have been the asylum's dispensary. This Holmesian deduction was made possible by the discovery of a broken ceramic door sign that, when put together, read DISPENSARY. It may also have doubled as a physician's examining room and a place to perform minor surgery, as the asylum's collection of instruments lay scattered amid the rubble. Among them were an

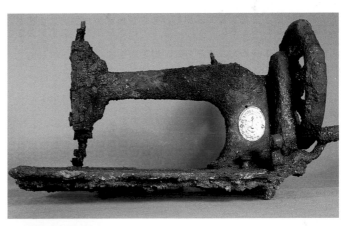

Though major staff changes rocked the hospital in the years before the fire, matron Miss M. A. Wootton weathered the storms. Among relics believed to have fallen from her third-floor apartment were a stencil bearing her name and a tea service for one in pseudo-Japanese stoneware (top). Below a sewing room was strewn a scattering of pins, buttons, and a Singer sewing machine, the latter seen here before and after cleaning. A box of brass cell-door keys (left) enabled a lock to work after both had received laboratory treatment.

Ivor Noël Hume

ophthalmoscope for examining the fundus of the eye, a range of dental forceps, two scarificators for bleeding patients, several unattractive tools for groping after stones, and a uterine sound. Presumably an essential component of such a kit was the brass buckle from a restraining strap.

More appropriate to a dispensary were a balance, several glass measuring tubes, a great variety of pharmaceutical bottles, and, miraculously undamaged amid the rubble, a pair of ceramic papboats for feeding the aged and infirm. Although the papboats showed no evidence of fire, rows of bottles against the west wall had melted into a grotesquerie of shapes, graphic evidence of the heat that had consumed virtually everything that could ignite.

Although the burning dispensary floor must have collapsed into the basement storeroom, causing anything flammable in it to catch fire, rubble plaster had fallen soon enough to smother the flames. Consequently, much survived that would otherwise have been totally destroyed—including the still readable remains of a

stack of 1885 newspapers. The asylum's annual report for that year named eight daily and 24 weekly papers available to the patients, but none of those identified in the storeroom was among them. These included several copies of the *Chicago Daily News*, the *Chicago Tribune*, the *Philadelphia Times*, an unidentified San Antonio paper, numerous editions of the London *Times*, and the remains of a New York mail-order catalog. These Northern papers presumably belonged to a member of the staff, and it is tempting (if academically unsound) to see them as fuel for the post-Civil War rancor to which Dr. Moncure alluded.

The charred remains of several crates stood on the floor, each containing large quantities of new and used glass bottles, one box holding more than 300. Other crates contained single bottles for the storage of acids or other chemicals, the fragile vessels cushioned in straw, some of which had escaped the flames. Clear evidence of how the fire had burned in the room was provided by the remains of a butter churn with wooden sides and a

Unused to digging amid the ruins of an 1885 mental institution, archaeologists found some artifacts at first difficult to identify— like the leg (right) of an upturned bed. Above: Another bed of the same type after laboratory treatment.

Ivor Noël Hume

16

ceramic lid through which the plunger rose and fell. In the intense heat the sides were consumed causing the lid to slide down the plunger's shaft to land on its perforated wooden disk, smothering the fire and preserving it—carbonized but intact.

How does one explain the presence of a butter churn in a dispensary storeroom? Perhaps someone faced with the task of preparing purgatives for four hundred or more patients decided he needed mechanical help. The butter churn enigma was not foremost in our minds as the excavation progressed; more pressing was the problem of clearing the plaster dust from around the hundreds of bottles without disturbing them. We solved it by abandoning brushes in favor of a vacuum cleaner. The same technique was used to expose the room's most unexpected feature. In the center of the floor, and in marked contrast to the orderly storage of the crated bottles, lay a heap of broken beer bottles, their fragments radiating out from the central pile as though dropped one by one from above. There seemed to be but

a single explanation: Access to the old maximum-security cell had been through a trapdoor in the room above, and this continued after it became a store below the dispensary. Someone who controlled access to the store used it to hide the evidence of secret boozing in the medical room above. Almost automatically the finger of suspicion points toward the man whose drinking a joint committee of the Virginia General Assembly concluded was "not only reprehensible in the extreme, but dangerous to the welfare of the institution, and hazardous to the comfort and safety of the unfortunate inmates." Within a year, Dr. Moncure's second assistant physician was no longer an officer of the asylum.

It has become an archaeological cliché that archaeologists use artifactual evidence to reconstruct the past in much the same way that police detectives assemble clues to identify miscreants and their crimes. In the asylum's dispensary store, however, we may have been both archaeologists and detectives, uncovering the evidence of misbehavior—just a century too late.

The east wing of the hospital shows the burned basement floors (left) and to their right crushed iron beds still in a cell that had housed two patients. Above is the hospital's main cellar, the upper stories' fallen walls reducing beds to a tangle of bars and straps and crushing matron Wootton's tea set and windowsill flowerpots. Of sterner stuff, cast-iron radiators fell unbroken one on top of another.

Dave Doody

Custis Square

The Williamsburg home and garden of a very curious gentleman

Courtesy of Washington/Custis/Lee Collection, Washington and Lee University. Photo by Dave Doody

Courtesy of Tudor Place Foundation, Inc.

John Custis IV was a man of many moods and more surprises, and a rarity in that his portrait was painted twice. Each included a different book but each with its pages embellished with the words "Of the Tulip." Each has a flower beside it, but neither painting shows him in the same clothes or in the same pose. The site of his Custis Square home (opposite) remains equally perplexing.

MANY YEARS AGO I wrote an article titled "Archaeology: Handmaiden to History," but when I came to Williamsburg in 1956, archaeology was handmaiden not to history but to architecture. From the first days of John D. Rockefeller, Jr.'s, restoration, most of Williamsburg's archaeological needs had been served by an architectural draftsman supervising a crew of laborers drawn from the pool of landscape gardeners. Not until the early 1960s would archaeology be recognized as a separate discipline with its own standards and procedures. But even then, its project schedules continued to be dictated by those of the architectural office. So it was that in 1963 I was advised that the architects had a mind to reconstruct the John Custis House and gardens and that

my department would spend the next summer digging for the remains of the most controversial and "unWilliamsburgy" dwelling ever built here in the 18th century.

We were to find foundations—bricks, mortar, window fragments—not to search for clues to the peccadillocs of John Custis and certainly not to the character of Martha Washington. But the joy of archaeology is that you never know what you're going to find until you dig. And that was never more true than at the place that came to be known first as "Custis Square" and later as the "Six Chimney Lot."

John Custis was the fourth of that name and the son of John Custis of "Wilsonia" on Virginia's Eastern Shore. He married Frances, the daughter of another wealthy landowner, Colonel

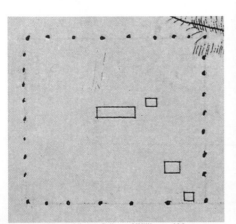

Daniel Parke of Queen's Creek plantation in York County. Custis detested Frances with a vehemence that still burned fiercely 34 years after her death. His 1749 tombstone at Arlington in Northampton County carries an inscription that only he could have chosen for it, declaring that he had lived "but Seven Years, Which was the space of time He kept a Bachelors house on the Eastern Shore of Virginia."

In 1712 planter William Byrd noted in his diary that Frances Custis was trying to "prevail with her husband to live at Williamsburg," which in John's mind was almost certainly the best possible reason for not doing so. It is likely, therefore, that it was not until his wife died in 1715 that he purchased or built a brick house on what was then the outskirts of Williamsburg and which today lies immediately east of Nassau Street adjacent to the Public Hospital.

A small brick building still stands on Custis Square's

eight-lot block, a structure long known as "Martha Washington's Kitchen" and still as the Custis Kitchen. Neither is correct—as we would discover when we found the remains of the real, and larger, Custis kitchen partially beneath it. The existing building seems to have been built no earlier than 1790, when the property was owned by Dr. James McClurg, professor of "Physick" at the College of William and Mary. The old Custis House was then still standing.

The McClurg-era kitchen is unusual in that it possesses an easterly gable end capped with coping bricks of the kind so often found on enclosure walls like those around Bruton Parish Church. But though unusual, the parapet, or modified Flemish gable, is not unique among Williamsburg buildings of the post-Revolutionary years, for a similar detail is to be seen on the 1812 Roscow Cole House on Market Square. Nevertheless, rather than being a product of that early 19th-century renewal of interest in Jacobean-style architecture, the McClurg-period kitchen could be a reflection of the 17th-century Flemish character of John Custis's brick home.

Though a voluble correspondent, Custis said little about his house beyond ordering in 1717 "good Commicall diverting prints" to hang in "the passage of [his] house," and noting in 1724 that it was "as strong and high as any in Govenmt [and] stands on high ground." Only from much later references do we learn anything about its plan and interior. When John's grandson John Parke Custis offered it for sale in 1778, the *Virginia Gazette* notice stated that the "house is in tolerable good repair, having two good rooms and a passage on the lower flower [sic]." However, in a letter to George Washington, he admitted that "the Houses on My Lots are in a wretched Situation; and are not fit to live in, and it will never be worth my while either to build or repair."

But Dr. McClurg, who bought the property, seems not to have felt that major repairs were necessary, and in 1779 he was content to have four rooms and two passages whitewashed, the cellar window frames repaired, a cellar door bricked up, and attention paid to the building's offset water table. It was a project that required 650 bricks.

Thirty-two years later the property was bought by lawyer Samuel Tyler, who promptly died, leaving his widow with "the houses and lots in the City of Wmsburg called the 6 chimnies [which] is in a ruinous & decaying state, the house not being habitable & can not be rented for anything." Historian Lyon G. Tyler in his book *Williamsburg, the Old Colonial Capital* (1907) would write that the Six Chimney Lot "gets its name from the six chimnies which once stood there, the houses to which they belonged having perished by fire." Tyler could never have seen the chimneys or he would have known that they were part of a single house. Consequently, his statement that they—it—burned may be no more reliable. It seems certain, however, that by the time Custis Square was absorbed into the Public Hospital's holdings in 1849, the old house had succumbed. Archaeological evidence would suggest that its remains were dismantled and its wall bricks salvaged in the 1820s.

To readers unacquainted with Williamsburg's historical sources, it may seem strange that so little is known about a property that once had been so prominent. The explanation is one that has affected every house and lot lying on the south side of Duke of Gloucester Street, falling as they do within the County of James City. During the Civil War and believing that its court records would be safer in Richmond than in Williamsburg, county officials shipped them there—only to add fuel to the flames, when in April 1865 the retreating Confederate government set

Sidney King's reconstructive painting (opposite, top right) of a house at Jamestown suggests the shape and character of John Custis's brick home that once stood in the space electronically outlined opposite. The author stands on the site of the garden well (opposite, bottom left). The detail from the 1781 Frenchman's Map of Williamsburg (opposite, top left) shows a larger house, its eight lots flanked by dot-defined trees.

General John H. Cocke claimed that his 1836 "cottage" at Bremo Recess in Fluvanna County (opposite, bottom right) owed its architectural style to Custis's "six-chimney" house in Williamsburg and to Arthur Allen's 1665 Bacon's Castle in Surry (left).

Ivor Noël Hume

fires that ignited the city. Consequently, we have neither the deeds nor probate inventories that have been so helpful in reconstructing house histories for lots lying north of Duke of Gloucester Street in York County and whose Civil War-era clerks were less fearful for their records' safety.

That no official documents relating to the Custis House survive does not mean that private documents are entirely lacking—as the *Virginia Gazette* notice and Dr. McClurg's bill in builder Humphrey Harwood's ledger attest. Now and again, however, the documentation can take unexpected forms. A wine bottle in the Colonial Williamsburg collection bears a glass seal with the name IOHN CUSTIS and the date 1713. More informative, however, is an attached silver plaque engraved with the following message:

Found 1810 in the Cellar on the "Six Chimney Lot" the oldest residence of the Custis family in Williamsburg Va and Presented by Mrs E Galt to Jas W. Custis. 1852.

Was Mrs. E. Galt the wife of William T. Galt who bought the property in 1824? If so, can we deduce that she had been treasure hunting in the cellar when the house belonged to the Richmond-residing Dr. McClurg? With the exterior cellar entrance bricked up in 1779, one can deduce that interior stairs to the cellar were still usable in 1810 before the building fell into the "ruinous & decaying state" described five years later.

When we removed the rubble from the cellar, we found no

bottles. Indeed, the building had been robbed almost to its last brick. Almost, but not quite. Small sections of the cellar foundations survived and, where they did not, the impressions of their bricks told us where they had rested. Part of the nine-inch-square brick tile flooring also remained, a paving material often encountered in late 17th- and early 18th-century buildings.

Much better preserved was another feature common to early 18th-century Virginia cellared homes—a brick drainage tunnel running away from a corner. This one headed north toward the natural slope to Francis Street and was interrupted by an equally well-constructed manhole. Though intended to enable a small slave to keep the tunnel clean, in the early 19th century it had served the opposite purpose, providing an opening into which trash was dumped—including, along with wine bottles, tumblers, and Chinese porcelain, a European-style chamber pot made by reservation Indians and sold, so I believe, for use by Custis Square's black servants.

I cannot resist adding that the Custis tunnel provided me with one of my Williamsburg career's more memorable and vocally colorful moments. I got firmly stuck halfway down it.

The remains of a bonfire at the cellar's east end, sealed beneath the rubble, at first suggested that the building had been demolished in the winter and that the workers may have burned interior woodwork to keep warm. But a closer inspection of the ashes revealed that small tree limbs had provided the fuel, prompting us to conclude that we were seeing the residue of site clearance after the house had been stripped of its bricks.

Ivor Noël Hume

Excavations in 1963 uncovered the remains of a dairy south of the still-surviving but incorrectly named "Custis Kitchen" (opposite). Beyond lay the partially explored basement of the "six-chimney" house, while in the background stood a late 19th-century block of the Eastern State mental hospital. Descent into the 40-foot well (left) was an adventure no less gripping than becoming wedged in John Custis's drainage tunnel (below).

Colonial Williamsburg

The below ground rectangle described by the cellar's real and ghost walls measures only 48 feet 9 inches by 23 feet 3 inches—hardly the 70-foot-long, or more, mansion suggested by the Frenchman's Map of 1781 but much closer to the dimensions shown on a contemporary map drawn by another Frenchman in the aftermath of the Revolution. The startling difference between them is hard to explain, but it serves to demonstrate that historical as well as archaeological evidence should always be treated with caution bordering on suspicion.

The Custis House measurements turned out to be closely paralleled by those of a brick dwelling excavated at Jamestown whose foundations measured 48 feet 6 inches by 21 feet 6 inches. National Park Service archaeologists first dated it to the third quarter of the 17th century, but researchers now put it as late as 1720—after John Custis's house had been completed in Williamsburg.

Regardless of its disputed date, Jamestown's Structure No. 6 has been interpreted as standing only a story-and-a-half in height, and it may be this shared feature that provided the Custis House with a link to a most unlikely informational source, namely a remodeled ca. 1803 "cottage" in distant Fluvanna County.

In 1844 General John H. Cocke wrote to the *Southern Planter* offering its editors a picture of "a cottage of my own building at Bremo-Recess" which he had completed in 1836. "The stile," he explained, "is copied from the only two specimens of the like building I ever saw—the well remembered, old Six-chimney House in Wmsburg once the property of the Custis

family—and Bacon's Castle in Surry."

By no stretch of the imagination is the imposing two-story Bacon's Castle a cottage. But it does possess two exterior stacks capped by three separated chimneys at each end—in short, a six-chimney house. The Custis House, on the other hand, must have provided a different inspiration. The surviving Bremo-Recess house has its six chimneys flanking its central hall; but it does have Jacobean-style gable ends; and those, along with the story-and-a-half height, may be the extent of the Bremo-Custis connection.

The Custis cellar showed that its chimney stacks had been internal—not in the center, like Bremo-Recess, but one at each end. Burning in the easterly hearth area suggested that that part of the basement might have served as a kitchen when the house was first built. Writing at the beginning of the 18th century, Robert Beverley noted that in the homes of Virginia gentlemen kitchen and laundry activities were by then "perform'd in Offices detacht from the Dwelling-Houses, which by this means are kept more cool and Sweet." Was this, therefore, a clue to the building's early date and to its construction in the 17th century before John Custis came to town?

Unlike conventional historians, who have access to usually verifiable written data, archaeologists rarely can say anything with absolute certainty. Instead we weigh apples against pears and are dismayed and surprised when our conclusions look alarmingly like grapefruits.

We discover the burned hearth inside the house and identify

it as evidence of kitchen activity and by extension use it to postulate a 17th-century construction date. But a few weeks later we excavate under "Martha Washington's" kitchen, and what do we find? We find the plan of an earlier kitchen, one of its rooms floored with the same nine-inch tiles as those in the dwelling's cellar. Surely, one can argue, the kitchen and the house are of the same date, in which case the "early" feature of the basement kitchen hearth is nothing of the sort.

If, therefore, John Custis did not buy an existing old house, it follows that he had it built around 1715 in a deliberately archaic style. Again we ask, why?

Perhaps he remembered his grandfather's home on the Eastern Shore, the Arlington mansion to which he would return to

Dave Doody

John Custis designed his own tomb that stands sentinal behind the graveyard wall. Beyond it archaeologists uncover and ponder the remains of his family home at Arlington, on the Eastern Shore (opposite).

end his days. But did that possess Jacobean gables and tall, separated chimneys? Alas, the only surviving description comes from William Byrd's diary for November 9, 1709, calling it "a great house within sight of the Bay and really a pleasant plantation but not kept very nicely." Diarist Byrd would have been hard put to be less specific.

The Arlington site is now within a housing development and has been excavated by the Virginia Company Foundation. We hoped that if we were lucky—and luck is the principal ingredient in most archaeological successes—the digging would reveal structural details that can help solve the mystery that still enfolds Williamsburg's House of the Six Chimneys. Unfortunately no obvious parallel emerged.

John Custis may have been singularly parsimonious in describing his house, but he was voluble when discussing his gardens. This obsessional hobby seems to have developed in 1716, before he wrote to his London agents asking for "handsome striped hollys and yew trees" explaining that he had "lately got into the vein of gardening." Twenty-six years later he would refer to his "very fine yew balls and pyramids which were established for more than 20 years," while bemoaning the fact that they had been seriously weather damaged on their south sides and might never recover. The Bodleian Library's copperplate of the College of William and Mary, which was engraved at about the same time that Custis was writing about balls and pyramids, shows how similarly clipped plantings graced the college forecourt.

Still standing in Custis Square is a single yew that some writers believe may be a survivor of the Custis garden plan. Others, like Lyon G. Tyler, recorded that it was "said to have been planted with Mrs. Washington's hands."

Colonial Williamsburg's director of landscaping Gordon Chappell reminded me that there is a comparable yew tree in the Bruton Parish churchyard, but although both are "very ancient," there is no way of determining how ancient—short of cutting them down. The likelihood that Martha Washington's gentle hands planted the Custis tree is small indeed. She was not, as they say, "into" gardening and had absolutely no love for anything to do with Custis Square—as our archaeological researches were later to suggest. But I am getting ahead of the story.

Early one July morning in 1720 Custis's brother-in-law Colonel William Byrd was persuaded to walk with him in his garden, where he had put down gravel paths. Five months later, on a December evening, Byrd again walked there with him and did so yet again in the following March, when he found the garden much improved. Back once more on a cold day in April, it can have come as no surprise to Byrd when in the evening his host proposed another garden stroll. Major Custis, Byrd recalled, "was very gallant"—an attribute for which the major was not widely renowned.

Writing to London merchant Robert Cary in 1725, Custis described his creation as "a pretty little garden in which I take more satisfaction than anything in this world and have a collection of tolerable good flowers and greens from England." He went on to say that he had bought a hundred tulip bulbs from a supplier in Battersea, but that they had arrived too late in the year and only two or three were blooming. It was at about this date (when Custis was in his 45th year) that he had one of his two known portraits painted. In it he is shown holding a book whose fore-edge inscription reads "On the Tulip." Beside it on a table perches a single, curiously elevated bloom.

Later letters to Cary focused more on plants that arrived dead than on Custis's planting successes. Among the losses were flowering honeysuckle and yellow jasmine (killed by being shipped on deck and doused with salt spray), carnations and auriculas (put in steerage and savaged by a dog). In a 1730 letter to naturalist Mark Catesby, Custis mentioned that he had at least two five-foot dogwoods in his garden. However, it is not these scattered letters on which John Custis's reputation as a gardener rests but rather on a 12-year correspondence with the London haberdasher, botanist, and horticulturist Peter Collinson that began in 1734. In that year Collinson suggested Custis should plant horse chestnut trees against the street because they "would have a fine Effect."

We know Collinson did send Custis the chestnuts and they arrived in good enough condition, for two years later Collinson wrote that he was "glad to heare the horse chestnuts grow." Although nothing is known about the layout of John Custis's garden—beyond the formality indicated by the gravel walks and yew trees—the Frenchman's Map of 1781 shows Custis Square flanked on all four sides by 31 tree dots, which may or may not mark the placement of the chestnuts Collinson thought would provide so fine an effect.

Although Custis grew or attempted to grow many kinds of flowers, his failures caused by transportation and the extremes of Virginia's climate prompted him to confess that even if he was "a great lover of all sorts of fine flowers . . . they, like all delightfull things; are very short lived; now fine trees," he went on, "are not only very entertaining but permanent; so I think are to bee preferd and all variegated trees and plants most hit my phancy."

The summer of 1737 had been particularly hot and dry, so much so that Custis "was obliged for severall weeks to keep 2 lusty men all day long to draw water and put in tubs in the sun to water my garden." A year later he would remember the task slightly differently: "I kept 3 strong Nigros continually filling large tubs of water and put them in the sun and watered plentifully every night [and] made shades and arbors all over the garden allmost; but abundance of things perished."

The 1964 excavations discovered rows of deep-set postholes we tentatively identified as supports for grape arbors—before reading the letter that said they were built to shade Custis's dying plants. In the same area we found two well shafts, the first short and subsequently replaced by a second almost twice as deep—another of Custis's attempts to keep his garden alive if not growing.

The second well seems to have been dug in the arid summer of 1737, when the first, relying on surface drainage for its water, dried up. Wrote Custis to Collinson: "As you are a very curious gentleman I send you some things which I took out of the bottom of A well 40 feet deep; the one seems to be a cockle petrefyd one a bone petrefyd; [this] seems to have been the under beak of some antediluvian fowl."

Skillfully brick-lined, the replacement well turned out to be 40 feet 1 inch to the bottom, where we found a bed of water-seeping marl whose multitude of fossils, alas, included no

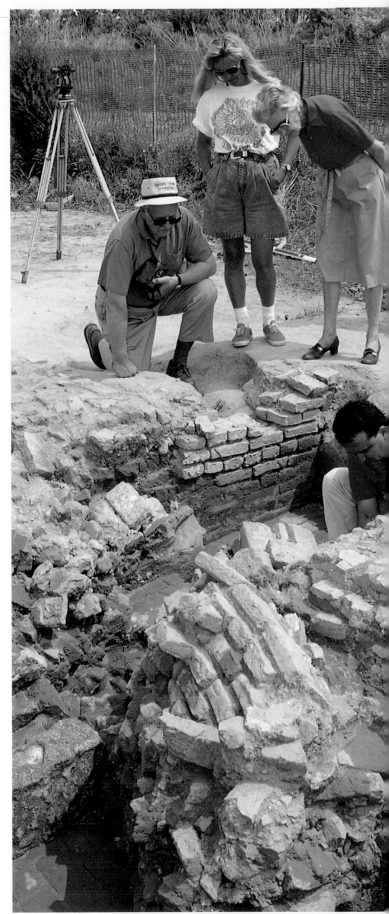

Dave Doody

25

Custis's garden is among the best documented of any in the annals of colonial America. Although archaeologists would not discover his lead figures of Venus and Apollo in his garden well, they would find a reminder that in 1735 botanist Peter Collinson had dubbed Custis a "brother of the spade." When digging the well, Custis had found fossil shells and bones, one of which he described as resembling "the underbeak of some antedeluvian fowl." Hardly antediluvian but certainly fowl-like were the skulls and beaks of ducks and chickens excavated from the well's filling. More surprising was the preservation of twigs, nuts, and the still-green leaves from Dutch box and American hollies. Alas, no well-held evidence survived of the ball and pyramidical yews that had mirrored those in the forecourt of the College of William and Mary (below).

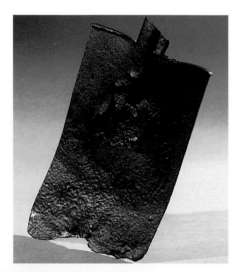

Ivor Noël Hume

Ivor Noël Hume

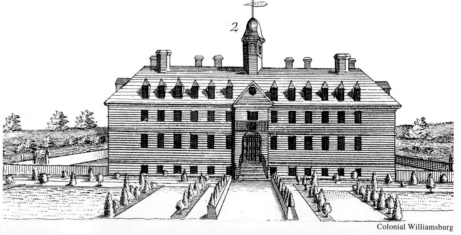

Colonial Williamsburg

Ivor Noël Hume

Treasures from John Custis's well: some of the named and dated bottles (left), one of them shown with the matching example salvaged from his cellar in 1810 (below); and to the left the bottle whose seal Martha may have mutilated. Other finely preserved relics from the well include a silver shoe buckle, a bell-metal skillet, and an iron door latch.

Ivor Noël Hume

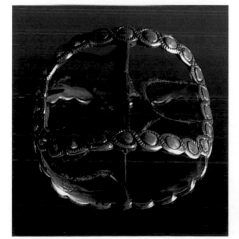

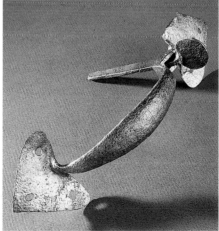

Colonial Williamsburg

pre-Noah chicken beaks but did yield fragments of ten-million-year-old whale bones. The late Dr. Earl G. Swem in his book *Brothers of the Spade* noted that as late as the 1930s Custis's well wonders were in the collection of the Mill Hill School in North London, which stands on the site of Collinson's home and gardens. But the school denies any knowledge of them and reports that the only surviving American connection is provided by some of the trees in the garden.

Much more important to us than the source of Collinson's shells was the discovery in the well of splendidly preserved examples of 17 different types of plants, shrubs, and trees cited in the Custis-Collinson letters. Among them, and still green after being immersed for nearly two centuries, were leaves of American holly and Dutch box, the latter showing the marks of the scissors or shears that had trimmed them.

The Custis well was to yield the finest hoard of historically important artifacts yet discovered in Williamsburg, virtually all of them in the filling's lowest four feet. Lying amid the fragments of 60 glass wine bottles were two intact examples bearing the same JOHN CUSTIS 1713 seal that Mrs. Galt had found in the house cellar. Other bottles attributable to the 1730s were marked simply I CUSTIS—the I being a common means of drawing a J in the 17th and 18th centuries. These last may have been among the bottles ordered by Custis from London merchants Lloyd and Cooper in 1737:

> *I sent for 3 gross of quart bottles by Rumsey markt I. Custis; I hope you will see yt that they hold full quarts since ye price you say is ye same.*

John Custis was sure that if anyone could cheat him, they would.

One of the I CUSTIS bottles had had its seal deliberately ground down, so that the name was almost entirely defaced. Could this have been done by someone with an abiding hatred of the man? The question was asked half in jest, but it was one that would later merit closer attention when the character of Martha Dandridge Custis Washington became an element in the Custis Square story.

Among the many artifacts recovered

Colonial Williamsburg

28

from the well was the finest collection of early 18th-century drinking glasses found in Williamsburg, children's wooden spinning tops, a pistol barrel converted into a pennywhistle (which can still yield a tune), a tin cup, a bell-metal skillet, flowerpots, fragments of a garden ornament, and, most intriguing of all, a silver shoe buckle, its decoration worn down on one side perhaps by a man (John Custis?) who habitually crossed his feet.

The discovery of the silver buckle was a reminder that John Custis had given to Anne, the wife of local tavern keeper Mathew Moody, a pair of buckles made by John Coke of Williamsburg and engraved "In Memory of John Custis." He had also given or loaned to her silver and pewter wares bearing the arms and crest of the Custis family, and which after his death she brazenly displayed in her "public house" on Capitol Landing Road.

The relationship between John Custis and Anne Moody did not end with pewter or shoe buckles, for in his will (along with a monetary endowment) he left her "the picture of my said negro boy John otherwise called Jack," perhaps because he knew of no one else who would be willing to take care of it.

The poignant and little-known story of Jack is of enormous interest, as we today better try to understand attitudes toward enslaved blacks in 18th-century Virginia. In his will, Custis stated that Jack was "born of the body of my slave Alice" and had been freed by a deed of manumission recorded in York County. Seeing that Jack was all right had become one of John Custis's major concerns, and in a will whose transcript runs to 88 lines, Jack's well-being occupies 23 of them.

Custis willed to Jack an estate on Queen's Creek with instructions that Custis's son Daniel Parke should build him a "handsome strong convenient dwelling house" to a plan drawn by John Blair and completely finished inside and out. Not only that, it was to be furnished with Russian leather chairs and couch as well as feather beds and black walnut tables.

Jack's age at the time John Custis died in 1749 is uncertain, but the will stated that he was "to live with my son until he be twenty years of age and that he be handsomely maintained out of the profits of my estate given him." In an earlier passage that perhaps sealed young Jack's fate, Custis had stated that "after the death of the said John otherwise called Jack I give all my estate heretofore given to the said John otherwise called Jack either by deed or otherwise to my son Daniel Parke Custis."

Opposite: Examples from the fine collection of drinking glasses (top) believed discarded at Daniel Parke's death in 1757, and three delftware cups and as many wooden spinning tops (center and bottom). Together they only hint at the diversity of wonders from the well in Custis Square.

Said to be a portrait of William Byrd III (left) and attributed to Charles Bridges, the painting is unusual in that it includes an evidently sympathetic background portrait of a black youth, suggesting, perhaps, that John Custis's "John otherwise called Jack" may have sat for the same artist. If one seeks symbolism where it may not exist, it is possible to read into the Byrd painting a fraternal relationship exemplified by the arrow of affection.

Colonial Williamsburg

Beneficiaries of John Custis's curious legacy, Daniel Parke and Martha Dandridge Custis (opposite), were portrayed by John Wollaston around 1756. Martha, 20 years her husband's junior, is represented as she was between the births of her third and fourth children.

Courtesy of Washington/Custis/Lee Collection, Washington and Lee University

Two years later Jack's architect, John Blair, would write in his diary for September 18, 1751, that "abt 1 or 2 in ye morng. Col Custis's Favourite Boy Jack died in abt 21 hours illness being taken ill a little before the 18th wth a Pain in the back of his Neck for wch he was blooded." Thus, so conveniently, was the burden of Jack's presence lifted. If anyone was suspicious, it is hardly likely that Daniel Parke's peers would have been so indelicate as to mention it. In any case, there is a valid medical explanation for what might have happened. Jack's neck pain could have been a symptom of meningitis, and if the boy also suffered from sickle-cell anemia, the bleeding could have killed him.

No one knows if Jack lies buried somewhere on the Custis Square lots, but while we dug there in the rubble of the house where he had lived and where his portrait had hung, "slave Alice's" son remained for us a real and tragic presence.

When Daniel Parke Custis went to law to try to get the family plate back from Anne Moody's tavern, she told the court that it had been given to her because John Custis was adamant that it should not fall into the hands of "any Dandridge's daughter." It was small wonder that Martha Dandridge Custis had no love for her father-in-law or for anything that had been his.

Her husband's death in 1757 left Martha a very wealthy widow—to the tune of £23,500. Still only 25, she considered herself "a fine, healthy girl," and no gentleman would have confused her agreeable plumpness with fat. In short, Martha Custis, who others had said possessed fine teeth, superlative tact, and an "infectious gentleness," was the catch of the day—as George Washington obviously recognized.

The widowed Martha, who John Custis had deemed "much inferior to his son," evidently wanted to retain little from his Williamsburg house. Scarcely four months after her husband died, much of its contents were put up for auction, among the lots no fewer than 137 of John Custis's precious pictures. The short list of things that she decided to keep included no pictures, perhaps validating John's concern for the survival of his painting of "John otherwise called Jack."

We can reasonably conclude that the trove of Custis relics found in the well were the product of Martha's clean sweep in the autumn of 1757. Is it stretching imagination too far, therefore, to see a fine-toothed, tactful, and gentle woman, later to be the first First Lady, taking a rock to grind away the name of John Custis from his bottle before symbolically casting it down the well? Remembering what John had thought of her Dandridge family, she may have derived no less gentle pleasure when in 1760 her new husband George rented Custis Square to her brother Bartholomew Dandridge.

Dandridge did not stay long, and by the autumn of 1762 Washington had leased Custis Square to William Byrd III, who made several unspecified repairs. In August 1769 the property was back on the rental market. After a brief tenancy by the Reverend Michael Smith, the house and lots were rented by Williamsburg's then current jack-of-all-trades Joseph Kidd. Among his several skills were those of paperhanger, floorcloth painter, upholsterer, gilder, lodging housekeeper, auctioneer, and appraiser. But most pertinent to us was his calling as a plumber and leadworker.

From a poem advocating vine growing penned by Robert Bolling, we learn that in addition to its ball and pyramidical yews the Custis gardens were graced by lead statuary that included figures of Apollo, Venus, and Bacchus. Such ornamentation was popular among England's landed gentry in the late 17th and early 18th centuries, and in the first quarter of the latter (when John Custis was creating his garden) lead castings from semiclassical figures sculptured in London by the Dutch artist John van Nost were greatly prized. It is conceivable, therefore, that van Nost was the creator of John Custis's figures. What is certain, however, is that Joseph Kidd eyed them less as a connoisseur of the undraped human form than as a lead-hungry plumber. Presumably without Washington's knowledge or permission, Venus and Apollo disappeared into Kidd's crucibles, and by 1773 only Bacchus survived.

The discovery of brass-working waste on the floor of the colonial Custis Kitchen recalls that by April 1773 Kidd was gone and the property was being rented by coachmaker Peter Hardy, some of whose activities were akin to those of his predecessor: gilding, painting, and brass foundry work. It is safe to conclude that Kidd had turned the old kitchen into a metalworking shop and that Hardy continued to use the building in that way. This raises an obvious question. If, as his *Virginia Gazette* advertisements attest, Kidd had coupled his many activities with running a lodging house at John Custis's old home, why would he have converted the kitchen into a workshop?

The answer may be that it was in his time that the easterly basement hearth of the brick house was put to use as a kitchen, thus explaining the hitherto enigmatic scorching we found there.

What, we may ask, had become of John Custis's beloved gardens during this time of change and apparent arboreal indignity and vandalism? Curiously, the boxwood trimmings and much of the twiggery we found in the well were deposited after Daniel Parke's death, perhaps even 10 or 15 years after—which puts them into the Smith-Kidd-Hardy era. One senses, nevertheless, that little tender, loving care was forthcoming, and the yew trees had been allowed to grow to such unruly shapes that they obscured the plinths and spaces left by the purloined Venus and Apollo. Kidd's advertisement for lodgers offered them no evening strolls through one of America's great gardens, but only "excellent clover pasture adjoining my house, well secured."

Today the site that had been the scene of some of the most extraordinary and tempestuous relationships in the history of Williamsburg is once again a pasture—for Colonial Williams-

Courtesy of Washington/Custis/Lee Collection, Washington and Lee University

burg's oxen. It lies vacant and waiting—waiting for the renewed archaeological work that can enable John Custis's garden to be reconstructed. Whether enough evidence can be found to justify the reconstruction of his anomalous "Six-chimney House" remains to be seen. But even if the reincarnation must be limited to rebuilding its foundations, the opportunity for visitors to walk with the ghosts of John Custis, William Byrd, the great naturalist Mark Catesby, and botanist John Bartram, not to mention Martha and George Washington, along gravel paths flanked by ball and pyramidical yews (and the occasional saucy statue), offers what may well be the most exciting prospect yet to be realized in Williamsburg.

Ivor Noël Hume

Lasting Impressions: Graffiti as History

Victorian vandals or homespun historians?

Shattered statues of Pharoah Rameses II at Thebes inspired Shelley's original ode to Ozymandias. Perhaps foretelling that their town would one day rank alongside the monuments of Egypt as a historical shrine, early Williamsburgers made sure that their names would not be forgotten. Opposite clockwise: At the Courthouse, CH 1915 rubs bricks with the 1878 of E. M. Lively, who the following year became a local hero when he put out a fire in the roof of the President's House at the College. At Carter's Grove an owner's son, William Henry Booth, finds himself in crowded company. Below, a trio of Wallers made their mark at the Public Records Office and at Bruton Parish Church. The 1790s seem to have been ripe for Public Records Office graffitists with a nice line in lettering. RC had less compliant brick to work on at the church, but a Union soldier from New York's 81st Regiment failed to make the most of his opportunity at the Records Office.

Ivor Noël Hume

And on the pedestal the words appear:
"My name is Ozymandias, king of kings!
Look on my works, ye Mighty, and despair!"
Also the names of Emory P. Gray,
Mr. and Mrs. Dukes, and Oscar Baer,
Of 27 West 4th Street, Oyster Bay.

"Ozymandias Revisited" by Morris Bishop

WHY? WHY WOULD anyone do that? I have been asking the question ever since I encountered T. Lowell of Boston and D. Bushnells of Ohio—names scratched on 3,500-year-old painted walls in Egypt. They were among the many wealthy American and European tourists who sailed the Nile in the 1830s and '40s in search of who knows what. Like the birds of prey, the original culture vultures happily destroyed what they enjoyed. Unlike the many who revealed their English origins only through their names, the Americans wanted posterity to know that proud citizens of Boston, New York, or Ohio had done the deed.

These people were by no means the first nor the last to leave their marks on Egypt. In a recent graffiti photographing trip there I bagged Ancient Greeks, Romans, Copts, Napoleonic scholars, a British consul, French and British archaeologists, a Jesuit priest, Belgians, a German Prince, and modern Russians, not to mention a miscellany of Arabs, some enshrined in valentine-style arrow-pierced hearts.

What was it, I asked myself, that made generally affluent and educated people feel comfortable defacing the very monuments they had come so far to admire? And why, later, would someone else deface the defacers leaving only the cities to take the blame? Was it possible that the original graffitists regretted what they had done and prevailed upon subsequent Nile traveling friends to hide their guilt?

While reflecting on these questions, I turned my attention closer to home and to the name droppers of Williamsburg and Carter's Grove. There being no inviting sandstone colossi or tomb murals on which to practice their art, only the colonial brick buildings have offered their surfaces—none more invitingly than the doorway of the Public Records Office. One of the noblest entrances surviving from 18th-century Williamsburg, its pilasters

Colonial Williamsburg

At the Courthouse of 1770 (below) today's visitors can find more names carved into the brickwork to the right of the steps than to the left. Early photographs (right) offered clues to who sat where—with time on their hands.

are covered with initials, names, and occasional dates. One would like to think that all are the work of boys who used the building during the 19th century when it served as an adjunct to the Williamsburg Grammar School, but not so. Several of the dates belong to the colonial years when Virginia's public records were housed there.

When I spotted "VE 81 Regt" I was sure I had landed a genuine British military vandal from those ten days in the summer of 1781 when Lord Cornwallis's army encamped in Williamsburg and left "Pestilence and Famine" in its wake. But I was wrong. The British 81st Regiment of Foot never got closer to Virginia than Ireland. Instead, the credit belongs to a later occupying force. Union troops held Williamsburg from May 5, 1862, to the end of the war, and two northern (but no southern) states had raised regiments numbered in the 80s—Pennsylvania and New York. And when you get the light just right you can see faintly below the incriminating "N. Y."

The Public Records Office was built after the Capitol was destroyed by fire in 1747, and we reasonably can assume that the quality of its rubbed brickwork was reflected in the new Capitol building that would be the scene of so many great events leading to Independence. Alas, that building burned in 1832. How many famous names might we not have found carved into its doorways had it survived? An unworthy thought, you say. Thomas Jefferson, who loved architecture more passionately than any other American of his day, would never have stooped to mutilating it. Perhaps not. But whose T. J. initials are carved in the gallery rail in Bruton Parish Church?

Church guides have long claimed them as Jefferson's, carved when a student at the College of William and Mary, but T. J. are by no means uncommon initials. An experimental search

Graffiti at the College of William and Mary: To the left of the Wren Building's east door is a plethora of 19th-century inscriptions (detail below). On the impost block beside the door the name of student F. W. Southgate (1828–31) defies us to know how he reached so high.

Ivor Noël Hume

through the *London Directory* for 1793 turned up 41, including 11 Thomas Joneses and one Thomas Jefferson—owner of a petticoat warehouse in Cheapside. At the northeast corner in the church's north transept one can find R. C.—twice. We know that Robert "King" Carter of Corotoman ordered wine bottles from England bearing seals impressed with those initials, but it's a rash graffitologist who claims Bruton's for his.

The church's west entrance is fairly liberally incised with the names of lingering worshippers, but the most prominent doorway, the one facing Duke of Gloucester Street, remains as clean as the day it was built—or rather rebuilt, for this brickwork was replaced during the restoration of 1939. If the old bricks were scarred by names and initials, as the west doorway makes likely, I have been unable to find that anyone considered copying them onto the new work or even keeping a record of what they were.

Archaeologists, of course, are renowned for taking the long view, and look at both past and future a little differently than most people. Consequently, the notion that relatively recent mutilations will have further historical value raises no eyebrows. In this writer's view, worthily or not, many of the countless travelers' names that mutilate the monuments have been there long enough to become part of their history. So how long is long enough? If we point with pride to a questionably 18th-century T. J. or an R. C., what value do we place on a "C. H. 1915" on the Courthouse? That surely was long ago and far away from the world as we now know it, and therefore a legitimate relic of Williamsburg's past. But what about a tourist's 1970 legacy on the north side of the same building? If the Courthouse is to be restored to its 18th-century appearance, should not this and all other 20th- and 19th-century graffiti be ground off just as one would remove a noncolonial window or chimney cap?

The philosophy of preservation is constantly evolving and is as changeable as women's hemlines. In 1681 the poet John Dryden expressed one point of view—one that would ensure the graffitists their immortality:

If ancient fabrics nod, and threat to fall
To patch the flaws, and buttress up the wall,
Thus far 'tis duty; but here fix the mark:
For all beyond is to touch our ark.

In a hundred years' time, today's garbage will have become an archaeologist's treasure, and an abandoned New York subway a cultural monument patrolled by guards to prevent graffitists from damaging the graffiti.

Those on the Williamsburg Courthouse posed an intriguing problem. Most, as one might expect, are on the front of the building, but rather than being incised into the doorway itself, most range along the water table on either side of the steps. That, too, is to be expected, for this is where lawyers, clerks, witnesses, plaintiffs, defendants, and their friends gathered on court days. Less expected was my discovery that many more graffiti are to be found to the east of the steps than to the west. I guessed that a tree offered more shade on that side, but my wife had a better idea: "Could it be the product of segregation," she asked, "black people assembling to the west and white to the east?"

The suggestion made sense, and if correct, could turn the rarely noticed scratchings into a page of Williamsburg's black history. I called Judge Robert T. Armistead, who had been a law student in Williamsburg prior to 1932 when the Courthouse ceased to be used as such. He remembered it well, but said that he had no recollection of any such exterior segregation. Once

35

Did William Byrd order this brick? Was it really put in place beside a window of the Brafferton Building in 1723? These are just two of the many questions posed when one scratches the surface of Williamsburg's largely unexplored graffitological archive.

inside, he added, a dividing rope sent black people to the left and white to the right.

"Isn't it possible," I persisted, "that if that division existed inside, it would continue informally outside?"

Judge Armistead did not think so. But an hour later he called back to tell me that he remembered that there had been benches on either side of the door, and maybe the blacks and whites did sit on opposite sides of the steps. He suggested that I look at such early photographs as might survive to see who was sitting where.

Colonial Williamsburg's newly expanded library quickly demonstrated its retrieval capabilities, producing five photographs taken between 1897 and 1907, one of them showing to the right a speeding cow and lounging on the steps to the left as likely a trio of potential graffitists as one could hope to find—all of them white. None of the pictures showed Judge Armistead's benches. Alas, the course of research does not always run straight and true.

You would expect that of all Williamsburg's inviting brick walls, those at the College of William and Mary would have provided the most irresistible challenge. But if so, time and restoration have taken their toll. The east face of the Wren Building is surprisingly short of enrichment and what little there is raises questions to tax the ingenuity of the best brain in Baker Street. Why, for example, is the name F. W. Southgate large and alone on the central doorway's left impost block? Records show that he was a student at the College between 1828 and 1831, but not that he was nine feet tall! Did he climb onto the flanking railing to reach the brick, and if so why did he go to such conspicuous trouble when there were so many invitingly reachable bricks lower down?

Then there's the mystery of the massed graffiti beneath the flanking left window where several courses of heavily burned bricks are laid in non-colonial bond, and all covered with large and deeply cut initials. Too far out to be reached from the porch and too high to be attacked from the ground, they may have been salvaged from other parts of the building, perhaps after the fire of 1862, for there seems to be no record that Colonial Williamsburg's restoration team created this gaggle of graffiti.

Not all incised inscriptions are the product of ego-tripping vandals, and a brick in the Brafferton building is one such exception. Architectural historian Marcus Whiffen in his book *The Public Buildings of Williamsburg* declared that the date of the Brafferton "is established by an inscribed brick to the right of the window on the west side of the south door." The brick reads W B 1723, and some authorities have identified the W B as William Byrd who was then on the Board of Visitors.

The Brafferton brick differs from the usual run of graffiti in that the brick seems to have been inscribed *before* it was kiln baked—a state known to archaeologists as *ante cocturam*. This,

then, was akin to a foundation stone, and to make sure that it would be noticed, the deeply incuse letters were filled with fine white mortar. On the other side of the same window, there is another date: 1863, recalling the time when the College was in Yankee hands and the Brafferton building looted. That date was carved into an already fired brick (*post cocturam*), and like the rest of Williamsburg's graffitological legacy, could have been applied at any time *after* the brick was baked, but not before—whereas the 1723 digits had to be as old as their matrix.

Unfortunately, too few original brick buildings survive in Williamsburg to provide valid statistics, but such evidence as we have suggests that public buildings were more likely to be graffitistically enriched than were private. Thus, for example, the three principal private homes, the Wythe House, the Palmer House, and the Ludwell-Paradise House, remain virtually clean, though the Ludwell-Paradise House bears the incised date 1776.

But why state the obvious? Public buildings would inevitably receive more traffic and be gathering places for people waiting to pray, to be taught, or to be reprimanded. What home owner would allow would-be graffitists to lurk about his door?

That argument is as sound as a bell—until one looks at the riverside doorway to Carter's Grove. Both pilasters are liberally embellished, one of the largest and clearest additions provided by the son of Edwin G. Booth, Jr., who inherited the plantation in 1885 and kept it until 1905. William Henry Booth the graffitist was barely 20 when the family moved away, and it is likely that the Kappa Alpha and Kappa Sigma fraternity initials gracing the doorway were contributed by fellow students from the College of William and Mary following in their host's inscriptional footsteps. Like tourists on the Nile, Carter's Grove visitor R. F. W. wanted us to know that he came from "Wash. D. C."

So here we are back at the beginning, still asking why? To claim that like bored students carving on their desks, monument mutilators are really nice people with too little to do is an argument thin to the point of emaciation. Closer to the truth is the notion that just like the world's big names, the little ones yearn to be remembered—openly through their progeny, or their school yearbook, or secretly in far-flung historic places where immortality seems better assured.

Thus, in some distant millennium, long after our civilization has crumbled into an uninterpretable tangle of rusted steel, shattered plastic, and dead batteries, and after the Egyptian sands have again wound the Nile's monuments in their protective shroud, archaeologists from the planet Pluto may rediscover the temple at Dendera. What, we may wonder, will they make of a tiny silver plaque that they'll find secreted between two of the stones, a plaque engraved

AUDREY & IVOR
NOEL HUME
Williamsburg, Virginia
Were Here
February 20
1986

"Why?" they may ask themselves as they rub their antennae together, "Why would humanoids have done something like that?"

Coming to Grips with "Granny"
A case of mistaken identity at Wolstenholme Towne

TO BE WRONG is appalling, but to admit to being wrong is suicidal. So said colleagues when they opened the *Washington Post* one day in June and saw an Associated Press dispatch that read: "An archaeologist says he made errors in interpreting data from his excavations at 17th-century Wolstenholme Towne, one of the earliest excavated Colonial settlement sites in America." I was that archaeologist and, yes, I had changed my mind—and I'll probably do it again before we conclude our researches into the archaeology and history of the plantation at Carter's Grove the first settlers called Martin's Hundred.

Although the colonial history of the land now occupied by restored Williamsburg (previously known as Middle Plantation) goes back to 1633, the numbers of 17th-century artifacts found here are pathetically few. Indeed, it was not until 1963 that we had an opportunity to investigate our first clearly pre-18th-century site—one 20 miles away on land that did not belong to us.

The place was Denbigh plantation near Newport News. Once the home of 1630s Virginia revolutionary Samuel Mathews and his governor son, the land had been purchased by developer L. B. Weber, whose interest in local history prompted him to appeal to Colonial Williamsburg for archaeological help. The resulting excavations uncovered the remains of two large 17th-century houses, much pottery and glass, arms and armor (including part of a helmet), a brand of the Virginia colony, a silver saucepan lid bearing Mathew's initials, and the only copper watering can known to survive from the 17th century. In short, the Mathews Manor excavations provided us with a dry run for the discoveries we would make 13 years later at Carter's Grove.

Although the Denbigh artifacts were exciting and had been recovered in associated groups deposited at specific moments in time, we still knew too little about the dating of 17th-century objects to be sure which group belonged to what date. In spite of our Denbigh experience, therefore, we were not much wiser when our work at Carter's Grove commenced in the spring of 1976.

For the next five and a half years we dug there almost continuously, excavating sites associated with Martin's Hundred whose core settlement at Wolstenholme Towne was destroyed in an Indian uprising in March 1622. What we found ranks among the most important collections of early 17th-century structures and artifacts yet discovered in the New World. However, it's a well-worn archaeological adage that three months' digging generates nine of post-excavation research; yet we had dug for close

Richard Schlecht

They found her in the pit amid her kitchen trash. She lay as though sleeping, but when they came closer they knew that there would be no awakening this side of heaven. Too late for the niceties of burial, they left her where she died.

Opposite: A life-preserving spring rises in the now-wooden gulley that separates reconstructed Wolstenholme Towne (background) from the heavily defended home of the Boys family. The green markers in the left foreground identify the resting places of its four male servants. Two more such markers beyond the Boys palisades locate the graves of women. Another, at left, partly hidden by the tree, marks that of Granny.

Joe Bailey, National Geographic Society

Although new thinking robbed Granny of her social standing, she remained the earliest Virginia female colonist to have been found (top) and the first identified as a victim of the Indian attack of 1622. An X-ray (center) shows the clue of the "ear iron" with its pewter knob in their original position round her skull. Granny was moved to the laboratory in three parts for further study. The Smithsonian Institution's famed physical anthropologist Dr. Lawrence Angel (above) measures her pelvis. Other human remains were transported in the same way, including the feet of a servant who had been wearing a single hob-nailed work shoe (bottom), its nail placement revealed by X-ray.

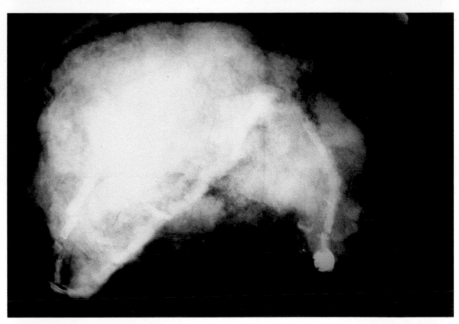

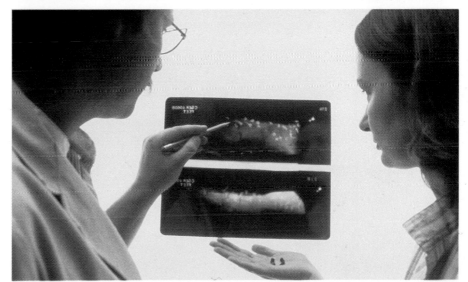

(opposite) photo by Dave Doody

Ivor Noël Hume

on 66 months with barely a pause for breath. To comply with the digging-to-thinking ratio, we would have to assume a position of intense cogitation lasting well into 1997!

That was not a well-received proposition. On the contrary, the National Geographic Society, whose funding had made the excavations possible, demanded a final research report within two years of the dig's completion. Its magazine's deadlines were even more immediate, needing publishable statements even as the fieldwork progressed. For our part, we were pleased to provide them, though carefully qualifying virtually everything we said with "perhapses" and "maybes."

Because archaeology is an increasingly costly business, its practitioners rely heavily on public approbation to warrant further investments. It was ever thus. In the 1920s, the great American Egyptologist James Breasted was described as being as skillful at digging on Wall Street as he was in Egypt. For us, the prospect of the enormous circulation attendant on the publication of articles in *National Geographic* was surely the best way to create and sustain public interest.

In tandem with two *National Geographic* articles (June 1979 and January 1982) came literally hundreds of newspaper stories as well as an award-winning film from Colonial Williamsburg's own studio. These, along with the publication of a popular book, all served to keep Martin's Hundred in the public eye.

The discovery in 1977–1978 of Wolstenholme Towne and its now famous fort led in 1980 to the excavation of a smaller site about 400 feet to the southeast, one comprising a single house protected by a more or less triangular stockade. It was there that we found the skeleton of a woman lying in a sleeping posture in the mud of a rubbish pit—a woman wearing a bent iron spring around her head. Identifying this as part of a hairdressing device popular in the early 17th century, I deduced that the woman was a person of some importance, probably the mistress of the house, and that she died in the pit while trying to escape in the aftermath of the 1622 Indian attack.

We called the woman "Granny" because she had lost her lower molars, though in reality she was only about 40 years old. Virginia pathologists and the director of a New York insomnia clinic agree that she had died in her sleep. We at first saw this as a symptom of hypothermia, but later the head of the Medical College of Virginia's emergency room pointed out that the same sleep-promoting symptom is characteristic of people dying from loss of blood. That made better sense, for such meteorological records as are available do not support the idea of dying of cold during daylight hours in Virginia in late March.

Because Granny's house stood alone and at some distance from the main Wolstenholme settlement, I saw it as a defensible outpost—and *outposts* by definition are extras or additions. I have to admit, too, that because her palisaded enclosure was small, and for the subconscious and totally invalid reason that we found it *second*, I slid like butter into the trap of concluding that lesser meant later. When the National Geographic Society's mapmaker needed me to give the place a name a bit more interesting than its archaeological designation as "Site H," I called it the "Suburb."

Although the 1982 *National Geographic* article had focused on Granny and her burned house, the site was hidden from the main Wolstenholme settlement, and so would not figure in our

later plans to present the big picture to Carter's Grove visitors. The story of how we came to invent a technique for the partial reconstruction of Wolstenholme Towne has been told elsewhere. All that matters is that the public responded well to it—save in one respect. Those who had read the articles or seen the film wanted to be shown where Granny lay buried. But we couldn't do so. Once excavations at Site H ended in January 1980, part was allowed to grow back into woods and the rest returned to the plow. Nevertheless, the visitors' wish was not forgotten, and when the Winthrop Rockefeller Charitable Trust undertook to help broaden the scope of Carter's Grove interpretation, Granny's house and palisade joined the list of new projects.

By the end of March 1986, her defenses were up and so was the horizontal and vertical outline of her house. Until this work began, Site H had been relegated to the back burner of our research schedule. First, we reasoned, we need to study Wolstenholme Towne and everything that we had found there. Now, however, the suburb again thrust itself to the fore. Visitors were arriving even before the construction was finished, and two barrel-housed narrative stations (we have nine on the Wolstenholme site) were waiting to tell them the where, what, and when of Granny's place. Project historian Audrey Noël Hume was

Archaeologists learn to convert dirty marks in the ground into mental images of the buildings and activities that once were there, but it takes a period-steeped artist of the caliber of Richard Schlecht to convert those images into recognizable reality. Here, through his brushes, the John Boys site with its home palisades, mounted artillery, and tree-stripped ravine, lives again as it may have done in the spring of 1621.

Richard Schlecht

hauled loudly protesting away from her assigned research to grapple with these questions.

As the name of our profession suggests, we had two lines of attack: historical and archaeological. The latter, in addition to providing the plan of the palisades and the remains of a burned house, yielded enough pieces of armor and weapon parts to indicate a strong military presence. More important, it gave us three graves—plus Granny in her trash pit. The largest grave contained the badly decayed remains of four skeletons buried head to toe like sardines, and on one of the feet we found the remains of a heavy, wood-soled, and hob-nailed, workman's shoe. The other two graves contained bones identified as those of women—though one was limited to a pair of femurs and could not have been identified as female had it not been for the presence of an iron key between these upper leg bones and a brass thimble to the right of them. It was common practice for women, particularly those with some authority in a household, to carry their sewing equipment in a bag or purse attached to a girdle and to hang their keys on a string from it.

So here was our cast of characters: one young woman unidentified and cause of death unknown, one woman of uncertain age but an authority figure, four people of low estate (one a single-shoed male, the others unidentified), and Granny with the fancy hair-do. Each was found outside the palisade, but none more than a few feet from it, suggesting that all were products of the same killing event. Although only Granny could be identified as a victim of foul play, it seemed logical to assume that the rest were too. The alternative for those in the multiple burial and for the "Key Lady" was that they were victims of communicable disease, hastily buried in the clothes in which they died. But would a sick man die with his shoe on? And why only *one* shoe? And there were other problems to tax us.

Why did we have *two* authority-figure females: Granny and the Key Lady? And if Granny was the mistress of the house, why was she left in the rubbish pit when even a shod servant merited a grave? Nobody could have missed seeing her, for the pit lay just outside one of the palisade's gates. Then, too, if the multiple grave contained only servants, what had become of their master?

No journals survive to describe what happened at Martin's Hundred on the "fatal Friday morning" of March 22, 1622. All we have is a general account of the Indian attack on the colony as a whole and a listing of the dead by plantation. It was to this last that Audrey had to go to find a household that lost four male (?) servants and three women. She had been through the exercise many times before and had come to the conclusion that the home of Thomas Boys (or Boise) was the most likely candidate. The list read:

> *Mast Tho: Boise, & Mistris Boise his wife, & a sucking Childe.*
> *4 of his men.*
> *A Maide.*
> *2 Children.*
> *Nathaniel Iefferies wife.*
> *Margaret Davies.*

Unfortunately, the list does not indicate where one household ends and the next begins, so there is no knowing whether Nathaniel Jefferies's wife or Margaret Davies was with Thomas Boys when they were killed. Nevertheless, if Granny was Mistress Boys, we should have uncovered the remains of her husband and of two, if not three, children. Yet we found none of them.

And there was another problem. Unknown when the list of the dead was sent to England was the fact that five men and about 15 women (most apparently from Martin's Hundred) had been taken hostage by the Indians. If that had been their policy when attacking Wolstenholme Towne, why did we find the skeletons of three women in its suburbs? That was just one of the problems we had pushed under the rug when in 1982 we tried to associate Granny with Mistress Thomas Boys.

The inability of archaeology to provide historically acceptable dating evidence was never more apparent than when we were grappling with this enigma. The circumstances of Granny's death, the burning of her house, and the fact that there was no evidence of rebuilding afterwards, led us to conclude that the suburb was destroyed in March 1622. But it did not follow that every skeleton we found there had been buried in the slaughter's aftermath.

We had ample documentary evidence that killing sicknesses made devastating inroads into the ranks of newly arrived colonists; so perhaps all but Granny had died of contagious disease. Even if the graves' filling had been rich in broken artifacts (which they weren't), unless the fragments had manufacture dates written on them, we would have been hard put to establish time brackets narrower than 10 or 20 years. Here we were dealing with but two.

In my book *Martin's Hundred*, I struggled with this problem, and in settling on Thomas Boys, added:

> *Archaeological reasoning is akin to trying to reassemble a watch that has lost half its parts. When you are through, it may look all right, but it still won't tick. Furthermore, if you do not fully understand the mechanism, there is always the chance of fitting the wrong cog in the wrong hole. In trying to reconstruct what happened and to whom on Site H, we had only to misread one clue to throw our reasoning hopelessly awry.*

Suppose, then, that I had been wrong in seeing all the dead as victims of the Indian attack? How would we read the list if, say, we eliminated both the Key Lady and the unknown young woman?

The household of John Jackson lost a child of unspecified age, and "4 Menservants," but no women. We had Granny and no child. A much more likely candidate was the home of another Boys (Boise):

> *Master John Boise his Wife.*
> *A Maide.*
> *4 Men-servants.*

The absence of a comma after "Boise" meant that not he but only his wife had been killed. Thus his losses amounted to four men servants and two women. We know more about John Boys than any of the others on the list. He was the senior civil official in Martin's Hundred (pending the arrival of Governor Harwood in 1620) and had represented it at the first Virginia Assembly at Jamestown in 1619. More important, John Boys was responsible for the distribution of land within the Hundred. One more thing: His wife's name was Sara—and a year after the attack the records state that "Mrs. [B]oyse (the Chiefe of the prisoners) [was] sent home appareled like one of theire Queens." Thus, if the four in our multiple grave were John Boys's men servants, Granny certainly was not the lady of the house. With Sara scratched from the list, she of the fancy hair-do would have to be the "Maide."

As this reasoning developed I expected at any moment to hear a voice in my ear whispering, "The butler did it!"

Granny's head-of-house status had been built around my belief that her hair dressing was elaborate and of a type that had been fashionable in the late Elizabethan era but which had lost favor around 1610. Thus, I saw her as an older person clinging to the quality English standards she knew and favored in her youth. Comforting support for my identification of her hair-roll spring would come from England, where a brass example survives in the Museum of London, each end terminating in a pewter knob. But Granny's has a knob only at one end, a twist of iron substituting at the other. Her head was small, and it appeared that the spring had been shortened to fit it. Would the mistress of the house settle for something so rough, or could it be that this was a hand-me-down being worn by a servant?

While we were still debating this point, a scholar from Holland, Dr. Jeremy Bangs, the newly appointed curator at Plimoth Plantation, paid us a visit. He had read about the hair spring and knew that we had found it bent round behind Granny's head—a position I had attributed to rough handling by an Indian attacker. "Were there any brass pins associated with the band?" he asked.

"Not as such," I replied. "But there *was* a thin copper stain at the base of the skull and in contact with the iron."

Dr. Bangs smiled. "That's what I expected." He went on to explain that in 17th-century Holland people of all classes, from burgers' wives to maid servants, wore a wire spring around the backs of their heads. Like the English hair-roll spring, its end terminated in pewter knobs and turned down (as did Granny's) over the ears and so was known as an "ear-iron." It held a plain undercap in place, to which a more decorative outer cap was secured with pins.

Granny's descent from mistress to servant was now a likely possibility. Such a conclusion would also explain why she was left in the pit where she died. The burial party discovered her muddy and blood-boltered body in the pit and, glad to be relieved of the task of digging another hole, they simply shoveled dirt over her and left her where she lay.

If Audrey was right in reassigning Site H with John rather than Thomas Boys, several other pieces in the puzzle would need to be rearranged. As warden and land distributor John Boys would have been one of the first to build there, meaning that this house and its defenses were erected soon after Martin's Hundred settlers reached Virginia in 1619—probably *before* rather than after Wolstenholme Towne was begun.

With this new picture emerging, another nagging problem disappeared. We knew from the records that Martin's Hundred possessed a cannon; and when we found a cannonball for a big gun called a saker, I concluded that that was the kind of cannon it was. However, the supposed cannon platform at a corner of the Wolstenholme fort was too small to take it. Besides, the fort was located at the back of the settlement and poorly placed for a saker to hit enemy ships approaching up the river. Since Spain was considered by the English to be more of a threat than the Indians, there seemed to be something very odd about Martin's Hundred's defensive planning.

As soon as new timbers began to rise in the suburb's post holes we realized that here was a far more substantial military structure than we had supposed. One of its two protective flankers faced the river and was sufficiently large to mount a cannon of saker size. Much closer to the James than the Wolstenholme fort, the fortified compound controlled access to a ravine which, today, provides the principal approach from the river. No less important, a freshwater spring flows through the ravine and must have served both the suburb and the main settlement. In sum, therefore, if Warden Boys was the first to stake his London sponsors' claim on the land they called Martin's Hundred, he could have chosen no more strategic location.

If you have stayed with me this far and have a flair for murder mysteries, you'll know that we still have a couple of bodies unaccounted for—the young woman and the Key Lady. Were they unlucky visitors to the suburb at the time of the attack, or did they live there and die at other times? Or—perish the thought—do we *still* have it wrong? Unlike schoolbooks that have the answers at the back, we have nowhere to look to check that our conclusions are right—at least, not now. But who is to say that in the attic of some English cottage, or amid the uncataloged manuscripts of a great private library, there may not lie a piece of brittle parchment inscribed in faded brown ink "A True List of the Names of those Seated in Martin's Hundred & a Mappe of the Places whereon they are Planted in the Yeere 1621."

Although, in the years since that hope was voiced documents relating to other Martin's Hundred settlers have surfaced, Granny remains a cipher. In 1989, conforming to the court order under which she was exhumed and which required that she be reinterred exactly where she was found—which could have meant burying her bones amid the trash where she died—she was laid to rest in a 17th-century-style coffin and with the kind of Anglican service we hoped she would have wanted. A silver plaque on the coffin lid and inside a sealed capsule provided by the National Geographic Society together told her story. I hope we got it right.

A time capsule provided by the National Geographic Society joined Granny in her coffin before the Reverend Richard May conducted the burial service at which (clockwise) the author, coffin-builder Woodrow Abbott, foreman Nate Smith, and archaeologist John Hamant bade her farewell.

Courtesy of National Geographic Society

Dave Doody

Martin's Hundred: The Search Continued

"What we don't know isn't so," so spake the experts

Ivor Noël Hume

Enter into his gates with thanksgiving, and into his courts with praise: be thankful unto him, and bless his name.

STANDING WITH HEAD BOWED, I barely heard the priest reciting the 100th Psalm. I could think only of what I hoped was awaiting us beneath the heavy stone slabs of the church floor. The quest that began in an open field in Virginia eight years earlier was about to end in the darkness of a burial vault beneath a tiny country church in England.

The workman standing beside me had no idea why he and his mates had been hired to lift the stones and dismantle a stone wall. But the rector of St. Mary's church in the parish with the strange-sounding name of Lydiard Tregoz well knew what we were seeking. He had read about the mystery of the colonial coffins from Virginia in the *National Geographic* article "First Look at a Lost Virginia Settlement," published in June 1979.

"I thought I'd wear this," said Reverend John Flory, pointing to his stole and the crossed nails symbolic of the Passion embroidered at its ends. With a smile he added: "It seemed appropriate."

The chain of events that led us to Lydiard Tregoz began in 1976 at Carter's Grove plantation in Virginia where I with my team of Colonial Williamsburg archaeologists had discovered the remains of the early English settlement known as Martin's Hundred. Although we knew that the discoveries could add immensely to our knowledge of life in British America in the early 17th century, we had no idea the project would capture the lasting popular attention that it did.

For years after the digging halted, people in the most unlikely places came up to me and asked: "What happened in the end? Did you ever find out who 'Granny' really was? Are you going to reconstruct Wolstenholme Towne so that people can visit the site? Will there be a museum where we can see the helmets? That weird blade you wrote about; did you ever figure out what it was? Did you ever find the coffin you were looking for—the one with the A-shaped lid?"

In archaeology very little can safely be assumed. Simple luck will often drop answers to seemingly insoluble questions neatly into your lap, while problems that should easily be solved resolutely refuse to cooperate. The mystery of the nails turned out to belong to the latter. It began when we found graves dating from the second quarter of the 17th century. In them were the remains of men, women, and an infant, each with a row of nails running down the center of the skeleton. Coffin lids normally (at least in later centuries) were secured only at the sides, prompting me to dismiss the Martin's Hundred burials as the work of an eccentric local coffin builder. But when other archaeologists working on sites of the same period elsewhere in Virginia began to record similar discoveries, I soon changed my mind.

Early and mid-17th-century illustrations of plague burials in England solved the problem—or so I thought. In every picture the coffins had gabled or peaked lids. As most of the heads of the nails we found along our skeletons lay in the same direction, I had little doubt that they had been used to secure the join of the two abutting boards. All I needed to prove it was to ask British church

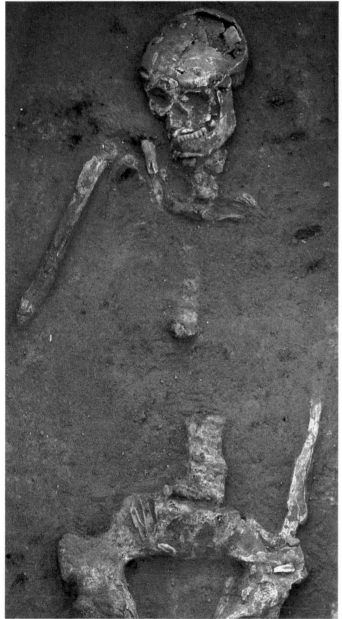

Ivor Noël Hume

Nails resting on the skeleton of this Martin's Hundred resident (above) provided the first clue that in the early 17th century coffins had gabled lids. Evidently buried in haste, the dead in Wolstenholme Towne (opposite) did not enjoy that luxury.

authorities for permission to examine an intact example in one of England's many church vaults. That was where I ran into trouble.

The librarian for Westminster Abbey wrote: "Nobody here seems to have any knowledge of 16th- or 17th-century coffins with A-roofs."

A research officer for the Council for British Archaeology answered from personal experience: "I have been involved with the recording of several family vaults in the last few years, including one of the period in which you are interested," he wrote, "but on no occasion has this type turned up."

The ecclesiastical historian for Britain's Council for Places of Worship made his point even more bluntly: "There is no hope of Mr. Hume finding an A-lidded coffin in any vault in England. Such coffins were never generally used in England, and I do not understand at all his reference to plague burials, for such burials were always un-coffined to minimize the risk of contamination."

Julian Litten, the Victoria and Albert Museum's specialist on funerary art, agreed. The coffins in my illustrations, he said, were not used for burial but only for carrying plague victims to the grave site.

So how was it that one of the pictures shows the coffins being placed in the grave? I convinced myself that I was right and everybody else was wrong. But how was I to prove it?

Our first break came when I learned that at Clifton in Nottinghamshire the Clifton family had been buried in the same vault since the 15th century. Better still, it was entered through a door and not by tearing up the church floor—and the vicar had a key!

Alas, when he used it, we found that so many later burials were jammed into the vault that if there had been gabled lids among the earlier coffins, they had long since been crushed beneath the weight of later arrivals. However, the journey to Clifton was by no means wasted. In the church we found the elaborately sculpted tomb of Sir Gervaise Clifton who died in 1669, the monument featuring a full-scale rendering of a gabled coffin.

In another *National Geographic* article (January 1982) I told how the trail next led to the Sackville family vault at Withyham where we found the lead liner for the casket of the infant daughter of the fifth Earl of Dorset—the inscribed lead plaque dated 1649 and folded over the ridge of a gabled lid.

That, I thought, should have been confirmation enough. Critical colleagues countered that the lead liner for a noble child could hardly be claimed as proof that less exalted people were buried in gabled wood. There was disagreement, too, as to whether all such lead caskets were originally cased in wood.

By this time I was finding more illustrations ranging in date and place from the Black Death in France to London's public gallows at Tyburn in the 1680s where four gabled coffins were shown on a wagon. These, however, differed from other English illustrations in that the lids had triangular ends, suggesting that they were meant to be opened and not just nailed shut. They probably belonged to the College of Surgeons who often took the cadavers of executed felons for teaching aids. If so, the Tyburn picture supported Julian Litten's conclusion that gabled coffins were reusable.

Although more than three years had passed since the Withyham chapter of this saga appeared in the *National Geographic*, I continued to hear from readers offering parallels for our Martin's

The modest exterior of Lydiard Tregoz Church in Wiltshire (below) belies the richness of the 17th-century monuments inside. Chief among its treasures is the 1615 painted triptych (right) commemorating Sir John St. John and his wife Lucy. The three painted coffins in the foreground were the bait that sent Williamsburg archaeologists delving beneath the church floor and into the St. John crypt (bottom, left). A later St. John tomb and monument stood above the crypt (bottom, right). The possibility that it might collapse when workmen breached the sealing wall below was a consequence not to be taken lightly.

Ivor Noël Hume

Ivor Noël Hume

A "resurrection" tomb: This 1634 monument (below) shows Temperence Browne sitting up in her gable-ended coffin beckoning us to the Church of St. Peter at Steane Park, Northamptonshire. Digging below her (lower, left), we found nothing but a finger bone and a fragment from the corner of her—or somebody else's—coffin.

Ian Yeomans, National Geographic Society

Hundred coffins. From Haifa, Israel, came a reminder that in 1982 the high priest of Samaria had gone to his grave in such a coffin. So had the Shah of Iran. Several Mennonites told me that members of their church are still buried in them, and a man in Indiana wrote to tell me that he had the wood for his coffin in his barn. It was to be gabled, he said, because his family had always had them made that way.

From West Germany came a photograph of an actual coffin—of the Tyburn type—but with long handles at the ends. Church records showed that it had been made in 1613 for taking plague victims to their graves. Another source turned up a hitherto unpublished sketch of Jesuit priests in Canada in the 1680s, two of them kneeling beside a gabled coffin concealed under a cloth pall. Yet another correspondent sent me excerpts from medical textbooks to prove that calcium phosphate crystals found in human urine are gabled and known as "coffin-lid crystals."

More pertinent was a letter from Australia. The writer wanted me to know that regardless of what British archaeologists might say, gabled coffins had been unearthed in Britain. His source: the second volume of a history of Edinburgh published in 1848. His was the first evidence to reach me of anyone ever recording such a discovery in Britain. Grateful though I was, I could not help wondering why anyone in Australia would want to read the *first* volume of an 1848 history of Edinburgh, let alone the second!

Among the many people to whom I had turned for help was Pamela Maas, national secretary to the National Association of Funeral Directors. It was she who told me that "Winchester Cathedral has some gable-lidded coffins stacked high above their altar," adding that "they are said to contain the bones of former Saxon kings."

I sought the help of cathedral librarian Canon F. Bussby, who promised to help but confessed that he considered the boxes to be "ossuary chests rather than coffins and were never used as we normally think of a coffin's use." Nevertheless, they had to be seen—which would not be easy. They stood atop stone screens

47

Proof of the pudding: In this mid-17th-century woodcut, bearers carry a pall-draped, gabled coffin to its grave (right). With less ceremony but still in gabled coffins, London plague victims went to their rest (below, right). As late as 1680 miscreants hanged at Tyburn were carried away to Surgeon's Hall in reusable gabled coffins (below, left).

Opposite: The Earl De La Warr opened his family vault for us, here examining the gabled lead coffin of an infant ancestor who died in 1649 (top, left). Below, the gabled tomb of Sir Gervaise Clifton near Nottingham beckoned to no purpose. A chest broken open by Cromwell's looters in Winchester Cathedral (center) had been made around 1525 to hold the bones of displaced English kings. At right, the Victoria and Albert Museum's Tor Abbey Jewel, shown actual size, dates from about 1600, its removable, gabled lid gloriously crafted in enameled gold. Lacking beauty but eminently practical, the handled and hinge-lidded reusable "pest coffin" was made at Schaafheim in Germany in 1620 for transporting plague victims.

Courtesy of Gardner Collection

Monarchy or No Monarchy, 1661

about 16 feet above ground.

I arranged for scaffolding to be erected to enable me to reach them, to examine their construction, and, with luck, to photograph the placement of their nails. But once atop the platform I could see that Canon Bussby had been right. The six chests were elaborately decorated and more closely resembled medieval reliquaries than they did coffins.

They had been made in the 1660s to replace mortuary chests constructed in 1525, when the Saxon kings' bones had been unearthed during renovations to the building. In 1642 the cathedral had been looted by Cromwell's troops. An 18th-century historian told how the soldiers "defaced many of the monuments, and pulling down some of the chests which contained the remains of the Saxon kings, they threw their bones against the painted glass, which they destroyed throughout the church."

It is hard to put up scaffolding in a cathedral transept without attracting attention. My wife, Audrey, a long-suffering partner

from the beginning, had declined to climb the poles and remained below fielding questions. An elderly guide to the cathedral told her, "He's wasting his time up there. I'll show you what he's looking for." He led Audrey away to another stone screen behind the altar. On the top stood a rectangular wooden chest without a lid and beside it another about three feet long, its gabled lid broken but intact on one side. Here at last was a genuine 16th-century coffin-shaped box, and almost certainly a relic of the Cromwellian looters who had broken into it in search of treasure.

Although the box was only about the size of the infant's coffin from Martin's Hundred, the method of its construction seemed to confirm our interpretation of the nails from the adult coffins. But still English critics insisted, as had Canon Bussby, that a king's mortuary chest could not be considered a parallel for a common coffin—even if it was the most simply constructed gabled box imaginable.

So the search went on.

Ira Block, National Geographic Society

Courtesy of Victoria and Albert Museum, photo by Ivor Noël Hume

Peter Eidmann

The previously skeptical Julian Litten now joined the hunt. He had seen our growing file of evidence—including a miniature gabled coffin in gold with an enameled skeleton inside it. Known as the Tor Abbey Jewel, it dates from the late 16th century, is cataloged as English, and is one of the treasures of Litten's own museum. Convinced that the Martin's Hundred people had indeed been buried in gabled coffins, and that the design was not an American oddity but an English tradition, Julian spent his spare time visiting rural churches hunting for monuments indicating that the owners buried in vaults below lay in *our* style coffins.

At Burton Agnes in Yorkshire he found a tomb topped with three gabled coffins, but tentative approaches left little doubt that permission to open the vault would not be granted. At Steane Park in Northhamptonshire he found the 1634 monument to Temperence Brown—shown sitting bolt upright in her lidless but gable-ended coffin. Here the omens were more favorable. Prolonged negotiations with family and diocese produced the neces-

sary authorizing paper to be nailed to the church door, a document received only hours before we began digging.

Preliminary magnetometer testing by a specialist from the Department of the Environment had assured Julian that the grave had not been disturbed by later burials. An area about three feet wide and six feet long lay below Temperence Brown's monument. There was just room for her between the wall and the adjacent 1721 tomb of the 18th-century Crewe family—but only if the church wall had no footings, and the Crewes no burial vault. The magnetometer reading notwithstanding, soon after we started down we hit first the spreading foundation and then the brick wall of the Crewe vault. All that remained of Temperence and her coffin were an iron corner reinforcement and one finger bone!

Back in Williamsburg I was ready to give up, but Julian kept searching. Six months later he wrote saying that he had a new candidate, the vault of the St. John family under the church of Lydiard Tregoz. What made it a good bet was a magnificent pan-

49

Using data from the Martin's Hundred coffins, in 1984 Michael Spreadborough made this one in oak (below) to receive a member of the ship's company lost aboard Henry VIII's flagship Mary Rose *in 1545. A requiem and symbolic interment (right) held in Portsmouth Cathedral on July 19, 1984, commemorated those who died in the* Mary Rose *disaster.*

Opposite: The idea for the partial reconstruction of Wolstenholme Towne (above, left) came from a temple site at Dendera in Egypt (right). There, stone gateways survive intact, while the soft brick walls have eroded away to ribbons of gray rubble. Below, strips of lead once used to secure glass in Martin's Hundred windows were elaborately pressed to record the 1625 date as well as the name and town of the man who made the glazier's vise (right, center). Once this practice was recognized, every piece of window lead reaching the lab was carefully studied (left). When the search extended to Northamptonshire in England, a fragment dated 1733 was found to have fallen from a window of the ruined Kirby Hall (bottom, right).

Courtesy of Mary Rose Trust

eled triptych against the north wall, dating from 1615. The painting showed members of the family and in the foreground three small wooden coffins, each of them gabled. Julian explained that the original 15th-century vault had been remodeled in 1748, at which time all the early St. John ancestors were sealed behind a new stone wall.

"I leave further decisions to you," Julian wrote. "Should we peer behind this rubble wall or would we be on a hiding for nothing?"

There was no way of knowing. But I was sure that if we passed up the chance to find out, we would be saying "what if?" for the rest of our lives. "We'll do it," I told him. Friends and colleagues shook their heads, but I had a feeling that this time we were going to be lucky.

As I stood beside the vault's stone cover listening to John Flory's prayers, past disappointments and the experts' rejection of our successes seemed distant and unimportant. The questions uppermost in my mind now were, "Why is John praying with a congregation of two? Where was the rest of the crew? Where was our photographer? And where in heaven was Julian?"

The quest that led us to Lydiard Tregoz had changed over the years. Beginning with a straightforward desire to explain and document details of the Martin's Hundred coffins, it had expanded to embrace more fundamental questions. Now we were asking why the English (and, it seemed, most Europeans) had buried their dead in coffins with lids more difficult to make than flat

ones. We wanted to know what people in Virginia thought about death, and more importantly, about life—*their* life on the frontier of European civilization.

Six years' digging had left us with many thousands of artifacts still to be processed and studied—small potsherds and pieces of corroded metal we jokingly classified as "probably part of something." Of course, being part of something is just as informative as being all of it—providing we are smart enough to know what it is.

Most tantalizing of the unrecognized metal objects had been a spikelike blade about a foot long and cruciform in section. Bent over and broken from something much larger, it may have been a weapon. But what sort of a weapon? Too heavy for a sword, too long for a dagger, it could only come from a pole-arm. Friends at the Tower of London agreed, and concluded that it had to be the point from a halberd; but although we searched the Tower's collection, nothing matched it. Researches in America and Europe were no more successful. By the time I talked to antique arms specialist Robin Wigington at Stratford-on-Avon, I had virtually given up.

"Have you ever seen a halberd with a point like this?" I asked, showing him a drawing of the blade. "Or a piece of armor like that?" So used to getting a negative answer, I had barely given him time to reply.

"Wait a minute," Robin cut in. "That's no halberd. It's a brandistock." He saw my blank look, and explained that it was a

Ivor Noël Hume

hollow staff containing a concealed blade about two feet long, and which, at the touch of a spring, could convert into a singularly intimidating spear. "Most of them are Italian," he added. "They're very rare."

"So where do I find one?"

"Upstairs."

It was true. Robin Wigington owned not one but two brandistocks, one with a cruciform blade exactly like ours. And he was right about their rarity. Even knowing what to look for, I have yet to find another with a comparable blade.

Remarkable though the weapon is in its own right, even more startling was its presence in Virginia in the second quarter of the 17th century. Although one brandistock could not change our view of history, it was not alone. As our study of the artifacts continued, more objects began to testify to a much more sophisticated standard of living in Martin's Hundred than we had hitherto supposed.

The more we studied the relics of Martin's Hundred the less comfortable we became with our stereotyped image of the rough-living pioneer colonists. Their homes, unquestionably, were modest, for at first they were constructed by people without much experience in home building. But it by no means followed that the furnishings they had brought with them were primitive or of poor quality. On the contrary, the artifacts pointed to a serious attempt to maintain English standards.

One might suppose that all we had to do was to ask British

Evenutally identified as the business end of a brandistock or officer's walking staff, this cruciform blade from the Harwood Site (below) proved to be a puzzle as long as the weapon it came from. The paralleling early 17th-century Italian antique is seen here with its blade extended. At rest in its retracted position, it projects only six inches beyond its pole-ax hammer and spike (right).

Ivor Noël Hume

archaeologists and historians to answer our questions about early colonial life. We were shocked, therefore, to find that they knew less about the archaeological record of early 17th-century English life than we did. In the absence of other correspondingly datable sites, Martin's Hundred had become for its period what Pompeii was for 1st-century provincial Roman life or Deir El-Medineh was for the Egyptians—a household-by-household look at a lost way of life.

In England students of arms and armor, museum curators, and 17th-century reenactment societies were turning to the Virginia discoveries for information. And so did Julian Litten as he shouldered a unique assignment. He was to design an appropriate coffin for the burial in Portsmouth Cathedral of one of the men whose skeletons were found aboard the 1545 wreck of the *Mary Rose*. Having concluded that it should be a Martin's Hundred-style box, Julian was now as anxious as was I to see and measure a surviving gable-lidded coffin—and to know what might lie behind the stone wall at Lydiard Tregoz.

By the time Litten and photographer Ian Yeomans arrived, the flooring slabs were up and the brick steps leading down to the vault uncovered. Shining a light into the entrance, I could see a stone table supporting crumbling coffins. Wooden sides had collapsed and lay in fragments on the floor, along with large brass-handle escutcheons, green with corrosion. A pile of similar coffin pieces had at some time been pushed under the table and had compressed into a soft brown mound. A sickly smell of compost hung in the air.

Once in the chamber we found several more coffins, their crumbling outer shells covering separately constructed lead liners whose weight had caused those beneath to buckle. To our right lay a second chamber so tightly packed with equally crumbling coffins that it was barely possible to get through the doorway without falling into them.

An engraved brass plate lying on the foot of a coffin to which

it did not belong bore the name of Sir Edward St. John and the date 1684. So there evidently were 17th-century coffins crushed under the later arrivals and had not been walled up in 1748, as had been thought.

The rubble wall said to conceal them was to the left of the first chamber, and proved to be far better constructed than I had expected. Indeed, the stones were as carefully dressed and the mortar as smooth as the walls of the church itself. Careful examination led me to conclude that rather than being built within a once much larger vault, it supported the barrel roof of both the 18th-century chamber and its entrance passage. What else, I wondered, did it support?

Quick calculations showed that just beyond and above it stretched the floor of the south chapel on which stood the huge marble monument to Sir John St. John and his two wives. I remembered that a brochure called it "one of the finest groups of monuments in the country," that it had recently been restored at a cost of £11,000, and that "the work is not yet fully paid for." I wondered what John Flory and St. John descendant Lord Bolingbroke would say if we dismantled the "rubble" wall and brought down the monument on top of us.

From childhood I had been thrilled by that moment in 1922 when Howard Carter had removed the top stones of the wall sealing the antechamber to Tutankhamen's tomb; how, as he peered through the hole, his partner Lord Carnarvon had asked: "Can you see anything?" What wouldn't I have given to have shared that first view and to have been the one to reply, "Yes, wonderful things!"

With that in mind, I asked Ian Yeomans to let his camera be the first to see what might lie behind our stone wall. If, at last, we were about to find our gabled coffin, it seemed only right that all the people who had helped us should share the moment of revelation. I asked how large an opening he would need. "About two feet square," he replied.

Marking it off in one corner close to the roof, I told the waiting mason, "Okay, let's start here." And for two hours the ring of hammer on steel chisel echoed through the church. The wall was as unyielding as it looked.

Of all our Martin's Hundred discoveries, one drew by far the largest number of letters. It related to an enigmatic inscription found impressed inside the folds of a fragment of casement window lead: "Iohn: Byshopp of Exceter Gonner: 1625." Not only did its discovery produce marvelously diverse interpretations of its meaning, it prompted Susan Hanna, U. S. National Park Service curator at Jamestown, to peer inside the lead found in excavations there. She came up with six different inscriptions dating between 1661 and 1690. A piece from Williamsburg was dated 1722, and another from Virginia's Lynnhaven House, 1724.

John Byshopp's message to posterity was no isolated anomaly. On the contrary, it looked as though dating the wheels of glaziers' vises (through which the lead was drawn) was relatively commonplace—perhaps even a legal requirement. If so, the law was English and should equally apply to English windows and houses. Questioning British architectural historians, curators, and restoration glaziers evoked the same smiles of disbelief that had greeted my gabled coffin inquiries. None had ever heard of dated window lead. But none had looked!

Looking would not be easy. I knew that few old-home owners would get ecstatic about having their windows taken apart. It could only be done when repairs were being made. Consequently, I could hope for no quick confirmation of my widow-dating theory. I knew, too, from the Jamestown study that most of the fragments found there bore no inscriptions. So one might examine scores of English windows without finding one whose lead was dated.

While in England in 1984 for the Lidiard Tregoze project I visited several great houses, one of them ruined Kirby Hall in Northamptonshire. Begun in 1570, and the home of Queen Elizabeth's Lord Chancellor, Sir Christopher Hatton, much of it had fallen into ruin by the mid-19th century. Surviving high in several attic windows—safe from prying fingers—I could see the remains of casements, their broken glass still hanging from the sagging lead. If only I could get someone in the Department of the Environment (which maintains the ruin) to get up there and look! The thought had barely formed when I looked down and saw lying on the ground a small piece of lead that someone had twisted into a ball and thrown aside.

I picked it up. "You know," I told Audrey, "this is the first time anyone has looked for a date in a piece of English window lead." Her skeptical smile was answer enough. The chances of this little piece being dated were microscopically small.

With the aid of my penknife I carefully pried open the crushed channel. Inside was the usual row of raised ridges—then some lines that weren't straight. "Here," I said, "your eyes are better than mine, isn't that . . . ?"

Audrey peered into the fold. "Yes, I think so."

And it was. The lead was dated 1733. With that astonishing piece of luck already in the bag, I was sure that in the vault at Lydiard Tregoz the omens were no less propitious. I watched the mason and his helpers working in relays as they slowly, tantalizingly slowly, chipped their way through the wall. They were almost two feet into it. "Listen! I think it's sounding hollow!" said the hammerer.

I put my ear close to the wall and told him to bang again. He was right; but a trickle of sand and black dirt from above made me suspect that the hollowness was coming from the loose fill under the chapel floor.

At 11:40 a.m., after more than two hours of chipping and levering, the mason broke through—into packed rubble and dirt. There was no coffin-filled chamber behind the "rubble" wall. Our luck had run out.

Or so it seemed.

Two months later Julian Litten wrote me a "guess what?" letter. That morning he had received a telephone call from architect François Jones, who was supervising repairs in Exton church in Somerset. While removing a 19th-century floor, the ground under it collapsed into a clay-walled grave. In it lay the skeleton of a man—around him the decaying, brass-studded, and red-velvet covered wood of his *gabled* coffin. A nearby ledger stone put the date of burial at 1608.

If we needed a punch line, Julian's penultimate sentence said it best: "All good things come to those who wait."

Courtesy of François Jones

Ending a chain of research that had spanned nine years and led to four continents, a grave of 1608 was accidentally discovered during renovations at Exton Church in Somerset. Although the coffin was badly damaged by the collapsing floor, its all-important gable end survived intact.

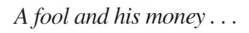

A fool and his money . . .

Coins and traders' tokens of gold, silver, copper, and even of lead, circulated widely in a colony perennially short of small change.

For Necessary Change

or penny problems in the private sector

"The prospect of finding an archaeological treasure was raised when six inches from the surface of the first trench emerged a large and perfectly preserved silver coin of Louis XV of France dated 1719. This half-écu seems to be the coin of the highest denomination yet found in colonial Virginia."

THE SITE was Rosewell plantation and I wrote those words in 1962. To my knowledge the coin still remains the second largest silver piece found in Virginia (left, above). In contrast, the most recent discovery is one of the smallest—yet imbued with far greater historical significance. Found in ongoing excavations at Jamestown, the Elizabethan silver half-groat is the earliest closely datable coin to be found there. In reality it is only half a half-groat, though fortunately it happens to be the right half—the one that bears the mint mark.

Many English silver coins of the Tudor reigns were undated, but like domestic silver they bear a mark that records where and when they were made. In this instance the mint mark took the form of a hand and was used in London between 1590 and 1592. Found in a pit we believe to have been filled around 1610, this coin was excitingly supportive, if not confirming evidence that our dating was correct.

That the coin had been cut in half (left) had not rendered it worthless but served only to halve its value. A groat was a fourpenny denomination and theoretically worth one-eighth of an ounce of silver. Thus a half-groat was worth twopence, and by halving that you had a penny or a penny's worth of silver. Queen Elizabeth's treasury did mint penny coins and another even smaller worth three farthings, but, being so small and light, they were easily lost and caused English shopkeepers no end of trouble.

In Virginia a shortage of small change of any kind persisted throughout the colonial centuries. At home in England the problem was addressed by Elizabeth's successor James I in a manner characteristic of the man: In 1613 he gave the franchise (and the problem) to a favorite courtier, allowing Lord Harrington of Exton to mint a private token coin at the one-farthing level. To give them the reassuring appearance of silver, Harrington's copper farthings were coated with tin and were required to weigh no

Dave Doody

When coins were worth their weight in gold or silver, a merchant couldn't be too careful. Such was the case with Colonial Williamsburg's Ryan Fletcher in the guise of John Greenhow in his store's counting room.

Sir John Harrington's tinned copper farthing (below) of 1613 (obverse and reverse) generated dismay when found in the 1620 fort at Wolstenholme Towne. Small though the farthing may be, it is large by comparison with a James I silver penny, the smallest of small change (right). Not yet found in Virginia is Bermuda's hog money (bottom), but Spanish coins cut into pieces of eight reals (right) are relatively common.

Dave Doody

less than six grains. When they were found to tip the balance at but five, his Lordship was faced with a recall situation.

Although a minor glitch soon overcome and a mere footnote in the long history of British numismatics, Harrington's "mistake" was to promote cardiac arrest when one of his lightweight farthings turned up in the 1620 fort in Virginia's Wolstenholme Towne (above).

Minted in May of 1613 and withdrawn in July, the farthing token should have been telling the archaeologists that it must have been lost in that year and that the fort had been built seven years earlier than we thought. The historical record made nonsense of that interpretation, and so, regardless of the fact that we had no confirming documentation, we could only conclude that rather than being melted down and restruck, some of Harrington's underweight farthings were shipped to Virginia to address the settlers' need for small change.

Perhaps learning from early Virginia's penny problems, Bermuda (then called the Somers Isles) obtained its own token coinage in 1616, the year that Captain Daniel Tucker arrived as its new governor. It is likely, therefore, that he and the money landed together. Struck in thinly silvered copper alloy, the denominations ran from a shilling down to a twopence or half-groat. Captain John Smith in his *Generall Historie* recalled that "they had for a time a certaine kinde of brasse money with a hogge on the one side, in memory of the abundance of hogges was found at their first landing." A ship on the reverse probably commemorated Sir George Somers's building there of the *Deliverance* after the wreck of the *Sea Venture* in 1609.

Known to numismatists—for self-evident reasons—as "hogge money," 15 of the coins were found by archaeologists from the College of William and Mary in 1993–1994 while excavating in the vicinity of Bermuda's King's Castle. Rather than being buried as a hidden hoard, the tokens were scattered through a layer of trash dating to the mid-17th century. It might be con-

Courtesy of Smithsonian Institution

strued, therefore, that the 1616 hogge money was still in circulation 30 or so years later. But if so, the discovery contradicts John Smith's statement published in 1624 that the money had been tender only "for a time" prior to that date.

In view of the close relationship between Bermuda and Virginia, it is possible that hogge money reached Jamestown and circulated in the colony until more intrinsically reliable currencies became available. That, however, remains to be proven, for as yet no hogge money has been found here.

Although genuine coins from more than one die are known, copies of the Bermuda shilling exist, reputedly made not to deceive but to provide collectors with examples of a coin too rare to be acquired.

In London, in 1636, Virginia's Governor Sir John Harvey complained that there was still little or no money in his colony and so petitioned the king to have a supply of token farthings sent over. Although by then tobacco had become a much used currency, Harvey pointed out that between the time when one crop was shipped and another ripened, masters had no alternative means of paying labor.

The scarcity of money of any value was such that at the Virginia General Assembly of March 1661, an act was passed prohibiting the exporting of "Money out of this Country, above the sum of Forty Shillings," and that "if any shall exceed the same Sum, to forfeit double thereof."

Cutting up large coins to make little ones was an accepted solution and continued through the 18th century, predominantly using the cob coinages from the Spanish Mexico City and Peruvian mints of Lima and Potosí, whose pieces of eight were cut into halves and quarters. Because Spanish and other European coins were found to contain better silver than those from the English mints (a charge hotly denied by the mint master), several laws were passed in Virginia making it illegal to refuse English money and inflating its value proportionately based on the five-shilling silver crown, which in 1714 was to trade at five shillings and tenpence.

Although European copper coins were unac-ceptable currency in Virginia, anybody's gold or silver coins were worth their weight regardless of whose head adorned them. The previously cited 1714 act of the Virginia Assembly specified that foreign gold coins should "pass and be current, according to their respective weights," and listed "all Spanish or French coined Gold, all Pieces of coined Gold of the [Holy Roman] Empire, all Chequeens and Arabian Pieces of Gold, and Moidores of Portugal, and all lesser pieces of that Species."

At that time, unlike the products of Spanish-American mints, all English coins were made in a press mill, hand-hammering having been abandoned in 1662. The so-called milling process had been tried during the reign of Elizabeth I, using a screw press introduced by Frenchman Eloye Mestrelle, but although the quality of the coins was superior, his process was unacceptably slow and was abandoned in 1572. Six years later, still in the money-minting business, the disappointed M. Mestrelle was arrested, charged with counterfeiting, and hanged.

The question of how long old coins remained in circulation is one often debated by archaeologists, for each one found in the ground gives us a date after which it had been lost. The problem, however, is how long after? A silver thaler of the Habsburg Empire dated 1697 (the largest silver coin yet found in Virginia) provided an answer if not *the* answer. It was found at Yorktown in a Revolutionary War context and may perhaps have been lost by one of Lord Cornwallis's Hessian soldiers.

About 20 years ago a silver groat of Henry VII (1485–1509) was shown to me. It was said to have been found during construction on Williamsburg's Richmond Road. But whether it came from someone's collection or had been lost by a colonist can be anybody's guess. The fact remains, nonetheless, that gold was gold and silver silver, no matter how old. It was no less a fact that while hand-hammered (pre-milling) coins came from the mint at the mandated weight, the enterprising use of sharp scissors soon rendered many of them significantly lighter. By trimming a scarcely discernable amount from the edge of each shilling that passed through one's hands, one eventually collected enough shavings to make another invariably lighter-weight shilling from bogus dies.

Although the crime of counterfeiting or clipping the king's coinage was punishable by death—hanging or drawing and quartering for men, burning for women (the last in 1788)—the practice remained widespread as long as hammered coinage continued to circulate. Thus, in the 1714 act, heading the list of coins that were to be exchanged by weight rather than face value were "All Pieces of British Gold Coin, not milled"—clear proof that hammered gold coins minted prior to 1662 were still in use more than 50 years later.

Thirteen years later still, in 1727, another act of the Assembly regulated the exchange value by weight of Spanish pieces of eight, French écus, Portuguese crusadoes, and Flemish duccatoons, and ordered that all English milled silver should circulate at an inflated rate of six shillings and threepence per five-shilling crown. Although the use of hammered coinage was prohibited in the reign of William III, by specifying "English milled Silver Money," it seems likely that 17th-century (and even Elizabethan) hammered coins were still around.

The crowns, écus, and duccatoons were, of course, the currency of the big spenders and buyers, but even they were unlikely to have been happy to tender a shilling for a threepenny newspaper only to be told "sorry, we're out of change." Lesser folk, for whom the purchase of a halfpenny loaf necessitated having a halfpenny to spend, were no less frustrated by the scarcity of small denominations.

As early as the 15th century, English monasteries paid for labor in what was called "Abbot's money"—in reality, lead tokens that, when enough were earned, could be exchanged for real money. Although in 1613 James I banned the casting and circulating of lead tokens, the practice evidently continued much later, the discs being molded in private homes and businesses as interim payments to servants and apprentices. One such token (above) has been found in excavations at Thomas Jefferson's birthplace at Shadwell and may have been used not as payment but as a tally to account for produce harvested or shopwork completed.

Like silver, the humble lead was of value—as bullets and

Lead tokens, like this (left) found at Thomas Jefferson's birthplace at Shadwell, belong to a class paralleled on the Thames foreshore (center), and by a hoard found under a floor of an almonary at Evesham in England. With them was a piece of waste lead and a limestone mold for casting several designs (bottom). All date from the 17th or 18th century.

Ivor Noël Hume

Courtesy of Evesham Town Council and Vale of Evesham Historical Society

fishing weights. It is not surprising, therefore, that few examples have been reported from Virginia. The largest surviving numbers have been recovered from the foreshores of the Thames at London (above, center), one of them dated as late as 1714. Evidence of their local manufacture has been provided by an example that failed to fill its mold—a mold probably like a stone example found along with 17 tokens under the floor of an old house (now the museum) at Evesham in England. In a 1613 proclamation, James I had banned the use of lead tokens while admitting that there had hitherto been "some toleration" for their use.

Other coinlike pieces common on most early sites in Virginia, from Roanoke Island to Jamestown and the James River plantations, are brass counters intended as mathematical aids in conjunction with counting boards, the latter ordinarily set into or marked out on shops' counters—thus giving them that name. In coin-hungry Virginia it is possible that such counters were also used as tokens. The majority came from Nuremberg and bear the names of makers the dates of whose working lives are known, thus providing archaeologists with valuable time markers. Two examples recently found at Jamestown in association with the previously mentioned halved half-groat of 1590–1592 were made by Hans Krauwinckel the Elder, who had died in 1586 (right).

In the mid-17th century, perhaps motivated by the expected disruption of coining from the royal mint during the English Civil War, English merchants, from goldsmiths to tavern keepers, minted their own halfpenny and farthing tokens in copper and brass, and one of these has also been found at Jamestown, as has a later version of the Harrington farthing. Whether they circulated in Virginia as currency or were discarded by arriving colonists who had no further use for them will never be known.

The English Civil War did indeed disrupt the production of coinage. Denied access to the Parliament-held mint at the Tower of London, and well aware that his loyalist army would remain so only if paid, Charles I set up mints at Oxford, Exeter, Bristol, Truro, Worcester—anywhere that he had supporters with family silver to be melted down. In the Commonwealth period that followed (1649–1660), a small number of silver coins were minted and so, from the beginning, semi-official mints produced farthings that declared themselves on one side to be made from 1/4 OUNCE OF FINE PEWTER (really 98 parts tin to 2 of lead) and on the other as being FOR NECESSARY CHANGE (left).

The urgency of that need was apparent to the new regime that took control with the 1660 return of Charles II and the restoration of the monarchy. But instead of recognizing the merit of the large tin farthings of the Commonwealth or the ubiquitous copper and brass tradesmen's tokens, it reinstated the old hammered silver coinage with denominations down to the diminutive penny. Not until 1672 did it get around to issuing finger-friendly copper halfpennies and farthings. Perhaps the best Virginia example of the latter (dated 1675) was found during repairs under the entrance tower at Bacon's Castle.

Besides copper halfpennies and farthings, Charles II's reign saw the production of both values in tin, this in an effort to assist the declining Cornish tin-mining industry. But because these base metal coins were likely to be counterfeited, the forger's job was made more difficult by inserting a copper plug in the center of each coin. The result was not pretty, and although many survive, few are in good condition.

The short reign of Charles's successor James II (1685–1688) failed to produce any copper small change but did mint more of the plugged tin versions. However, the reign is of numismatic interest in Virginia, because it led to the issuing of the first (and only) official low-denomination coinage designed to address the southern plantations' small change crunch.

In August 1688, the king's secretary wrote to the officers of the mint seeking their approval for the design of a tin farthing created "on behalf of the Tynn farmers," and inscribed as being worth 24 PART REAL HISPAN. The designers had explained that "the said coynes are intended to pass in his Majesty's Plantacons & such parts of his Dominions where they only take Spanish money & value all coynes by that Measure, Soe that without that Inscription those people will not take them." Someone did take one (or left one) at Jamestown, and I found three in London's Billingsgate Dock, where the smaller ocean-crossing ships sometimes moored.

Britain's second revolution, the one that ousted James and enthroned William and Mary, saw renewed minting of the poorly wearing, copper-plugged tin halfpence and farthings, followed by a single issuance of copper in 1698. In Virginia, however, the joint reign is dramatically recalled by a silver half-crown found under a floor during the restoration of a small brick house in Charles City County. Perhaps hidden beneath a board by someone who had no right to it, the half-crown was the equivalent of a considerable amount of labor or merchandise. It is unlikely, therefore, that it had been placed between the joists when the house was built as a good luck token—as sometimes was done with coins of lesser value.

In Virginia the 18th century brought little or no alleviation of the small change problem, although English copper halfpennies and farthings are not uncommon from Williamsburg archaeological sites. During the reign of George I (1714–1727), one William Wood obtained a patent to produce copper tokens for the American colonies, ranging in value from twopence to a penny. Each bore the king's profile on its obverse and a rose on its reverse under the inscription ROSA AMERICANA.

Issued between 1722 and 1724, for reasons that are not clear, the Wood solution was not warmly embraced in the colonies, and I know of none having been found in Virginia. Wood also made coins for use in Ireland, and two examples of these have been found in Williamsburg, and another in Prince Edward County.

Ivor Noël Hume

Obverse and reverse of a Schwartzenberg silver thaler of 1696 was found at Yorktown. The largest coin yet unearthed, it may have been brought over by one of Lord Cornwallis's Hessian mercenaries.

No more successfully, and certainly unlawfully, Messrs. Rigault and Dawson of Gloucester County, Virginia, issued their own brass shilling token in 1714, three examples of which survive—along with an army of reproductions produced in 1973. Although hailed by a past governor as "the oldest money in the United States," the Gloucester token is hardly that. Massachusetts had begun minting its own coins in shilling, sixpenny, and three-penny denominations in 1652.

Of the English copper coins found on 18th-century archaeological sites in Virginia, many, if not most, are forgeries. But few are as badly made as two lead attempts at George II halfpennies found in excavations on the site of Williamsburg's Printing Office.

Through a seven-year period in the mid-18th century the solicitor to the Tower Mint recorded 650 prosecutions for counterfeiting. In an effort to avoid the ultimate penalty, one forger changed the king's name from George II to Claudius Romanus and George III to Brutus Sextus. Indeed, it was said that in England in the 1770s more forgeries were circulating than were the

real thing. That, coupled with the fact that through three long stretches (1701–1717, 1721–1727, and 1750–1770) no official copper coins were minted in England, may have prompted the Virginia General Assembly in 1769 to petition the crown to purchase £2,500 worth of good copper halfpennies—60,000 of them.

Prolonged negotiations with two successive secretaries of state finally resulted in the creation of a halfpenny minted specifically for Virginia and dated 1773. The coins' eventual arrival were reported in the *Virginia Gazette* on February 23, 1774, giving the impatient citizens of Williamsburg every reason to expect that within days the new halfpennies would be clinking in their pockets. But Treasurer Robert Carter Nicholas, and presumably Governor Dunmore, believed that they lacked authority to issue the coins without a royal warrant, and none had accompanied the money. In response to Lord Dunmore's complaint to London, the warrant was eventually dispatched. Dated November 16, 1774, it announced that five tons of the coins were "now ready to be exported to our said Colony of Virginia." Somebody had forgot-

Ivor Noël Hume

A 16th-century German woodcut (above, left) by Hans Burgkmair shows an artisan hand-hammering coins between steel dies. More efficient was the later process of stamping coins from milled sheets by means of a screw press (right), here illustrated by Denis Diderot in 1765.

Fingers cradle a 1606 silver shilling of James I that shows evidence of extensive clipping. Nuremburg counters (left, top) are found on many early 17th-century Virginia sites. The silver penny and twopence of the Commonwealth period (1649–1660)—shown flanking a scale-depicting dime—were no more user friendly than their royal predecessors. Copper farthings of Charles II (left) were less easily lost. Both are dated 1675 but from different dies, that at the left found at Bacon's Castle in Surry County, Virginia.

Heads and Tails

The "rose" copper farthings of Charles I were issued in 1636 (a); James II's tin farthings of 1687 (b) each had a copper plug in the center to discourage forging. But, as at right, many fell out. In 1688 James also issued a tin token made for the American plantations and worth one 24th of a Spanish real (c).

The William and Mary silver half crown of 1692 (obverse and reverse) was discovered under a floor in Charles City County, Virginia (d). The copper token halfpenny of 1723 (e: obverse and reverse) coined for the Irish plantations by William Wood under a patent from George I, was found in Prince Edward County.

Forgeries were also abundant: This halfpenny of George II (f) was found at Wetherburn's Tavern in Williamsburg. Across the street at the Printing Office someone was trying his hand at copying the same coin (g: obverse and reverse) in lead!

In England counterfeiters of the George II and III halfpence outwitted the law by changing the inscriptions, here reading CLAUDIUS ROMANUS and BRUTUS SEXTUS (h). The 1773 George III Virginia copper halfpenny (i) was found at the shop of cabinetmaker Peter Scott on Duke of Gloucester Street. Fire had destroyed the shop in 1776.

Coined in Birminghams's Soho Mint in 1797 and worth their weight in copper, these massive twopenny and penny pieces (j) were designed to defy counterfeiters— but didn't, as the lead penny (below) demonstrates.

Ivor Noël Hume

ten to mention that they had been there in their unopened kegs for the past seven months.

The royal proclamation was finally published in the *Virginia Gazette* on February 23, 1775, giving the crown's critics a splendid opportunity to demonstrate that the king and his ministers were hopelessly out of touch with the problems of their American colonies. The same edition of the *Gazette* included a news item from Surry County stating that its Committee of Safety had sold embargoed goods seized from the ship *Thomas* in exchange for £138 11s. 9d. in "halfpenny Virginia currency." From the first days of issuance, therefore, the new copper money was being acquired for hoarding rather than circulating.

With the winds of impending war already stirring the tobacco fields of Virginia, wise colonists could conclude that hard cash—even of copper—could weather the storm better than would paper money or promissory notes for crops that might never be harvested. Nevertheless, there is evidence that some Virginia halfpennies did reach the pockets of the needy—who lost them into the Williamsburg earth for archaeologists to find. One of the best-preserved examples has come from the rubble-filled cellar of the Peter Scott House on Duke of Gloucester Street that burned in January 1776, due to "the Negligence of some of the Soldiers who had been quartered there."

This ends the story of small change in colonial Virginia. The new nation's new currency was created on April 27, 1787, when the United States Congress authorized the Board of Treasury to contract for "three hundred tons of copper coin of the federal standard." Meanwhile, back in England in the same year, the master of the mint admitted that only 8 percent of the copper coins then in circulation "had some tolerable resemblance to the king's coin."

England's solution to its counterfeiting problem has to have been one of the most bizarre in the annals of world coinage. Using James Watt's recently invented steam press, the new coins would not only be worth their weight in copper but would be so uniformly made with thick raised edges and incuse lettering as to be impossible to counterfeit successfully.

Issued in 1797, these so-called cartwheel one-ounce penny and two-ounce twopenny pieces would go down in history as the fattest and least pocket-friendly small change ever produced. If returning travelers brought any of them to Virginia, they may have done so only as paperweights or to demonstrate that at the century's end the idiocies of treasury bureaucracy were still alive and well in King George's England. As for the counterfeiters—they kept right on counterfeiting.

. . . and Copper Penny Inserted

Ivor Noël Hume

THE LOCAL ESTATE auction's full catalog entry read "173. 1 English Carved Wooden Box with Date of 1670 & Copper Penny Inserted and Iron Hardware." Why, I asked myself, would a box dated 1670 have had a copper penny inserted into it, when the first English copper pennies were those "cartwheel" monstrosities of 1797?

Intrigued by that question, I went to the auction's preview and was instantly captivated by Lot 173. It isn't often that I see something that I simply have to have no matter what, but this was just such a something. Tarnished and yellowed by old wax, the copper penny proved to be a fine hammered shilling of Elizabeth I. Its mintmark put its date at some time between 1593 and '98. It was true that the coin had been inserted, but not later as I had expected. Instead, the lid of the heavily carved oak box was designed around it, the shilling set between the 16 and 70 of the date.

To the left of a central crosslike device were the D J initials of the person for whom the box was made, and on the back the E K of its maker. And that was not all; hiding in much lower relief on either side of the cross and encompassed by foliate scrolls, two small, seemingly demonic faces leered up at me. They seemed to be saying, "We know what you don't know!"

And no doubt they are right.

Who was D.J., and why did he have his box designed around a shilling that was 70 and more years old? Was it perhaps given to his father by Good Queen Bess herself as payment for some small service? Was it the first shilling that D.J. earned? Or are those secretive faces the key? Is it possible that the box had some role to play in witchcraft or demonology?

If, "Dear Reader," you know of other such coin-set boxes or have any suggestions as to its meaning and purpose, I shall gladly—as we used to say—offer a penny for your thoughts.

Tarleton at Carter's Grove
In every legend there's a seed of truth

I MET Mrs. Archibald "Mollie" McCrae only once, but it was an experience never to be forgotten. In a two-hour conversation (mostly hers) and a tour of Carter's Grove in October 1956, she introduced my wife, Audrey, and me to the legends of her home. Most memorable among them was her account of the dashing British cavalry officer Colonel Banastre Tarleton riding his horse up the mansion's staircase in an effort to rouse his sluggardly troops billeted on the second floor. To make his presence more forcefully felt, he slashed at the banister rail with his sword and finally broke off its tip by driving the blade downward into the rail beside the newel post. If I needed proof of this remarkable exploit, there was the blade tip still impaled in the wood.

It seemed churlish to observe that the slightly protruding blade fragment was surrounded by what looked suspiciously like the marks of the hammer used to drive it in place. Then, too, the coincidence that Banastre should be whacking away at the banisters seemed a shade too great. Furthermore, it would have been impossible for Tarleton to hold his saber in such a way as to drive its blade vertically downward from the back of a horse unused to climbing stairs. But Mollie McCrea was a formidable yet gracious hostess, and it would have been impolite to question her story. Nevertheless, both Audrey and I were convinced that the Tarleton tale was total fiction.

It had its origin, it would appear, in 1915 when Robert A. Lancaster wrote in *Historic Homes and Churches of Virginia* that "along the handrail may still be seen the gashes made by the sabers of Tarleton's men, who paid their respects to Carter's Grove when raiding Virginia during the Revolution." The story acquired new details in 1927 in Elsie Lanthrop's *Historic Houses of Early America,* when dashing Colonel Tarleton became "the savage General Tarleton" and "rode up the broad, low stairs on his horse, hacking at the banister rail . . ."

In truth, there was no unequivocal proof that Tarleton had camped at Carter's Grove, let alone billeted his troopers in the mansion. It is true that he was quartered in or near Williamsburg in late June of 1781, and that on the 26th of that month he was at Burwell's Ferry on the James about four miles upstream from Carter's Grove. But that did not put him in the mansion—at least not until 1970, when the evidence for his presence was discovered by archaeologist Bill Kelso.

Digging behind the line of fence post holes that marked the garden's westerly perimeter, Kelso found a large brass insignia molded in relief with clouds and a sunburst below the motto

Although it is unlikely that the shining metal protruding from the banister at Carter's Grove (below) is really the tip of Colonel Tarleton's saber, the oval brass medallion (left) unearthed behind the garden fence leaves little doubt that he or his men were there.

Ivor Noël Hume

POST NUBILA PHOEBUS, meaning after the clouds the sunshine. Only four English families are known to have used that motto, and Tarleton's was one of them.

The oval ornament had been attached to leather, but whether it came from a trooper's saber belt, from the winker of a horse, or something more personal like the colonel's dispatch box, no one knows. But one thing is certain: Banastre Tarleton's men *were* at Carter's Grove in 1781. Of course, Mollie McCrea knew that all along!

Digging at Bruton
Much ado about nothing?

Her beauty makes
This vault a feasting presence
full of light.

S O WROTE THE AUTHOR of *Romeo and Juliet* as his hero laid the murdered Paris alongside Juliet in the tomb. That Elizabethan dramatist had a thought, a phrase, a line for virtually every occasion, and 400 years later we use them still—sometimes rendering ourselves the cleverer, the wittier, the more well read by citing our source. "Once more unto the breach, dear friend! Shakespeare."

But how much did William Shakespeare, the son of a provincial glove maker and a farmer's daughter, really write of the play first titled *The Famous Victories of Henry the fifth: containing the Honourable Battell of Agin-court*? Did he write any of it? How could a man whose formal schooling ended at 14 have acquired the breadth of classical, legal, historical, political, and court knowledge to write 37 of the world's most enduring plays, and to do so in the space of about 23 years? And what had he been doing with his life during the 12 years before he allegedly wrote his first play—the third part of *Henry VI*?

Such questions as these were kicked around as early as 1769, but raised few scholarly eyebrows until 1848 when they surfaced again in a singularly improbable venue—J. C. Hart's New York publication *The Romance of Yachting*! Eight years later, English philosopher and playwright William Henry Smith was the first to suggest that Francis Bacon might have been the real author of the plays attributed to the "Stratford actor."

Over the years several other candidates have been proposed, always an elitist group, well educated, and who moved in aristocratic circles. They include the 15th Earl of Rutland, the 6th Earl of Derby, and in 1920 the 7th Earl of Oxford, this last the candidate of one J. Thomas Looney. Although the Baconian theory was launched by Smith in England in 1856, it found its home in the United States through the writing of Judge Nathaniel Holmes titled *The Authorship of Shakespeare* (1866–1886), and in the past century infinitely more words have been written about Bacon-alias-Shakespeare than it took to write the plays.

In 1938 the controversy reached Williamsburg in the personable person of philosophical and cryptological student Marie Bauer. She explained to the surprised vestrymen of Bruton Parish that beneath their church lay a vault containing the literary legacy of Sir Francis Bacon. Sealed in copper cylinders would be found

the proof of his authorship of all those plays—plus a formula for establishing world peace. To skeptics who asked "Why us? Why our church?" the explanation went something like this:

Queen Elizabeth (whose "not until we're married" philosophy provided a name for our Commonwealth) had secretly wed the Earl of Leicester whose equally secret son was adopted by Lady Ann and Sir Nicholas Bacon and grew up as Francis Bacon. After years of sycophantic support of Elizabeth's successor James I, Bacon (by then elevated to Viscount St. Albans) fell from favor and found himself imprisoned in the Tower. Meanwhile he had acquired a son named Henry Blount who in 1635 was dispatched to Virginia carrying his father's documents to safety.

It is unclear whether Francis was supposed to have so instructed. An early experiementer in refrigeration, in March 1626 he caught cold while stuffing snow into a chicken and died a few days later—leaving us to puzzle over the fate of his manuscripts between 1626 and 1635. When Henry Blount reached Virginia, he changed his name to Nathaniel Bacon—perhaps or perhaps not the same Nathaniel Bacon who rose to become president of the Council and even the colony's acting governor. Surviving Virginia property records between 1623 and 1666 include no one named Henry Blount nor a Nathaniel Bacon until 1652.

Be all that as it may or may not be (and probably isn't), the key "fact" is that Henry Blount aka Nathaniel Bacon hid his father's papers first at Jamestown and later in a vault beneath the new church at Middle Plantation—later to become Williamsburg—where they remained, waiting to be unearthed by Marie Bauer.

Who, you might ask, directed her to Williamsburg? Answer: George Wither.

For the benefit of the readers who admit to never having heard of him, George Wither (1588–1667) was an editor, satirist, and poet of modest talent (a contemporary called him a "hack rhymster"), who was hired in 1635 to add illustrative verses to a book originally published in Holland in 1613 and titled *Nucleus Emblematum Selectissimorum*. An ever-vigilant cryptologist, Marie Bauer found coded in Wither's text the fact that "Under the first brick-church in Bruton Parish, Williamsburg, Virginia, lies Francis Bacon's vault."

In 1628 Wither had published a *Prophecy of our present calamity (and lest we repent) our future Misery*, but was he able in 1635 to prophesy that in faraway Virginia and 39 years later two parishes would unite to be named Bruton, or that in England the Stuart succession would be replaced by a Dutchman in 1689 and cause Middle Plantation to be called Williamsburg?

Ignoring such picayune problems and beguiled by the personality and earnestness of their visitor, the Bruton vestrymen allowed her to dig a hole within their church tower and only called a halt after she had dug so deep a pit that someone suggested that the tower was likely to slide into it. Curiously, no one had mentioned that the church was not begun until 1711 to replace the second Middle Plantation church of 1683 where, if anywhere, the vault would have been located.

Nothing daunted, Marie Bauer returned to her drawing board—or more precisely to the floor of her rented apartment across the road in the Custis-Maupin House, where she and student volunteers from the college laid out sheets of brown paper covered with her drawings of 18th-century inscriptions on tombs and ledger stones in the churchyard. Crawling around on the floor helping the lady researcher was recalled by one young Williamsburg resident as the best fun he could remember. But for Marie Bauer, this was serious stuff.

The 1749 stone of "Ann Wife of Graham Frank" only needed a little juggling to shout "anagram!" while, to the eye of a skilled cryptologist, the tomb of Governor Edward Nott could be induced to declare "This marble marks the South East End of gentil old Bruton's foundations." It would have been unsporting, one supposed, to mention that Nott died in 1706 while the gentle old church was still standing.

Convinced of her facts but lacking a permit, Marie Bauer and a few of her Custis-Maupin crawlers embarked on a program of probing with an iron bar around the Nott tomb in search of the 1683 church footings. And she found them. Early on August 26, 1938, and still without a permit, Marie Bauer and her cohorts began to dig.

The history of archaeology is replete with chance discoveries and successful results of amateurs' outrageous theories. It drives professional archaeologists green with envy and red with fury, and although the facial hues of Williamsburg's city fathers when they discovered what was going on is not recorded, they were in no mood to hand out medals. Nevertheless, there was no denying that the remains of one of Virginia's most historic 17th-century buildings had been found.

Having demanded that Marie Bauer desist, two days later the vestry voted funds to enable the excavation to continue. A gang of laborers was brought in and, armed with picks and shovels and employing methods scarcely more archaeological than Marie Bauer's, they trenched along the outline of the building, found it to measure 66 x 29 feet, made quick drawings, and took a few photographs. Two days later the trenches were backfilled.

Spurred on by her discovery and encouraged by Colonial

Colonial Williamsburg

Williamsburg assurances that if she could locate the vault by means other than digging Colonial Williamsburg staffers would help her, she enlisted the support of a New York mining researcher, Mark Malamphy. He arrived in Williasmburg in November and made "an equipotential survey of the churchyard" that detected a buried anomaly about ten feet square and between 16 and 20 feet down—a conclusion endorsed when more sophisticated sensory techniques were employed 48 years later.

Again Marie Bauer had made her point. True to its word, Colonial Williamsburg provided the labor; the vestry voted the money, and, under Malamphy's supervision, the dig began. But at a depth of only five feet, spades struck the corner of a brass-studded coffin. The vestrymen saw themselves being accused of desecrating a Christian burial and quickly changed their minds. The dig was stopped, the dirt thrown back, and, sadly but no wiser, Marie Bauer left town.

Close on half a century would pass with only an occasional stirring of the Bruton/Bacon pot and then only in the retrospective pages of newspapers and books. But on the other edge of the nation, in Mrs. Marie Bauer Hall's home state, a legend was growing—the myth of "resistance by the Rockefeller Foundation" that had thwarted her when the truth was within minutes of being revealed. That charge was repeated in 1987 when the California-based Veritat Foundation was created to push, once again,

for the vault to be opened and America's "founding parents' secret plan for the enlightenment of humanity" to be revealed. The "Stratford actor" and his plays no longer were the prize, their pride of place usurped by even more heady possibilities.

In 1985 (two years before the Veritat Foundation focused again on Marie Bauer's 1938 researches), a package containing an audio tape reached me from Mrs. Ethel L. Cordingley of Cobourg in Ontario. In 1974, while in Vancouver, a psychic, Mrs. Sheila Conway, had provided her with what she described as "a life reading." In the midst of a session focusing directly on Mrs. Cordingley, the psychic told her something totally irrelevant. Taken from the original recording and interrupted by much coughing, a dog barking, and extraneous sounds, this is what she heard:

. . . there are retainers . . . and they followed him over on foot . . . stand up that it may be seen. We see that there are special sights being given to little bands of people . . . at the time of the Armada. And we see that your group was one of them . . .

There is a little place. It is in the New World. And it is on the border between the Carolinas and Virginia. We wish to say to you that there is an aspect of this life which is not known to many. We wish to bring it to your attention for it is that there is a churchyard.

Rarely in the annals of archaeology has a small patch of grass stirred such controversy. Photographed in the summer of 1992, this seemingly vacant space in Bruton Parish churchyard gives scarcely a hint of what had been found there 54 years earlier. The same view in 1938 (opposite) shows the uncovered foundations of Williamsburg's first brick church. Built in 1683, it was in use until the present church was completed in 1715.

The tomb in the middleground of both pictures is that of Ann Frank, allegedly a key piece in the Baconian puzzle. Beyond and to the left, the obelisk tomb (now partly hidden by the tree) and the large table tomb to its right were erected by the Bray family. The ornate tomb of Governor Nott (1706) stands behind that of Ann Frank in the 1938 photograph.

Marie Bauer's calculations placed Bacon's vault within the 1683 church between the foreground foundation and Ann Frank's tomb.

Dave Doody

Somebody asks: Why is the churchyard important?

Because there is in that churchyard of this little town, is a box. It is a metal box containing maps and papers, and the papers some are written in standard English print, and some are written as puzzles. We say to you that when you ask about this, you will find the information regarding this, for this box was brought to this little town. It is . . . the name of the town . . . It is on the outskirts of the town an old church and a graveyard. And the little town . . . the nearest town is called Durham. The box with its contents belonged to Sir Francis Bacon.

Mrs. Cordingley died in 1991, but in correspondence with her in 1985 she wrote agreeing that "the story is very far fetched, but," she added, "it did arouse my curiosity, and if I had not read [your book] *Here lies Virginia*, I doubt the tape would have been played again." Asked whether Mrs. Conway was associated with the Rosicrucian movement (which through Marie Bauer had an interest in the Bruton vault), Mrs. Cordingley replied, "I would

be very surprised if she was interested in the Rosicrucians. The society was never mentioned."

Had Mrs. Conway known about Bruton Parish church and the Williamsburg vault thesis, and had she wanted to renew attention to it, moving the scene to Durham, North Carolina, and not mentioning a vault, would have been an odd way to go about it. Then again, the references to the time of the Spanish Armada and to "little bands of people" and to North Carolina pointed not toward Jamestown but to Sir Walter Ralegh's Roanoke Island "Lost Colony," which vanished in 1588—the year of the Armada.

Mrs. Cordingley's original letter ended with these words: "Hope you get something from this if it's only a laugh." But, in truth, the 1974 Vancouver recording is no more outlandish than virtually everything else that has been written about Sir Francis Bacon's American legacy, and as such it belongs in the record.

In 1991 two students of Mrs. Hall's doctrine, with a local resident as their spokesman, arrived in Williamsburg and on September 9, under the cover of darkness, resumed where Mark Malamphy left off. Apprehended, and amid the inevitable blaze of publicity, they explained that the vault contained Francis

Ivor Noël Hume

Opposite: The Bruton box theory was at last laid to rest when Colonial Williamsburg archaeologists revealed the full outline of a typical 18th-century coffin. The open slot across its width shows that the studded lid had collapsed into it under the weight of the backfill.

William Hogarth's 1736 engraving from his Harlot's Progress *series (right) shows her coffin to be similar to the Bruton example, but of better quality than most prostitutes should have expected. Many 18th-century coffins had an engraved lead or copper-alloy plate attached to the lid identifying the occupant, like those shown above in the vault of an English nobleman. Alas, no such plate was found on the Bruton coffin.*

Bacon's original drafts of both the U. S. Constitution and the Declaration of Independence, unspecified "works of the Apostles," missing English Crown jewels, Bacon's translation of the Bible—and his birth certificate proving him to have been Queen Elizabeth's illegitimate son.

Although legally barred from entering the churchyard, the diggers returned on November 27 and by 4 a.m. had dug a seven-foot hole before being interrupted by a Colonial Williamsburg security officer. Warrants were issued for their arrest, but by then they had left the state. Church authorities breathed easier; but in many a Williamsburg home, families debated whether a professionally conducted excavation might be the best way, once and for all, to resolve the Bruton vault controversy.

Writing about this issue in 1962, I ended with the following thought:

It is to be hoped that one day it will be possible to re-examine the foundations of the church and its surrounding wall in an attempt to answer some of the many questions that are still not resolved.

Thanks to the interest regenerated by the Veritat Foundation and to the somewhat unseemly events of 1991, on August 17, 1992, and at the vestry's invitation, Colonial Williamsburg archaeologists began excavations "to recover significant information about the appearance of the first church," a project that I have waited 30 years to see.

At the month's end, press reporters tired of watching earth being scraped from an apparently barren hole, were briefly whipped to a modified frenzy when a fragment of brass-studded wood was rediscovered in Marie Bauer's backfill. To anyone acquainted with 17th-, 18th-, or 19th-century mortuary art it looked like a sliver from a fairly standard coffin and not a document-concealing box.

As the archaeological digging progressed, the source of the fragment was revealed. It was indeed the side of a wooden, fabric-covered, brass-studded coffin of 18th-century type, one of several found more or less along the line of the old church's nave. Unfortunately, as soon as Mrs. Bauer Hall's 1938 filling had been removed, the excavation was abandoned—its point made. Consequently, there is no certainty whether the burials were interred during the life of the early church (1683–1715) or were buried in the churchyard years later.

No new architectural information emerged from the reexcavation of only the church's northwest corner, but it did make one very pertinent point, namely that many more Williamsburg citizens lie in the churchyard unrecorded than the presently visible stones and table tombs suggest.

Lest future critics should argue that the archaeological team had failed to dig deep enough—earlier sonic testing had reported an "anomaly" as much as 20 feet down—William and Mary geology professor Gerald Johnson took core samples deep into subprehistoric clay levels and found not a trace of anything manmade. He did, however, encounter a geological anomaly at almost exactly that depth and in the northwest corner of the church that left him in no doubt that this, and not a Baconian vault, was the source of the earlier readings.

With their theoretical legs dug out from under them, does it follow that the last has been heard of the proponents of the Bacon's buried box theory? At the risk of being burned at the heretic's stake, I rather hope not.

Our world will be infinitely the poorer when every last myth is exploded and every mystery solved. Do we really need to know that the Yeti's huge footprint is only that of a small mountain ape melted large, or that the Loch Ness Monster's photographed flipper was merely a floating leaf? Similarly, do we really want to be sure that when the 1683 Bruton church was torn down, Bacon's utopian blueprint wasn't dug up, perhaps to be buried again in a churchyard near Durham, North Carolina?

One thing at least is certain: A strikeout in Williamsburg did not, and could not prove beyond all possible doubt that Francis Bacon was not a ghost writer for Anne Hathaway's husband. So, just as Marie Bauer's studies reportedly led her first to the old church at Jamestown and only when that proved fruitless she turned her attention to Williamsburg, future Baconian theorists may be inspired to renew their quest elsewhere—and that, in the view of many Bruton parishioners, is As They Like It.

The Folgate Street Experience

Never show 'em the monster

Early on Saturday morning a ghastly murder
was perpetrated near Spitalfields Market. . . .
The latest deed of ferocity has thrown
Whitechapel into a state of panic. . . .
London Daily Telegraph
September 10, 1888

ON A DRIZZLING, September evening almost a century after the Jack the Ripper murders began and as abruptly ended, my wife and I made our way through the gathering darkness into the Spitalfields area of London's East End. There on a damp step in Folgate Street two silent and melancholy men sat staring at the door opposite. Small piles of straw lay strewn among the weeds flanking the stone doorstep—the straw an ancient reminder to neighbors that there was death in the house. Over the door, the wavering flame of a gas lamp cast shadows across the entrance to Number 18 and illuminated the rusting iron bars of a pair of prisonlike bird cages whose single occupants occasionally shuffled uneasily on their perches. The 19th-century human prisoners of the Whitechapel slums had had a passion for song birds.

"Are you waiting for Mr. Severs?" I asked the men. One nodded, the other looked blankly at me as though he did not understand. Their faces appeared pale, even haunted, in the gaslight. In silence we stared at the dark and shuttered windows of the house across the street, wondering what lay in store for us when its heavy green door opened.

In 1988, in the Ripper Murders' centenary year, their story continued to fascinate, as was demonstrated by the publication of at least seven books on the subject, each thrashing over the familiar evidence and promoting its own candidate for the killer. Gruesome though the five murders were, they have long since been eclipsed in both number and ferocity. What makes them perennially intriguing is the fact that the murderer was never caught. Consequently, his name, his motive, and his fate have remained food for endless speculation and flights of imagination. And it was to be an exercise in imagination and not a desire to walk the streets that Jack trod that brought us into his hunting ground on that wet September evening.

Shortly after Audrey and I joined the Colonial Williamsburg

Ivor Noël Hume

research team in 1957, I uttered the then heretical proposition that the restored and reconstructed 18th-century buildings were no more than frames for pictures of colonial life, and that it was the prospect of experiencing the life of the past that motivated a sizable percentage of our visitors. The Restoration was then directed by architects, and archaeology was no more than an architectural tool functioning out of the drafting room. Not surprisingly, therefore, several years would elapse before the leadership would get seriously to grips with Williamsburg's broader educational opportunities and responsibilities.

The notion that there was more to historical preservation than saving buildings was by no means new. Writing about the surviving homes of Philadelphia as long ago as 1912, H. B. Eberlein had said this:

The story of a single house is ofttimes the history in small of all the country roundabout. It is only by studying history in small that we shall ever know its full meaning. It is only by marking well the homely things bound up with the daily life of the men of aforetime that we shall ever see the great facts of history in their true light and realize the full extent of their significance for us.

The Reverend W. A. R. Goodwin, the father of restored Williamsburg, shared Eberlein's foresight—though there is no proof that he read the latter's book—and saw the buildings as a means to "help us to understand more fully the social life of a given period, for after all," Eberlein had added, "that is what counts most." Dr. Goodwin was romantically conscious of the colonial ghosts who haunted the little city's streets, and he envisaged them being brought to life by means of costumed hosts and hostesses

Straw at the door and a ghostly watcher at an upstairs window warn that 18 Folgate Street is no ordinary London house.

There are said to be ghosts in Williamsburg, and in the Palace cellars one can well believe it. Speakers hidden behind barrels and under

who would walk the Palace gardens and greet visitors arriving at the Raleigh Tavern by carriage from the railroad station.

Peopling the reconstructed past has been—and always will remain a problem—not because the actors may play their roles poorly, but because their audiences cannot forget that they *are* performers. In some historical re-creations visitors do not communicate with the actors but simply view them as they would a play—watching from the outside and not from within. At Plimouth Plantation in Massachusetts, the players take another approach, willingly conversing with the visitors but professing ignorance of the world since 1627. Intriguing though the premise is, the visitors themselves cannot escape from the 20th century. They see actors, albeit educating actors, but actors just the same. More important, they see themselves. Like it or not, they remain the ultimate and inescapable anachronism. Until one is free of one's fellow 20th-century man, woman, and child, the time machine's door remains frustratingly closed.

Before coming to Williamsburg I had gained some experience writing and reading for radio. Indeed, I was weaned on it, having learned to shiver at the shriek of a howling wind and to look fearfully over my shoulder at the sound of a creaking door. Although reading remains the most direct stimulus to the imagination, radio provides a second, aural stimulation that brings us closer to physical participation.

In the early 1970s, I had an opportunity to experiment along those lines in the wine cellars of the Governor's Palace, whose flagged floors and original walling have always seemed to me to be the single most evocative place in all of Williamsburg. Using multi-channeled tape recordings and several widely spaced speakers known as transponders, we were able to re-create the voices of the archaeologists as they uncovered the cellar steps, and then slip back in time to hear the footfall of the governor's butler as he came down them, walked through the basement passages, read the labels on the cellar doors, then opened a door and went in. The effect was eerily realistic. Our ears were telling us that if we had looked a little harder we should have seen the butler walk past us. We had set at least one foot aboard the time machine.

Unfortunately, the technique had problems—problems of wiring and of maintenance. But the biggest drawback of all was the presence of visitors who might not come in at the beginning of the experience or who would talk through it. To succeed, the audience had to be controlled—i.e., arriving together and staying together—silent, and receptive. But short of making the cellars part of a guided tour, there was no way to do that.

"Are you all waiting for Mr. Severs?" The newly arrived couple who had joined us were in their early 60s, and American.

Ted Hooper

tables helped create the sound of the governor's butler's footsteps approaching and passing us on his way to another cellar.

"Boy, this is a tough place to find," the man added. "How did you hear about it?" I asked him. "From our travel agent," he replied.

But before I could question him further, we were joined by a single middle-aged woman, a New England furniture expert who knew me. I looked at my watch. I thought it said 7:29 and remembered being told on the phone by Mr. Severs that he would open the door at 7:30, and he would not open it again for late comers.

"They say he's very eccentric," remarked the New England lady.

I wondered how "they" knew. He had sounded rational and rather engaging on the telephone, though very clear about what he expected of us. On the other hand, when I had written to him from Williamsburg, the reply had been signed "Dominic Basher (footman)"—which admittedly was unexpected.

At 7:30 precisely, the door across the street opened, silhouetting a small and rather stolid figure against the warm yellow light at his back. I half expected him to be footman Basher in knee britches and powdered wig. Instead, the 38-year-old and none too closely shaven Californian who crossed Folgate Street to greet us wore an open-necked shirt and jeans. "Hello," he said, "I'm Dennis Severs."

After brief introductions he led us into the candlelit hallway

and down to the basement kitchen where a fire burned cherry red in the cast-iron grate, and a black cat languidly stretched and stared at us, its eyes gleaming in the yellow candlelight. "You sit here," Severs ordered, pointing each of us to chairs ranged along one wall. "You sit there. You there. That's excellent. And you, here. No, not there; here" and so on. For the next three hours we were to be putty in his hands—and silent putty at that.

"I have to have your complete attention," Severs told us. "I'm not a teacher. I'm here to entertain you. But I want you to remember that this is my house. I live here. It's not a museum. I warn you that I can get angry. If I don't think this is working, I may ask you to leave."

His approach was far removed from Colonial Williamsburg's concept of visitor relations. But afterwards we realized that what we were about to experience was dependent on total absorption on our part and split-second timing on his. Should we fail to sit quickly and silently where we were told or break into his narrative to ask questions, the spell would shatter and the time machine would self destruct.

The four-storied house is the last in a row of once affluent Spitalfields dwellings, an area that in 1685 became home to émigré Huguenot weavers and the center of London's silk industry. Severs had created his own Huguenot family, the Jarvises, and was about to follow them through five generations to 1901 and the death of Queen Victoria—whose silk funeral robe was to be the last royal order placed with the dying Spitalfields industry.

Our journey through London's history would begin 1,600 years earlier beneath the cellar floor where a Jarvis boy had found fragments of Roman pottery—which Severs extracted from the hole to show us—reminders that here once was a Roman cemetery. But the real story began in the early 18th century and took us from room to room through the house, up to the garret and down again as we followed the rising and declining fortunes of the Jarvises and their neighborhood. We heard and sensed the family around us. We listened to their voices in the next room and their servant's footsteps on the stairs. We heard the clatter of 19th-century looms overhead as poverty forced the family to bring the workplace into its once elegant home.

In better days Mrs. Jarvis entertained her friends for tea in the parlor, and a whispering Severs asked us to wait until he could get them to leave. When he succeeded, and we entered the room, steam was still rising from the half-empty teacups. A sudden draft made us shiver, and a few minutes later we were being told about the problems of ill-fitting windows. We learned how Mrs. Jarvis and her affluent Spitalfields women friends used their fans, and we may or may not have noticed one lying on the seat of her chair by the fireplace—until, as the fire burnt itself out and the shadows lengthened, the fan slipped from the empty chair onto the floor. Mrs. Jarvis had left the room.

The Folgate Street experience went beyond sight and sound. Each room had its own special smell—of herbs used in sweeping the 18th-century floors, of the cloying aroma of hair powder and perfume, and in the ragged 19th-century attic the stench of oil lamps and penury. Throughout the journey Severs provided a continuous commentary—in person, as we entered and left each room, but much of the time as a disembodied voice that left us to focus only on the room and its furnishings, while he slipped

William Hogarth, *The Industrious Apprentice* series

away to prepare the next.

He flooded his audience with such a wealth of political and social history, weaving important events with antiquarian trivia and entwining both into the daily activities and problems of his Jarvises, that the sheer volume of fact and fiction became overwhelming and indivisible. Before long we were forced to lay aside our mental paper and pencil, recognizing that few of Dennis Severs's "facts" would be accurately remembered tomorrow. All that would endure would be the impression of having spent three hours in the changing Jarvis world—which, of course, is what he intended.

But while our information-storage faculties may have short-circuited, other senses (those usually dormant in historical exhibits) stored memories that are unlikely ever to fade: the shiv-

Gustave Doré, *The Bull's-eye*

In the 1730s the clatter of looms meant prosperity for the Huguenot weavers of Spitalfields (opposite); but by the 1870s changing fortunes had turned once-elegant Folgate Street homes into tenements for the helpless and the hopeless. Somewhere in the darkness beyond the police patrol's lanterns Jack the Ripper watched and waited.

Below: The sights and smells, first of affluence (opposite) and later of poverty, brought generations of Jarvises stunningly and memorably alive.

er from the draft, the smell of dirt in the garret, and the sounds of feet on a fog-shrouded night in September 1888. As we sat in the semi-darkness in the Jarvises' cluttered Victorian parlor, a distant police whistle warned that the Whitechapel killer had struck again. Moments later we heard the police at the street door demanding, over Mrs. Jarvis's protestations, to search the house. We heard their boots and voices on the stairs, and as we sat holding our breaths for fear that we, too, might be discovered, we instinctively shrank back into the shadows as a constable's bull's-eye lantern probed the yard outside our window.

For those in Severs's audiences familiar with the paintings and engravings of Hogarth, Zoffany, Rowlandson, Cruikshank, and Doré, the total experience had to be the more stunning, for we had stepped through the frames into the pictures to touch the face of history—at least some of us had.

The elderly male tourist had banged his head on the staircase moments before the end and stayed behind to be repaired, and so was unavailable for debriefing. As for the two melancholy men, one explained to Severs at the door that while he had enjoyed the experience, he couldn't speak for his friend who didn't understand a word of English. "I'll explain it all to him later," he added.

I would have liked to have heard him try; but the men had no desire to linger and hurried away into the wet night. Only the lady from New England remained to share her reactions with us. She proved to have been distinctly less entranced. Unable to overlook drapes incorrectly hung or a bed not really "of the period," she concluded that although the experience was good theater (albeit an hour too long), it had little or nothing to do with muse-

Courtesy of Dennis Severs

ums. For me, however, every moment had been magical.

Dennis Severs claimed to be neither educator nor actor, only an artist. In reality, he also was a psychologist, teacher, performer, technical wizard, and master of that basic (and nowadays ignored) rule of suspense film-making: "Never show 'em the monster." But while earning our admiration, he also has to endure our jealousy for having created something that we, as professional historical communicators appealing to large numbers of independently minded visitors, know to be beyond us.

Perhaps the closest we ever came to the Severs approach in Williamsburg was to be found in the James Anderson House archaeological exhibit. There the artifact-documented reconstruction of the candlelit Traveler's Room was presented as though the guest had just left his disheveled bed. The fire's dying embers still glowed in the hearth, and the remains of his supper lay on the table beside it. The flaking whitewashed walls were gray with soot, leaving ghost images where pictures once hung, and in the corner the room's silence was broken by the ticking lantern clock. Visitors who remember the penultimate

scene in Hogarth's *A Harlot's Progress* may have recognized the stoneware mug on the mantel shelf and the labeled medicine bottles on the dressing table—though the traveler's piece of bread on the toasting fork was strictly his own.

The difference between this and 18 Folgate Street is that, although the Williamsburg room was authentic in 84 subtle yet archaeologically documented ways, its visitors, because of their numbers, remained outside the frame, never stepping into the picture, never quite able to believe that at any moment the 18th-century traveler would return and get back into bed to dream of the absent-minded lady who left her hat as his trophy. But for those of us who have been his landlord since he halted his journey at the James Anderson house in 1973, our amorous tenant was as real as the Jarvises of Spitalfields. Well, almost.

The James Anderson House archaeological exhibit was dismantled soon after the Winthrop Rockefeller Archaeology Museum opened at Carter's Grove in 1987. The house is now used as office space—but perhaps is still home to the restless spirit of a colonial traveler looking for his bed.

In the "Traveler's Room" at the James Anderson House archaeological exhibit, visitors came as close as is possible in Williamsburg to sharing the Folgate Street experience. Eighty-four excavated artifacts, ranging from the tiles on the hearth to the chamber pot, warming pan, and blanket on the bed, provided precedents for everthing in the room— save for the phantom lodger himself.

Ted Hooper

In Pursuit of the Loch Ness Mouse
The quest for a better mousetrap

IT WAS JUST a flash. Well, not so much a flash as a darker darkness that zipped across the back of the hearth and was gone—if it had been at all.

"We've got a mouse!"

"Where?"

"In the house. In the fireplace!"

"Nonsense," I replied. "There are no mice in this house."

Audrey, my wife, wasn't afraid of mice, or anything else for that matter. But she was keen on being right—particularly when she was sure she was. "We had mice in the attic last Christmas," she reminded me.

"Ah, yes. In the attic's different," I insisted. "But not down here. There's nowhere for them to hide." Which showed how much I knew about mice. Nevertheless, several years earlier I had decided to become a mousetrap collector. It came about like this:

We were on one of our annual research trips to England and stopped in the Berkshire town of Hungerford at an antique shop specializing in old tools. Amongst them was the most bizarre mousetrap I had ever seen. Not that that was a distinction hard to attain. The only kind I knew anything about was the standard spring variety, which promises to whack any mouse across the back of the neck should it be gauche enough to lean on its bait plate while lunching.

The Hungerford trap was infinitely more ingenious. It required the mouse to stick his head in a hole in a block of wood to reach bait impaled on a hook that, when pushed, released a spring mounted like a medieval catapult on top of the block, in turn jerking a loop of wire lying in the bed of the tunnel upwards to garrote the diner. I found it hard to believe that any sensible mouse would stick his head into such a hole. But the designer not only thought otherwise, he believed that *three* mice would fall for the same trick, for this was not a first-come first-served affair; it was a three-holer.

I learned much later that the garroting mechanism of the English three-holer was simultaneously manufactured here in the United States by the Victor Animal Trap Company whose "Choker Mouse Trap" was square with clipped corners through which the head holes were drilled. The shape had the advantage of placing the rash rodents further apart and at different angles, thus rendering their corpses less discouraging to late arrivals. The design must have been successful, for although the Victor Company of Lititz, Pennsylvania, is now the Woodstream Corporation, it still makes the old four-holer—but in plastic!

In 1792 cartoonist James Gilray lampooned Britain's attempts to establish a trade mission at the court of Peking. The envoy is shown trying to impress the Emperor Chien Lung with English novelties, among them a wire mousetrap of the kind sold by London street peddlers (left). The emperor answered: "I set no value on objects strange or ingenious, and have no use for your country's manufactures."

Being woefully ignorant of the ways of mice, I could not imagine that any sane rodent would stick its head into a vacant hole when what had befallen the previous diner was plain to see. And in the case of the English triple threat the prospect of a third squeezing between two corpses to take its turn at the cheese was too absurdly intriguing to be ignored. So that's how I became a mousetrap collector.

In a world in which we are constantly confronted by questionnaires asking why we bought this or support that cause, one is frequently asked to list one's hobbies. When I was younger I used to write in "Chamber pot collecting"—which was true, but a shade undignified. "Mousetrap collecting," on the other hand, sounds less sedentary and has more zap to it. Besides, it was nice, when asked by a tiresome reporter "How many do you have?" to be able to rather grandly reply: "One."

Unfortunately, I made the mistake of mentioning my collection to a London antiques dealer who several weeks later called me in Williamsburg to say that he had a line on an amazing Georgian mousetrap he knew I would want to acquire. Intimidat-

Below right: the three-holer that started it all. Colonial Williamsburg's deadfall thumper turned out to be younger than was thought (below) but, although relegated to the 19th century, the author's (right) proved triumphant in the presence of modern technology.

Opposite: more recent additions to the collection—a dual deadfall trap put together with 18th-century rose-head nails and, in front, Victor's wooden four-holer.

Ivor Noël Hume

Hans Lorenz

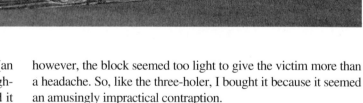

ed by the transatlantic phone call offering a mere mousetrap (an approach normally reserved for a Picasso or a Chippendale highboy), I failed to insist that my collection was closed. Thus did it grow from solitary grandeur to an ignominious two—made worse by the discovery when the expensive Georgian treasure arrived (I'm sure I also paid for the phone call) that it wasn't a trap but a mouse house complete with sleeping quarters, dining hall, and rotating rec-room.

The second real trap was added shortly afterwards, a reputedly 18th-century device paralleling another in the Colonial Williamsburg collection, both owing something to the derivative ingenuity of France's Dr. Guillotin. However, instead of a blade descending between two posts, the traps substitute a block of wood, its fall triggered by releasing a string tied to a peg held by pressure against a pivoting bait tray. When that is touched, the peg is released. And down comes the wood block with a mouse-flattening thump. At least that was the idea. To my eye,

however, the block seemed too light to give the victim more than a headache. So, like the three-holer, I bought it because it seemed an amusingly impractical contraption.

This, then, was the scope of the collection when the mystery mouse made its first alleged appearance. Still unwilling to believe that it existed, I nevertheless set the standard 20th-century spring trap.

The next morning the trap remained unsprung—but the cheese was gone. Three nights in a row the same thing happened: the trap set, the bait missing. Each night I devised more ingenious ways to ensure that the trap could only be approached from the right operating direction—no sideways sneaking up on it or attacking from the back. Short of descending from a rope or being dangled by a troupe of acrobatic friends, there was no approaching but by frontal assault. Yet each day the bait vanished, and the spring remained unsprung.

By the fourth day I had begun to question whether we were

dealing with a mouse at all, but rather with some lighter, more nimble, and certainly more crafty protagonist—like a cheese-eating cricket. Whatever it was, I could only hope that if the food supplies were appreciably increased, it might eventually grow fatter—and slower. However, the "maybe-it's-not-a-mouse" theory was destined soon to be discarded when careful inspection of a rejected bait fragment revealed a V-shaped pattern of teeth marks.

Captain Ahab had his white whale; I had what Audrey had dubbed the Loch Ness Mouse, a creature of infinite cunning and as elusive as a phantom. But I was not about to be defeated.

The wire springs of the three-holer were too fragile to be pressed into service. But the 18th-century falling-block device had no such frail parts, and after perhaps 150 years of benign inactivity, it returned to work alongside its 20th-century counterpart—both primed with identically delicious samples of Cheddar's best.

Three hours later, en route to bed, I crept into the darkened living room with a shielded flashlight in the hope of catching the competition at dinner. Too late! The modern trap's cheese was gone. Almost as an afterthought I swung the light beam over to the massive 18th-century structure. Its trigger string dangled free; the block had dropped, and from beneath it protruded a tail and two pink feet.

Triumph was tinged with remorse as I elevated the block to inspect its handiwork. That a piece of wood barely heavy enough to bruise had created so incredibly thin a mouse was hard to credit. The Loch Ness Mouse had been transformed into a novelty bookmarker.

Was it sheer bad luck that the 18th-century trap had scored when the modern version had been skunked again and again? One mouse, admittedly, was less than an infallible statistic.

The next morning Audrey was up ahead of me, leaving the door ajar between the still-darkened bedroom and the lighted corridor. Peeling one none too finely focused eye, I sluggishly prepared to follow her. It was then that I saw it. Silhouetted in the shaft of light, sitting up on its hind legs and wiping its whiskers was the Phantom of the Fireplace.

I knew that victims of violent death—beheaded queens, murdered nuns, people like that—have returned to haunt the places where they died. But a ghost mouse, and so soon? Nonetheless, to me, that possibility seemed no more improbable than that there could be a second mouse in a house where none could hide. Audrey, on the other hand, was less taken with the manifesting mouse theory, and although she could more easily accept that there just *might* be another live one, she preferred a more logical explanation: I was suffering from the delusions common to mouse murderers. Audrey's skills, however, were not limited to criminal psychology; she also was a practical person. "You'd better reset the traps," she told me.

And so I did—the new and the old, seven nights in a row. And seven more mice dined off the 20th-century bait tray before demonstrating how, in mousetrap terms, the future really can learn from the past.

Tailpiece

IN THE ANTIQUARIAN world things are not always what they seem—or are sold—to be. Although Colonial Williamsburg has only one falling-block mousetrap in its collection, the device is relatively common in the rural "bygones" galleries of English local museums, the seemingly oldest in the Elizabethan House Museum at Great Yarmouth. Mine was bought as 18th century, and Colonial Williamsburg's was cataloged as "Georgian"—which could mean any time between 1714 and 1830. Knowing that I would have to write a caption for the Williamsburg example, I asked curator Jay Gaynor whether he could be a little more precise. Meanwhile, I was searching paintings, engravings, and drawings from the 16th to the early 19th century for supportive illustrations.

I should have realized that something was wrong when an exhaustive search failed to yield any picture of the deadfall trap. All I could find belonged to two classes, both relatively mouse friendly—one a wire cage akin to a lobster pot and the other a wooden box that operated in much the same way as modern, humane cage traps. Not even Hogarth, whom one might expect to have enjoyed drawing a mouse thumper, offered anything like it. A phone call from Jay Gaynor explained why.

"We've just X-rayed our trap," he told me. "It's put together with wire nails."

Eighteenth-century nails were all handwrought. Following these through much of the 19th century were nails cut from sheet iron, and it was only toward the end of the century that machines using milled steel wire superseded the cut nail. It would be highly unlikely, therefore, that Colonial Williamsburg's "Georgian" trap could date before the 1870s. So where did that leave mine?

X-ray photographs would show that it combined both cut and wire nails—most of them wire. Clearly, therefore, both traps are of much the same date. Where, then, you may ask, does that leave all those Elizabethan and 18th-century traps in other museums and antique shops? Is it possible that the Loch Ness Mouse, in reaching for one more piece of cheese, has thrown the history of mousetraps into a globe-girdling frenzy of revisionism?

I do hope so.

"Sweete Themmes! Runne softly"
"Mudlarks" probe shore for antique objects, some tied to Carter's Grove

*Twenty bridges from Tower to Kew
Wanted to know what the River knew,
For they were young and the Thames was old,
And this is the tale that the River told . . .*

S O WROTE Rudyard Kipling in 1911. Nearly 80 years later the bridges or their descendants are still there, and the river continues to whisper its story to those with the time to listen—and look.

No other river has been written about over so many centuries with such affection by so many poets, or with such disregard for the truth. In 1501 William Dunbar, in honoring London as "The flour of Cities all," declared "Fresh is thy ryver." At the close of the same century Edmund Spenser begged "Sweete Themmes! Runne softly," and in the same year (1596) Michael Drayton described how "Down to fair Thames I gently took my way." Fresh, fair, and sweet were terms used throughout the centuries, and for poets who wrote of the river as it idled in its upper reaches or lunged below London into the open sea, the adjectives had validity. But in those miles that lapped the fetid shores of Westminster, Lambeth, the City, Southwark, Wapping, and the docks, such words as "foul" and "filthy" used by Victorian social reformer Henry Mayhew were closer to the mark, for the Thames at London was the city's unimpeded cesspool.

An anonymous contributor to *Punch* describing Queen Victoria's river procession in 1858 asked:

*Familiar with the river's smell
Who cannot fancy, all too well,
The odour which prevailed,
Which rose from the polluted stream
As thick, but not so white, as cream,
And in a suffocating steam,
The Royal sense assailed?*

In spite of the indignities suffered by the river at the hands of Londoners through countless generations, the Thames remained, as Sir John Denham wrote in 1642, "the most loved of all the ocean's sons." The river was Britain's principal artery as London was Britain's heart, and it was on the Thames's tides that most ships sailed for the New World—even if the first-class passengers preferred not to board until the vessels reached Deal, the Isle of Wight, or even Plymouth.

For Virginians doing business in London in the 17th and 18th centuries, the Thames made its presence felt, either as a barrier (there was only one bridge) or as the equivalent of an interstate highway. From Lord Mayor's barge and common coal carriers to Dutch eel boats and the river taxis known as wherries, a constant stream of traffic plied the river—except when winter fog blanketed it from shore to shore, and when it froze. Then, as if by

Low tide on the Thames near Southwark Bridge reveals 20 centuries of English history. For the author (opposite) sharp eyes and a surface-scratching trowel were his only tools. Today, professional salvagers (right) use metal detectors and shovels to reach salable treasures buried shoulder deep in the mud.

(opposite) photo by Ira Block

Ivor Noël Hume

A deep-digging mudlark shows his latest find, a 15th- or 16th-century iron padlock (left). Below, against a tapestry of shards and bones, a hobnailed shoe sole helped explain similar nails found in a grave at Martin's Hundred. Above the sole, two tile shards embrace more than a thousand years, the slashed red fragment coming from a Roman central-heating system, the blue-and-white shard from an early 17th-century fireplace.

Ivor Noël Hume

magic, the river above the London Bridge would be transformed into a frost fair.

In the winter of 1683–1684, the ice remained for two months and grew so thick that a whole ox was roasted on it. Stalls selling souvenirs, toys, food, and liquor stretched all the way from the Temple to London Bridge. A printing press was set up, jugglers juggled, bears performed, a bull was baited, and itinerant hustlers of both sexes and every variety had the time of their lives. Diarist John Evelyn called it a "Bacchanalian triumph, or carnival on the water." Unlike land fairs, where somebody had to be paid to pick up the trash, frost fairs had no problem with debris; it all conveniently disappeared into the river when the ice melted.

Using the river as a repository for trash had been commonplace since 43 A.D. when Roman Londinium began to develop on its north bank and the first bridge was built. London Bridge has remained in approximately the same location for more than 1900 years, providing since the Middle Ages a wall above which none but the smallest oceangoing vessels could pass. The rest moored just below the bridge at Billingsgate Dock or farther downstream beyond the Tower of London in reaches leading to the riverside villages of Wapping, Rotherhythe, and Deptford. By the early 19th century so numerous were the ships that from the Thames-side streets the river could be seen only through a web of spars and rigging.

William Drew, an American visiting from Maine in 1851, was astonished to find that "as far as can be seen, the river and docks are filled with sailing vessels, war-ships, and steamers, holding intercourse with all parts of the world. Such a tide of life as is to be beheld upon the Thames," Drew added, "is to be seen nowhere else on all the face of the earth."

Above London Bridge the boats were smaller but the traffic no less intense and, save in the moments of slack water at the top and bottom of the tide, steering one's craft between the arches could spell disaster for even the most experienced pilot. Over the years countless wherries and barges capsized, decanting their passengers and cargoes into the river, with the result that an entire profession was created to take advantage of other people's misfortunes. London dredgermen earned their living tonging, netting, and grapple-dragging for lost goods and drowned people; and as late as the mid-19th century, even if relatives offered no reward, a dredgerman could be assured of five shillings in "inquest money" for each corpse recovered. At that time it was well known but never officially explained that, though dredgermen brought in many victims, their purses and pockets invariably were empty.

Money found its way into the river in unexplainable quantities. Some was tossed there for luck, a rite going back to Roman times when travelers made offerings to the river gods, and some because the coins had already brought bad luck by being forgeries. But the presence in the mud of hundreds, probably thousands, of officially minted coins ranging from medieval silver pennies to 17th- and 18th-century copper farthings and halfpennies cannot be explained except as the product of countless accidents while persons were boarding and disembarking the wherries. Though the farthing and halfpenny denominations were small, they nonetheless represented wealth to the London poor, and we might suppose that no one would deliberately have discarded them. We might equally suppose that finger rings would be treated with no less respect. But such was not the case. One band recovered is engraved "I love v euer," and another, "LOVe THy TRV FRIND." Perhaps the friend wasn't true enough.

No matter how the treasures got into the river, most have one thing in common: They are still there, sealed in the silt waiting to be found, many preserved in immaculate condition.

Each day, as the tide goes down and the gray expanse of the shore begins to appear, a handful of professional searchers known as mudlarks can be seen descending the iron ladders and crumbling wharfside steps to begin their search for treasures that can be sold to museums or into the antiques trade. Theirs is a business whose history goes back to the early 19th century, when the poorest of the London poor, the shore rakers, salvaged coal, rope, copper nails, and the like and sold them to merchants for the pennies needed to feed their families.

In 1861 Henry Mayhew wrote of the "mud-larks" that they "may be seen of all ages, from mere childhood to positive decrepitude, crawling among the barges at the various wharfs along the river; it cannot be said that they are clad in rags, for they are scarcely half covered by the tattered indescribable things that serve them for clothing; their bodies are grimed with the foul soil of the river, and their torn garments stiffened up like boards with dirt of every possible description."

In this same mid-Victorian era, English antiquarians began to realize that the river was a treasure-house of relics. That awareness was heightened in 1857 not by the midstream dredging but from shoreline digging for new docks at Shadwell, about a mile below the present Tower Bridge. The laborers were then known as "navigators" (popularly shortened to "navvies"), and for the price of a beer and a few pennies they could be relied on to smuggle out of the docks anything their spades unearthed. The carriages of collectors are said to have congregated at the dockyard gates waiting for the navvies to emerge with the day's loot.

Two of these men, Charles Eaton and William Smith, reputedly doubled as mudlarks; and when the antiquarian market exceeded the supply, they opened up a manufactory of their own in a tenement near the Tower of London. So successful was the firm of Billie and Charlie that they soon gave up digging and shore raking to sell their products, not to the antiquaries (too risky) but to other navvies. Today, though their extraordinary creations fool no one, they are sought after as antiques in their own right; and one of the best collections in either Britain or America has been assembled by Williamsburg businessman Thomas W. Wood.

As the economic lot of the London poor improved, the mudlarks and dredgermen disappeared. So, too, did the wealthy private collectors. For the next 50 years or more such riverside

The Thames waterfront as Virginia's first settlers remembered it; drawn by J. C. Vischer in 1616. Dwarfed by St. Paul's Cathedral, the shores flanking Queenhithe Dock would become the premier hunting ground for historical mudlarks.

relics as were retained came from construction sites and found their way into the London and Guildhall Museums (now amalgamated into the Museum of London). Legend has it that the mudlarks' second coming occurred on the night of Sunday, December 29, 1940.

While German incendiary bombs rained down onto the city and into the Thames, and as the flames burst through the windows and doorways of the multistoried warehouses, turning the river into a shimmering orange sheet, Robin Green, a crewman aboard one of the fire-fighting boats, fell overboard. When he crawled ashore, he saw in the light of the fires that in his muddy hand he was gripping a broken clay tobacco pipe. Legend or not, it is a fact that in the years immediately after the war, Green and a handful of friends began a Sunday morning ritual of scouring the city shores in search of pipes, coins, rings, and any other small relics of London's history. The resulting collection was sold to the Guildhall Museum in 1949.

In those days the discipline now known as historical archaeology did not exist; consequently, the river's mini-treasures were seen as individual specimens able to inform only about themselves. No one looked beyond them to what they might have to say about the localities where they were found.

My own introduction to the archaeology of the post-medieval centuries began on the Thames foreshore in the spring of 1949. Among my first discoveries plucked from the mud beside Billingsgate Dock was a somewhat battered pewter coin minted in 1688 in the reign of James II for service in the American plantations. It proved to be an unrecognized omen, for six years after finding it I, too, would be leaving for "plantation" service with Colonial Williamsburg. Nevertheless, as for so many new Virginians through the centuries, memories of the "nobel Thamesis" endure. The sound of the lapping tide as it steals away from the shore, the pungent smell of the mud, the sight of sunlight glistening on the still wet brickbats, broken roofing tiles, and debris of 2,000 years are as indelibly printed on the senses as any camera can record on film. The thrill of spotting a 17th-century brass thimble or a Dutch tobacco box, or perhaps an 18th-century pewter cup, a Tudor toy lion, or an Elizabethan child's miniature pistol exact in almost every detail is neither easily described nor soon forgotten.

As an archaeologist, one is supposed to bury such pleasures under so many layers of professionalism that the excitement of

Ivor Noël Hume

Metals can survive in immaculate condition in the Thames mud, as these unconserved "brass" items attest. The coin (above), a 73 A.D. dupondius of the emperor Vespasian, was pulled up by a dredger below London Bridge. The Dutch tobacco box and latten spoon (right) date from the second half of the 17th century and are from Queenhithe, as is the Elizabethan toy pistol (below), its mechanism restored by Colonial Williamsburg gunsmith George Suiter.

the search and the breathless moment of discovery are as muted as an old man's love. But do that, and the past dies, too.

We are all finders at heart, and on any summer's day a new generation of professional mudlarks can expect to share the shore with a lawyer from New York, a priest from Long Island, a librarian from the College of William and Mary, or even a silversmith from Colonial Williamsburg. These amateurs seek only the gentle satisfaction of finding a few fragments of London's history to bring home as memorials to the place where Anglo-American history began. But the Thames shores have more to offer—more even than the modern pro-mudlarks recognize, for the social historian wanting to study London life and trade in past centuries has much to learn from the river's tidal shores.

Just as in the colonial centuries the Thames began the journey of people and goods to the New World, so today it still helps us reach out to them—even to solving 17th-century archaeological puzzles at Carter's Grove. A small brass box found on the Thames shore showed us what the parts of a similar box bearing the mark of the same Dutch maker found on our John Jackson site would have looked like when intact. Then, too, a potter working in Wolstenholme Towne produced vessels of an unrecorded shape, leaving us puzzling over where he learned to make such pots. A year later I found a fragment of just such a vessel at the entrance to London's Queenhithe Dock.

On that same September morning, an hour's search yielded a large and evidently antique boat hook, pottery ranging in date from Roman times to the 19th century, a German stoneware fragment matching the best Rhenish jug from Carter's Grove, 30 pence in modern currency, and a finely preserved 1807 penny of George III, its reverse struck from a rare die.

In Robin Green's day and throughout my youthful mudlarking, no electronic aids existed to tell us which bricks and stones to overturn. Indeed, by agreement with the Port of London Authority, digging was limited to a depth of six inches. But that restriction is no more. Today's treasure-hunting mudlark comes armed not with a keen eye and a deft trowel, but with shovels, sieves, bailing buckets, and beeping metal detectors. Shoulder-deep and coated in mud like his forebears, he is to be found in holes four and five feet in diameter, hacking his way down through the centuries in search of anything salable.

I interviewed one such digger whom I'll call Charlie. At first as suspicious as a gold prospector with a secret strike, Charlie

Ivor Noël Hume

An Elizabethan silver sixpence (above), a child's pewter cup from the early 18th century (top, left), and a collection of finger rings ranging from Roman gold to Victorian brass (bottom, left) leave us wondering why they ended their useful days in the Thames mud.

Buckles from shoes, spurs, and sword belts span the years from the 15th to the 18th century (below), while buttons range from those off Elizabethan doublets to 19th-century uniforms (right). Such small but informative objects are among the most common of the river's treasures.

Ivor Noël Hume

kept his head down as he bailed water. But eventually he began to talk about his uncertain and sometimes hazardous trade. "Some stuff you can sell and some you can't," he told me. "Coins is easy," he said, producing a small can containing the morning's haul: half a dozen farthings from the reigns of Charles II and William III. "They're how I know where I'm at in time," he explained, pointing to a layer of gray mud below a sealing stratum of chalk rubble. "Everything below that is going to be 17th century or earlier."

Charlie's was the basic archaeological reasoning, but for him it spelled only the difference between junk and jewels. A few minutes later his beeping detector proved his point. Reaching into the side of his hole he pulled out a 15th- or 16th-century iron padlock, so well preserved that it needed only a key to operate it. "That I can sell," he told me proudly. "But tools like hammers, drills, chisels, and stuff like that, there's not much call for them. But knives and spoons, you can move those—like that!" and he snapped his muddy fingers. I remembered that several years ago another of Charlie's confreres had offered to sell a collection to Colonial Williamsburg containing 290 knives and 30 padlocks.

84

Ivor Noël Hume

Relics of childhood are particularly evocative. These three toys in pottery (left) are from Queenhithe: a Tudor or Stuart dog, the torso of a Roman boy holding a dove, and a medieval or later lion.

When genuine antiquities were in short supply, Victorian mudlarks William Smith and Charles Eaton manufactured their own (below). Today, the works of "Billie and Charlie" are collectors' items in their own right. This selection from an American collection includes a key and dagger thought to be the work of a contemporary but unknown faker.

They would later find a home in the Museum of London.

The majority of that museum's best preserved excavated metal artifacts have come from the silt of the Thames and its tributaries, almost all of them purchased from navvies and mudlarks. Both the Museum of London and the Tower of London continue to do business with these people, believing it better to sup with the devil than to go hungry. Although curators and archaeologists rightly deplore the destruction of the important time relationships that prove which artifacts belong to what period, it is better to know what is being found and offered for sale than for the treasures to disappear into private collections, perhaps never to be seen again.

There is no denying that properly controlled, large-scale excavations more or less anywhere on the London foreshores could provide a wealth of information and enough marvelously preserved treasures to enrich any number of museums. But as Tower of London archaeologists discovered when they dug a modest trench in the autumn of 1986, major excavations would be technically difficult and prohibitively expensive. Instead, the mudlarks with their licenses to plunder dig on.

As I walked away from Charlie's hole on the Southwark shore, I caught up with one of his friends, who had listened to our conversation. "Here," he shouted, "let me show you something!" He pointed to a small black disk glistening on the surface of the mud. Slightly smaller than a dime, it was a silver halfpenny of Henry VI dating from the mid-15th century. "You see," said the finder, "we can still find stuff your way!"

With the coin admired and congratulations expressed, we parted, each on our stooping way peering intently at the mud for the hint of something round, pointed, or square-cornered, or the glint of brass or copper, or perhaps the protruding neck of a bottle. Some minutes later my new acquaintance caught up with me. "I'm off now," he said. "But before I go, I'd like to shake your hand."

"By all means. But why?" I asked.

"Because you're the one who started all this," he declared, waving his hand in the direction of the frantically bailing Charlie. "It was your book *Treasure in the Thames* what done it."

I don't remember my reply. The shock was akin to being praised for adding a moustache to the Mona Lisa.

"Yus," my friend added. "Your book's our bible. But it's got so rare that when one of us finds a copy in a library, we goes and nicks it."

The Mermaid Mystique

Go and catch a falling star . . . Teach me to hear mermaids singing

John Donne

The front & back View of a Mermaid.

Published as the Act directs, August 1793.

DO YOU HAVE any mermaids?" I asked the London shopkeeper. And two lady customers standing beside me glanced at each other and edged away down the counter.

"No, I'm afraid not," he replied.

"Wait," said his assistant. "I think we may have one in the basement." And the two women hurriedly left the shop. That was neither the first nor the last time that I would be suspected of *dementia sirenia.* You won't find that in the dictionary, but you can take it from me that it means mad about mermaids. In any case, my question was right in line with a long tradition of British antiquarian inquiry—like Robert Plot, who in 1678 sent out a questionnaire asking "Are there any Sepulchres hereabout of Men of Gigantick stature, Roman Generals or others of ancient times? Has there ever been any apparitions hereabout?" In short, the prospect of seeing a mermaid emerge from a Portobello Road

Courtesy of Museum of London

Above: Medallion from an English stoneware bottle made by John Dwight of Fulham for a "merman" tavern ca. 1680. A scientifically rendered mermaid (left) was engraved in 1793 to illustrate a volume of natural history.

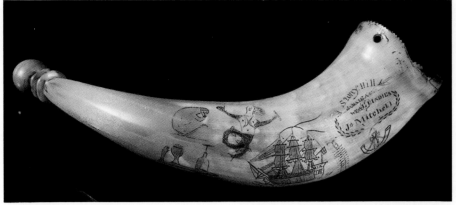

Ivor Noël Hume

Courtesy of National Geographic Society

The scrimshaw-decorated powder horn (left) shows soldier J. Mitchell's portrait of a mermaid as he saw her in a Jamaican lagoon ca. 1822. Below: N. C. Wyeth's romantic interpretation embellishes his mural of the Western Hemisphere, commissioned in 1927 for the National Geographic Society.

basement is something any antiquary can take in his stride. And I was sure I could—and would.

My quest, like so much historical research, was the product not of academically engendered intent but by a chance discovery. It happened like this: I had been pursuing historical and archaeological research in several Caribbean islands seeking parallels for colonial life and artifacts found in Virginia. A London dealer who knew of my interest offered me a powder horn made by J. Mitchell, a British soldier of the 33rd Regiment of Foot serving at Stony Hill, Jamaica, in the 1820s.

Mitchell evidently was both an artist and a naturalist, for although his engravings included the usual images that soldiers think about—a bottle, an overflowing glass, and a sailing ship to take him home, they also included recognizable renderings of local wildlife: centipede, scorpion, iguana, and a remarkably accurate sketch of an African Green Monkey, a species still to be seen on the neighboring island of St. Kitts. And then Mitchell drew a mermaid.

If you invite an average person to do that, the mermaid will invariably turn out to have a come-hither face and a titillating torso. But not Mitchell's. While his has the right tail and holds the traditional mermaid's comb and mirror, that's where tradition stops. Her face and head are unattractively pod-shaped, and her chest is as flat as a board. "Why?" I hope you'll ask.

Because the man who could draw a recognizable African Green Monkey likewise drew the mermaid as he actually saw her.

Although Mitchell's powder-horn engraving would seem to be the only surviving rendering of a real mermaid, he was

Below: The earliest portrait of a British mermaid adorns the tympanum of a doorway into the 12th-century church at Stow Longa, Huntingdonshire. She appears to be calling for help while being set upon by dogs. The concept of an undersea world inhabited by parallels to land creatures goes back into classical mythology. The 2nd-century Roman potsherd (top, left) is molded with a fish-tailed stag. Eleven centuries later an English tilemaker decided that a mermaid holding a fish would be acceptable to decorate a floor in England's Litchfield Cathedral (right, center). In 1491–1493 woodcarvers in Holland used Tritons and Sirens to enrich the church of St. Sulpice at Diest (right).

Courtesy of W. W. Rodwell

Ivor Noël Hume

Courtesy of J. A. J. M. Verspaandonk

by no means the first to encounter one in the Caribbean. On Wednesday, January 9, 1493, sitting in his cramped quarters aboard the *Nina* off the coast of Hispaniola, Christopher Columbus recorded that he "saw three sirens that came up very high out of the sea. They are not as beautiful as they are painted," he added, "since in some ways they have a face like a man." He went on to note that he had seen others along the west coast of Africa.

That there were African as well as American mermaids would be confirmed more than two centuries later by a highly reliable source—for who could doubt the objectivity of a Jesuit missionary? He not only saw them, he ate them.

The 1737 edition of Nathaniel Bailey's *Universal Etymolog-*

ical English Dictionary reported it this way: After first dismissing the mermaid as "a sea monster, which is described by painters and poets with the upper parts of woman, and the lower of a fish," the lexicographer went on to write his own rebuttal:

. . . whereas it has been thought they have been only the product of painters' invention, it is confidently reported that there is in the following lake, fishes which differ in nothing from mankind, but in want of speech and reason. Father Francis de Pavia, a missionary, being in the kingdom of Congo in Africa, who would not believe that there were such creatures, affirms that the queen of Singa did

see, in a river coming out of the lake Zaire, many mermaids something resembling a woman in the breasts, nipples, hands and arms; but the lower part is perfect fish, the head round, the face like a calf, a large mouth, little ears, and round full eyes. Which creatures father Merula often saw and ate of them.

That seems to have been the second father's only claim to fame, but Francis de Pavia's description of a creature with calf-like features gets us a step closer to the truth—and to Mitchell of the 33rd's Jamaican engraving, but not in the least like the mermaid of our imagination. For that we can look to Washington, D. C., and to the headquarters of the National Geographic Society where, in 1927, the great American artist N. C. Wyeth embellished his painted map of the Western Hemisphere with the quintessential mermaid, complete with flowing tresses, gilded mirror, and green nipples. On the other side of his hemisphere Wyeth painted her escort Neptune, a rather formidable fellow with a trident in one hand, a party favor crown on his bearded head—and red nipples, a reminder that to survive as a species through the centuries, mermaids needed mates.

Knowing absolutely nothing about them when my search began, I assumed that mermaids were created out of the imaginations of sex-starved sailors in the 16th century. Mermen, I must confess, never crossed my mind. But they should have, for the history of semi-human sea creatures goes back into the deeps of archaeological time, beginning with a Babylonian water god, half man and half fish, sculpted on an 8th-century B.C. relief at Khorsabad in modern Iraq.

The classical world had its sea gods, and the Greeks had a family of them who lived in the depths of the ocean: Poseidon (who for the Romans became Neptune and who has survived as the father of the oceans and the universal seafood deity), Poseidon's wife, Amphritrite, who became the Romans' sea goddess Salacia—almost certainly the prototypical mermaid—and their son Triton, all three of them part human and part fish. But in addition to this conventional family, mythology also gave us those menaces to mariners, the sirens whom Columbus equated with the creatures that rose up before him out of the blue Carib Sea. We meet them first in Homer's *Odyssey*, where they are not truly sea creatures but sit on an island "in a flowery meadow, surrounded by the moldering bones of men, and with their sweet song allure and infatuate those that sail by." They, of course, would live on in the German legend of the Lorelei, the Rhine maiden who lured fishermen to disaster. Although in antiquity the sirens were often portrayed as creatures of the air rather than of the sea, time set them squarely in the ocean.

Ancient logic dictated that if there were deities who lived in the sea, they would not be there alone, and out of that emerged the concept of an undersea world that paralleled our own. Not only were there merpeople but mer-animals, who relied on tail and fins for propulsion. It may well have been the Romans, there-

These tin-glazed Dutch tiles in the collection of the Victoria and Albert Museum are from two mid- to later 17th-century sets and evidently the work of different painters, one more spirited than the other.

Courtesy of R. J. C. Hildyard, Victoria and Albert Museum

fore, who took that concept to Britain, for in the first millennium A.D. the British were not a seafaring people. Be that as it may, it is a fact that pictures of tritons, sea horses, and even sea stags are to be found molded in relief on Roman pottery.

How European mermaids spent their time between being portrayed on Roman pottery and posing for a sculptor decorating a doorway into the tiny 12th-century church as Stow Longa in Huntingdonshire is anybody's guess. But that was where I went to photograph what is almost certainly England's earliest portrait of a mermaid. The vicar of Stow Longa, the Reverend Ronald Frost, showed me the doorway with its astonishing sculptured tympanum. The mermaid occupies most of it, her arms spread, her mouth open, her hair looking as though it were thatched, and her body from the waist down as fishy as it can be. My host had no idea why a mermaid should occupy so prominent a place, indeed, *any* place in a nowhere-near-the-sea parish church, and I had no suggestions to offer—at least not at the time. Now I think I do.

The Stow Longa mermaid dates from some time in the century that began in 1100 A.D., and in 1187, according to Chambers's *Cyclopaedia* (1738), "such a monster was fished up in the county of Suffolk, and kept by the governor for six months. It bore so near a conformity with man, that nothing seemed wanting besides speech. One day it took the opportunity of making its escape, and plunging into the sea, was never more heard of." In the 12th century Suffolk's government, and therefore its governor, was seated at Bury St. Edmunds, only 55 miles from little Stow Longa.

A century later and about 80 miles to the west, tilemakers at Lichfield included a fish-holding mermaid in one of their many designs. Paviors used the tile in a floor of the library at Lichfield Cathedral, where it remained unrecorded until recently rediscovered by architectural historian Dr. Warwick Rodwell. The captured mermaid of 1187 can hardly have been the inspiration for the Lichfield tile, but it might have prompted the carver of an arch in Bishop Alcock's chapel (1524) in Ely Cathedral, for that lies even closer to Suffolk than Stow Longa. Besides, we know that the 12th-century legend was still being told in the 18th century, when Ephraim Chambers compiled his encyclopedia. Though badly eroded, the Ely mermaid is the earliest in England to be shown with the now-traditional comb and mirror.

Across the North Sea in Holland, she was already well represented; in fact by the end of the 15th century mermaids had become stock characters among ecclesiastical wood carvers. My

Opposite: Colonial Williamsburg's London delftware charger of 1648 makes the most enthusiastic use of mermaids in 17th-century English ceramic art (center). Much stiffer, yet pleasing in their different treatments, are those on two London delftware plates (top, left, ca. 1720; top, right, ca. 1740). The ca. 1710 Bristol delftware charger's shell-blowing Triton (bottom, left) is more awkward. In an entirely different medium is the massive slipware charger (bottom, right) by Staffordshire's Ralph Toft (ca. 1666–1689), who forgot that Sirens sing.

illustrated examples were photographed by another architectural historian, Mr. J. A. J. M. Verspaandonk, in the church of St. Sulpice at Diest in Holland, and date from 1491–1493. Here we have not only the full-blown mermaid but also her mate, his human parts formidably encased in armor of the period. The earliest such pair is to be seen in the church of St. Peter, at Louvain, and dates from the period 1438–1441. Is it perhaps mere coincidence that that was another time that produced a captive mermaid? Once again Ephraim Chambers has something intriguing to offer.

In the year 1430, after a huge tempest, which broke down the dykes in Holland, and made way for the sea into the meadows, some girls of the town of Edam in West-Freezland, going in a boat to milk their cows, perceived a mermaid embarrassed in the mud, and with very little water. They took it into their boat and brought it with them to Edam, dressed it in womens' apparel, and taught it to spin. It fed like them, but could never be brought to offer speech.

Although spread across six centuries, these tales of mermaid sightings have one thing in common: The mermaids could not speak. And that's odd, because the sirens' principal attribute, as every classical scholar knew, was the quality of their singing. It seems fair to argue, therefore, that by the 16th and 17th centuries, for most people the siren connection persisted in name only—but not among scholars.

One of the earliest of English dictionaries, *The New World of Words* (1671 edition) contained the entry "*Meremade, or Maremaid, see Syren.*" If nothing else, that provided us with the common name's derivation: the Latin *mare* meaning sea, and *maid* (according to Bailey's dictionary, 1749) meaning "A virgin, a young or unmarried Woman; also a Fish." When one follows the *New World of Words*'s instruction to look up "Syren," there's no such entry. You find it under "Siren"—thus demonstrating the vagaries of spelling in the late 17th century.

Once there, the entry proves to be right on the traditional track: "certain Sea-deities, three in number . . . having their upper parts like maids, and their lower parts like fishes; they used by the sweetnesse of their voices, to allure Marriners to the Rocks, and cause them to be cast away." The writer then went on to recall the legend of Ulysses and his escape from the sirens' blandishments.

The sea deity or what might be termed a sensuous fish perception took artistic shape in Europe in the 15th century and coincided with the realization that the commercial world was a lot bigger than had hitherto been supposed. The sea was no longer a barrier but a conduit, and so for the allegorical craftsmen it needed a persona. At no time has that personality been more gloriously achieved than in the silver-gilt head table ornament made in Paris in 1482 known as the Burghley Nef. So named because it belonged to the Burghley family (a nef was a container for salt and napkins), it is built around a nautilus shell that formed the hull of a tall ship in full sail riding the sea personified as a mermaid. In another famed example of the silversmith's craft, this time made in London in 1610–1611, the mermaid plays a less allegorical role. As a pitcher paired with a silver basin, she busily combs her hair while dispensing water through her nipples.

Jewelers, too, found inspiration in the sea creatures, and the pendant called the Canning Jewel is among the finest ornaments surviving from the latter half of the 16th century. Made in Italy in the form of a triton holding a sword and shield, it was fashioned in enameled gold set and hung with rubies, diamonds, and pearls. No merman was ever better served.

With silversmiths and jewelers at one end of the artistic scale, English potters were pretty close to the other. But they, too, tried their hands at drawing and painting mermaids. The best surviving example is in the Colonial Williamsburg collection: a large London delftware charger dated 1648, its central decoration features the biblically correct theme of Susanna being interfered with by a couple of overly familiar elders. Perhaps it was drawing Susanna in the buff and combing her hair that prompted the painter to decide to surround the group with a motley of mermaids, for they, needless to say, had no place in the Biblical story.

In the second half of the 17th century, when Holland had become a major maritime trader, it was perhaps inevitable that Dutch painters of delftware tiles should feature their ship's driving force. Triton blowing his shell seems to have been a relatively common motif, and there are parts of two such tile sets in the Victoria and Albert Museum's collection. Not all depict Triton. Another portrays a merman frolicking (perhaps an understatement) with a female, and yet another in the same set shows her reclining naked and somewhat frazzled on his back. Needless to say, curators catalog these not as naughty pictures but as allegorical portrayals of Nepture and Salacia, probably unaware that *The New World of Words* defined "salacity" as "wantonnesse, or inclination to Venery" and attributed its derivation to "Salacia a goddesse of the water, whom the ancients held to be the wife of *Neptune*, and that she caused the fluctuation, or moving up and down of the sea."

Someone once said—it might have been me—that Dutch tiles provided design ideas for English delftware potters, and two mermaid plates in London delftware of the early 18th century seem to bear that out. Less Netherlandish in character is another delft dish, this one from Bristol and now in the Fitzwilliam Museum's Schreiber Collection where the motif is cataloged as a mermaid blowing into a conch shell. However, it was Triton who traditionally blew into a shell to direct the wind, thus making the Bristol merperson male rather than female.

In an entirely different medium, between about 1666 and 1689 the Staffordshire slipware potters Thomas and Ralph Toft, who specialized in large and flamboyant dishes, tried their hands at mermaids with virtually identical results—except in one instance when Ralph forgot to give her a mouth. Why both men would have made mermaid dishes remains anyone's guess, though like the London delftware plates they might have been made for the landlords of mermaid taverns.

In the 17th and 18th centuries, when a large percentage of the population could neither read nor write, identifying pictures hung over virtually every commercial doorway. Amid the multitude of painted signs, mermaids proliferated and served all manner of businesses from goldsmiths to grocers. In the mid-17th century at least 39 establishments issued mermaid-decorated token coinage, 18 in London and all but four of them inns and taverns. But whether or not the lure of liquor was thereby linked to the mermaid's invitation to disaster is something best left to

psychologists to ponder. The Mermaid tavern located between Friday Street and Bread Street was among the most famous in Elizabethan London, and is said to have been home to one of the first English clubs, the Mermaid (or Friday Street) Club founded by Sir Walter Ralegh. That Mermaid's patrons included many of the literary lions of the day: John Donne, Beaumont and Fletcher, William Shakespeare; and it fell to Sir Francis Beaumont to enshrine the tavern in the annals of English letters:

> . . . *what things have we seen*
> *Done at the Mermaid! heard words that have been*
> *So nimble, and so full of subtile flame,*
> *As if that every one from whence they came*
> *Had meant to put his whole wit in a jest,*
> *And had resolv'd to live a fool the rest*
> *Of his dull life.*

But not all of London's Mermaid taverns were as illustrious. And some could, indeed, lure unsuspecting customers to their doom.

Although the Great Plague that carried off more than 68,000 Londoners in 1665 had more or less run its course by the following spring, July of 1666 found the popular Mermaid tavern on Cornhill shuttered, under guard, and with a red cross on the door. A servant working there had taken sick with the plague and had been quarantined in the city pesthouse.

Yet another Mermaid tavern, this one in Paternoster Row, was described in the same year as "a dark back-house of small custom." That terse description is a far cry from the more easily imagined harbor-side Mermaid taverns crowded with jovial seamen and cleansed by the sea's salt air. Instead, it conjures up a shabby establishment jammed in behind other street-fronting buildings and recognizable only by its swinging mermaid sign—a sign whose faded paint first broke into bubbles and then into flame as the Great Fire of London swept up Paternoster Row to destroy the Mermaid and everything else in its path in the greatest and arguably the most necessary cleansing the city had ever known.

In the aftermath of the 1666 fire, and in spite of Sir Christopher Wren's far-sighted redevelopment plans, London's narrow streets and alleys were rebuilt more or less as they had been before. But there had been changes, among them a diminution of mermaids. The Mermaid in Friday Street, for all its literary fame, was not rebuilt. A survey of the city in 1676 listed only two: Mermaid Court, where the "dark back-house" had been, and a Mermaid Inn, located just south of St. Paul's Churchyard.

Seventeenth-century tavern keepers tried to keep track of their glass bottles by having their signs and initials stamped on glass seals and fused to their sides. Recent discoveries on the site of John Dwight's stoneware factory at Fulham have shown that in the 1670s he put similar tavern seals on pottery mugs and bottles: the George and Dragon, the Elephant and Castle, the Cock and Bottle—the Mermaid. Although this one was quite clearly male, there are no extant records of a Merman tavern, and so it is reasonable to assume that the seal was made for bottles ordered by the Mermaid by St. Paul's—unless, of course, it was a Triton or Nepture tavern. However, I have found no references to taverns with those names, although the 1676 London survey shows a Neptune Court in a suburb north of the ancient city walls.

That the Roman sea god and his son Triton were names still in common usage at the end of the 17th century was demonstrated by one Ned Ward, that era's version of the modern tabloid contributor. In *The London Spy* (1698) he described the tavern antics of a couple of drunken sailors, calling them "two Tritons," and "subjects of the pickled god Neptune."

In November 1738, Williamsburg readers of the *Virginia Gazette* learned of a triton or merman being captured on England's Devon coast:

Fishermen near that city [Exeter] drawing their net a shore, a Creature of Human Shape, having 2 Legs, leap'd out, and ran away very swiftly; not being able to overtake it, they knock'd it down by throwing sticks at it. At their coming up to it, it was dying, and groan'd like a human Creature; its feet were webb'd like a Duck's, it had Eyes, Nose, and Mouth, resembling those of a Man, only the Nose somewhat depress'd, Tail not unlike a Salmon's, turning up towards its back, and is 4 feet high. It has been publickly shewn here, by the Name of a Mermaid; *and Multitudes of People go to see it.*

Here, then, we have 18th-century evidence that the term "mermaid" could be applied to creatures of either sex.

Devon and Cornwall are the most legend-rich corner of England, and it is only to be expected that if a modern tourist is to meet a mermaid that is where to go—specifically to Zennor on Cornwall's rocky coast where the Atlantic batters its cliffs with foam-capped waves and banshee wind howls into Pendour Cove. But it is when, as they say in the West Country, the weather "fines away" and the sea gently caresses the rocks, that one may hear the voice of Mathew Trewhella singing to his mermaid bride. The legend has it that she heard the young man singing and lured him into the sea, and that although his body never washed ashore, his voice continued to be heard in Pendour Cove. The mermaid is still there, comb and mirror in her hands, carved, perhaps in the 16th century, on the side of a bench in Zennor church.

A correspondent writing to the magazine *Country Life* in 1996 recalled another mermaid sighting further up the Cornish coast at Bude. In 1825 she was seen and heard seated on an off-shore rock. Through several successive nights her presence drew ever increasing crowds until, at her last appearance she amazed the audience by singing "God Save the King" before diving off into the sea never to be seen again—at least as a mermaid. "She" was later revealed to be Robert Stephen Hawkes (not yet the Reverend) naked save for a wig of seaweed and oilskin fabric wrapped around his legs.

Whether the Reverend Hawkes got the idea for his hoax from the Mathew Trewhella legend or whether it was the other way round, we shall never know. But it is highly likely that the Zennor bench is much older than the tale.

Certainly both are a far cry from the dying monster described in the *Virginia Gazette* or from another surprisingly similar sighting off the French coast that was reported 12 years earlier in Boston's *New England Courant*.

The Monster is about eight Feet long: His Skin is brown and tawny, without any scale: All his motions are like those of men, the Eyes of a proportionate Size, a little Mouth, a large and flat Nose, very white Teeth, black Hair, the Chin covered with a mossy Beard, a sort of Whisker under the Nose, the Ears like those of Men, Fins between the Fingers of his Hands and Feet, like those of Ducks. In a word, he is like a well shaped Man.

These tales take us to the heart of the mermaid mystique: What do they tell us about the popular gullibility or the limits of human intelligence in centuries past? Before we pass judgment, however, we should consider the millions of shoppers who include a weekly dose of supermarket science in their grocery bags. Indeed, there is much else that we read or are taught that depends on quite prodigious leaps of faith.

In 1596, Sir Walter Ralegh, who was one of the most scientifically inquiring Englishmen of the Elizabethan Age, was prepared to accept as true (because native friends told him so) that in Guiana lived headless monsters "with eyes in their shoulders, and their mouths in the middle of their breasts."

"Not a word of truth in it!" we say. But are we sure? Are we equally sure that the report of fishermen pulling up a whole family of merpeople from the Indian Ocean was totally without foundation? That was in 1560 off the west coast of Sri Lanka, and was documented by affidavits from reliable (one might think) missionaries:

. . . some fishermen brought up at one draught of a net, seven mermen *and* maids; *of which several jesuits (sic), and among the rest, F. Henriques, and Dimas Bosquez, physician to the vice-roy of Goa, were witnesses. The physician, who examined them with a great deal of care, and made dissections thereof, asserts, that all the part both of internal and external, were found perfectly comfortable to those of men.*

Was the catch-of-the-day a fraud? Were the priests lying? And what about that other Jesuit, Father Merula, who had seen and eaten mermaids in Zaire? The answer, I am convinced, is no. There was truth in both reports, and the pictorial proof of it, I submit, is engraved on J. Mitchell's Jamaican powder horn. As had Columbus before him, Mitchell saw a mermaid rise out of the Caribbean water and rest in a basking position—like that of the Floridian manatee recorded by photographer Chris Maluka. Mitchell had drawn what he saw and took for granted what he could not.

The western hemisphere manatee is now a seriously endangered species, but has as its cousins the West African manatee (that provided Father Merula with his dinners) and, in the Indian Ocean and eastward to Northern Australia, the dugong or sea cow that gave physician Bosquez his anatomical specimens.

Although these mundane and disappointing realities identify Columbus's sirens and Mitchell's fish-faced and flat-chested mermaid, they do nothing to explain the English, French, and Dutch captures, for neither the manatee nor the dugong has ever been seen in Western European waters. Nevertheless, in 1608

European Renaissance goldsmiths and jewelers lavished their talent on mermen and mermaids to wondrous effect, as these treasures from the Victoria and Albert Museum attest. The Canning Jewel built around a baroque pearl (right) is Italian and has been attributed to the second half of the 16th century. The Burley Nef sails on a nautilus shell mounted in silver and parcel gilt (opposite), and was the creation of French goldsmith Pierre le Flamand, 1481–1483.

(above and opposite) Courtesy of Victoria and Albert Museum

and about as far north as a ship could get, explorer Henry Hudson's log recorded that off the coast of Nova Zembla

This morning one of our company looking overboard saw a mermaid . . . a little after a sea came up and overturned her. From the naval upward, her back and breasts were like a woman's, as they say that saw her; her body as big as one of us; her skin very white; and long hair hanging down behind, of colour black. In her going down they saw her tail, which was like the tail of a porpoise, and speckled like a mackerel.

If you are wondering what became of the mermaid who, at the beginning of our quest, was about to emerge from a London shopkeeper's basement, she (or rather he) did surface. The owner was a dealer in antique maps and prints, and what his assistant found you can see here. Engraved in 1793 to illustrate a natural his-

tory of the world, it was the scientist's attempt to rationalize something he feared to ignore, for who could then prove that out there, somewhere in the ocean depths, there might not be such creatures?

As late as 1861 some naturalists weren't sure. In his *Romance of Natural History*, the well-respected Philip Henry Gosse recalled the Hudson sighting and others somewhat like it and, after dismissing several zoological explanations, concluded that "it induces a strong suspicion that the northern seas may hold forms of life as yet uncatalogued by science."

In the summer of 1991 while on a fishing trip off the North Carolina coast, a sudden fog swept down on our boat, reducing visibility to a silent, shrouded circle scarcely 50 yards in diameter. The sky, the coast, the horizon, all were gone. Peering into the gray wall, the mate remarked, "I guess it's about time for the ghost ship to show up."

"More likely a mermaid," I replied. And the mate gave me a very odd look, put down his bait knife, and quickly went below.

Roanoke Island

America's first science center

EVERY ARCHAEOLOGIST DREAMS that just once in his life he'll find treasure. Mine substituted copper for gold and antimony for silver, and it came not from a sunken galleon or an Egyptian tomb but from Roanoke Island on the Outer Banks of North Carolina. There, in 1585, English and European scientists unpacked the equipment that would help determine the future course of American history. For me, finding the place where they set up their laboratory was to be the most exciting in a lifetime of discoveries.

Rarely, if ever, can one point to a piece of ground and say of it that the decisions reached there hundreds of years ago would impact today on the lives of us all. But a little patch of sandy soil on Roanoke Island is just such a place. Had the Elizabethan scholars working there concluded that Virginia held no economic promise, we would have had no Jamestown settlement in 1607 and no Williamsburg; indeed, no British presence south of New England. Instead, the southern British colonies would almost cer-

tainly have been settled by Spaniards—and Virginia might now be a Spanish-speaking, independent country akin to those of Central America.

I first visited the Fort Raleigh National Historic Site in the summer of 1957. Part of the Park Service's Cape Hatteras National Seashore, it featured the reconstructed, star-shaped fort whose remains had been known as long ago as 1817, when President Monroe visited the island. A ranger pointed to the grass-covered earthwork and told us "This was the fort built in September 1585 by Ralph Lane, the first governor of Virginia."

"Virginia?" asked a puzzled tourist. "But we're in North Carolina."

The ranger gave no hint that he had heard the question countless times before. The Elizabethan English, he explained, claimed the eastern seacoast from Cape Fear to Maine, and called it all Virginia.

"The fort's not very big," somebody muttered.

Richard Schlecht

Richard Schlecht

"How many people were there?" somebody else wanted to know.

We were told 108, though not all of them lived in the fort. That seemed just as well. Only about 50 feet wide within its earth rampart, a couple of dozen would have been plenty.

My archaeologist wife, Audrey, knew much more than I did about Ralph Lane's "new Fort in Virginia" and the story of Queen Elizabeth's "Lost Colony." She had read about it as a child and discovered that she shared the same birthday as Virginia Dare, the first English girl born in America. So thrilled by the mystery of the 1587 colonists' disappearance was Audrey that she begged her parents to change her name to Virginia. Little did she know that she would one day be standing where it had all

In June 1586, with their baggage tossed into the heaving ocean, Roanoke Island's first English settlers escaped to the storm-battered fleet of Sir Francis Drake (opposite). Artist Richard Schlecht's aerial view of the island (above) may have differed in the 16th century in that the deep indentation of Shallowbag Bay may have been less prominent than it is today.

The silver sixpence of 1563 (below) was found at the north end of the island and, being drilled above Queen Elizabeth's crown, it was almost certainly a gift from the English to a native American neighbor as a portrait of the latter's new queen over the ocean.

Courtesy of David Phelps, East Carolina University

97

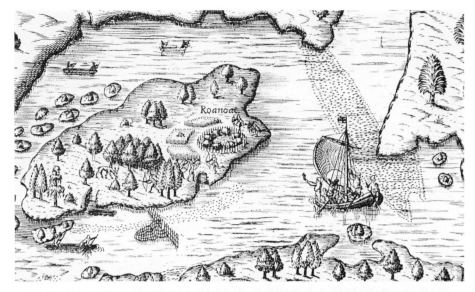

Theodore de Bry's 1590 engraving shows
Ralph Lane's settlers approaching the north
end of Roanoke Island, where an Indian
village already stood (right). The fort
reconstructed by the National Park Service
in 1950 (below) was long thought to have
been Lane's "new Fort in Virginia."

Ira Block

happened or that, later still, she would play a major role in reassessing what was known about the site.

When we first saw it, the earthwork was only seven years old. It had been reconstructed in 1950 following excavations directed by the father of historical archaeology in America, Jean C. "Pinky" Harrington. But he wasn't the first to dig there. In 1849 a visitor reported the finding of "glass globes containing quicksilver, and hermetically sealed." What became of them, nobody knows. But someone had unwittingly discovered the first relics of the metallurgical laboratory that we were to identify more than a century later. Union soldiers, camped nearby after the February 1862 Battle of Roanoke Island, had dug more holes in search of treasure—until ordered away by their commanding officer. Thirty-four years later still, Talcott Williams, an amateur archaeologist from Philadelphia, cut several trenches, some as much as nine feet deep, and although he found the site to be "singularly barren of debris" he pronounced it to be the right place.

That was enough to justify the Roanoke Colony Memorial Association, which had already bought the site, to erect a marker recording the birth of Virginia Dare and recalling that

THESE COLONISTS WERE THE FIRST SETTLERS OF THE ENGLISH RACE IN AMERICA. THEY RETURNED TO ENGLAND IN JULY, 1586, WITH SIR FRANCIS DRAKE.

The Association also erected a wooden fence to outline the fort—which was good thinking. Without it, nobody would have known where it had been, for nothing remained but the barely visible depression of its ditch.

The colonists who went back with Drake had been on the island little more than nine months, during which time they had turned the resident and neighboring Indians from "gentle, loving, and faithfull" friends into implacable enemies. With villages burned and their king beheaded, the Algonkian Indians of Roanoke Island were no longer considered "voide of all guile and treason." Instead, the English now saw them as heathen and dangerous savages, a perception that would color Europeans' relations with Native Americans throughout the colonial centuries. That, coupled with the failure of promised supply ships to arrive

from England, prompted Governor Lane to hitch a ride home.

England-bound after successfully attacking Spanish bases in the Caribbean, Drake had anchored off the North Carolina Outer Banks to deliver seized hardware and artillery, along with scores of Central American Indians and more than 200 black slaves he had freed from the Spaniards and who, he thought, would be helpful to the Roanoke colonists. Instead, neither window frames and cannon from St. Augustine nor a massive free labor force were what the colonists had in mind. Passage home was all they wanted.

Even as Lane and Drake negotiated, a hurricane of prodigious force raked the coast and scattered the fleet. Thunder shook the heavens, lightning stabbed the waves, hailstones the size of eggs rained down, and from time to time waterspouts linked sky and sea in murderous embrace. Although the worst had passed over by the time the hundred or so settlers loaded themselves and their baggage into the open boats, the weather was still "so boisterous" and the boats so often driven aground that sailors rowing

Ira Block

Ira Block

Courtesy of National Park Service

In 1965 archaeologist J. C. Harrington (left) discovered curiously shaped bricks that later turned out to be part of a scientific furnace (far left). He also found post holes that formed a pattern intriguing like those of the reconstructed 1620 watchtower at Wolstenholme Towne (above).

OVERLEAF: Richard Schlecht's interpretation of Ralph Lane's research center. Sir Walter Ralegh evidently provided his scientific team with European state-of-the-art equipment, but putting it to work on Roanoke Island must have been far from easy.

Excavations in 1992 revealed the remains of the laboratory set up in 1585 for scientists Hariot and Gans. Watched by the spirit of Hariot, archaeologist John Hamant uncovered chemical glassware fragments and a lump of worked copper (below) while the author and Dr. William Kelso (right) work to retrieve even smaller clues. The remains of a 1936 palisade post (bottom, left) being "eaten" by growing tree roots and (bottom, right) the author's sketch show how in time a post and its man-dug hole can be absorbed into a tree's root system to baffle future archaeologists.

Opposite: the "science center" in course of excavation and behind it the reconstructed fort (top) where renewed digging (below) yielded more relics of the 1585–1586 research.

Ira Block

Ivor Noël Hume

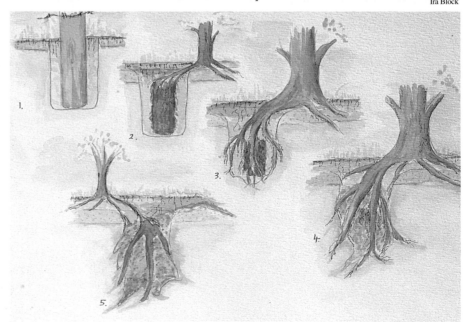

Ivor Noël Hume

them out through the Outer Banks shoals threw much of the baggage overboard to lighten the load.

The losses caused much lamentation at the time and would become an enigma to baffle future historians and archaeologists. How much did the fleeing colonists take away with them, and how much never reached the ships? To put it another way: How much was left behind for us to find?

A few weeks later the supply fleet did arrive. Its admiral, Sir Richard Grenville, found the place deserted, and left behind a tiny, 15-man garrison to hold the island for England. He would be back next year, he told his men. And with that assurance and their storehouse bulging with supplies, they were happy to be spared the discomfort of more months at sea.

The garrison's happiness was to be short-lived. Attacked by the Indians, with their storehouse in flames and their officer dead, they fought their way to their boat and headed south toward Pamlico Sound never to be heard from again. So ended the second English attempt to sustain a colony on Roanoke Island.

The third group arrived in August 1587, under the governorship of artist John White, whose daughter was married to fellow colonist Ananias Dare—the parents of my wife's would-be namesake—Virginia. Because the fate of White's people is unknown and because, for the first time, the settlement was home to women and children, the Lost Colony is the one that everyone remembers. But theirs, as the Park Service ranger told us, was not the fort that we were looking at. It had been built by their predecessors in 1585. John White's colonists lived inside a large stockade that he described as built from "great trees, with cortynes [walls] and flankers very Fort-like . . ."

It was those words that sent me back to Roanoke Island in 1989. I was then doing research on Virginia's fort at Jamestown, which in 1610 had been described in very similar terms. I had also learned that the only description of Lane's earlier defenses called them a "wooden fort of little strength," a structure that John White found to have been "taken downe" when he arrived in 1587. So where did the reconstructed earthwork fit into the sequence?

A solution had seemed in sight in 1965 when Pinky Harrington had returned to the site to investigate a "brick path" found by a Park Service maintenance crew laying a water pipe. The path turned out to be a cluster of bricks dumped into one of three pits, all of them inside a square wooden structure whose supports Harrington thought had been provided by conveniently located trees. Built barely 20 feet from the earthwork, Harrington called it "an outwork to Fort Raleigh" but was careful not to be more specific.

Twelve years later, after Colonial Williamsburg's archaeological team found the 1620 fort at Wolstenholme Towne, Park Service historian Phillip Evans noticed that the postholes of its watchtower almost exactly paralleled Harrington's outwork. Was it possible, Evans asked, that he had found a corner of Ralph Lane's wooden fort?

Excavations to try to find out were resumed in 1983, but although the digging yielded more broken pottery reportedly of the right period, it did nothing to solve the outwork enigma.

If that really was a corner of Lane's wooden fort or even, as Harrington had suggested, an outwork to the close-by earthwork, in military terms one would have been in the way of the other. At least that was how I read it. And what about the potsherds?

Ira Block

Ivor Noël Hume

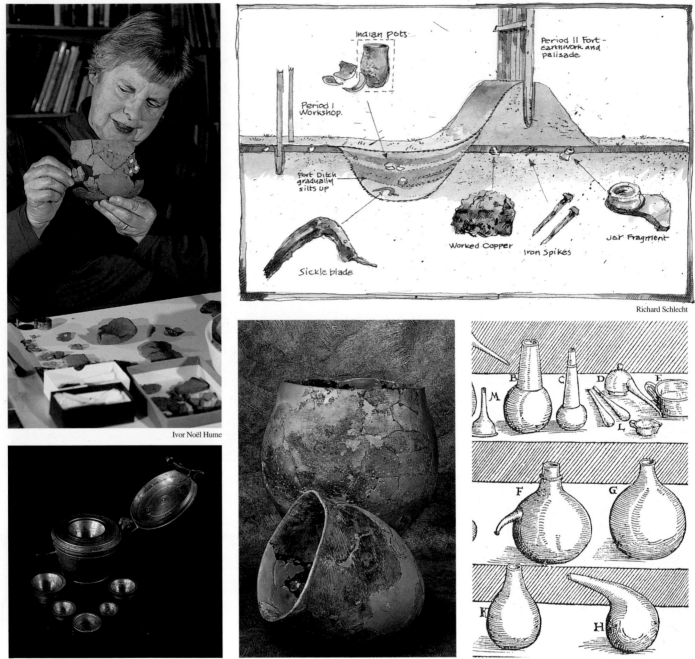

Richard Schlecht

Ivor Noël Hume

Ira Block

The placement of artifacts both in the fort ditch and under its rampart were crucial in determining what happened and when (top, right). Project curator Audrey Noël Hume pieced together an Indian bowl from the science center (top, left), one much smaller than had been found by Harrington in the ditch (center). He also found an apothecary's weight, shown here in front of a contemporary set (above). A fragment from the neck of a glass flask (right) matched a 1574 illustration (above, right) of the kinds of glassware used by assayers.

Ivor Noël Hume

Left, from top: A still-sharp fishhook came from the science center as did a curved bar of antimony used in assaying. The nails and worked copper had been found in the fort in 1949, but the lead seal (right) was an important new find. It is shown below with a scale-providing penny and to the right of it a better preserved seal of the same type found in the Thames at London. Below center: intact examples of the three basic ceramic types found in the science center—Normandy flasks, delftware ointment pots, and crucibles like those seen in a detail (bottom, right) from Hans Holbein's 1537 woodcut of an alchemist's laboratory.

Ivor Noël Hume

Ira Block

Richard Schlecht

Sir Thomas Grenville's 15-man garrison was soon attacked and driven from its blazing storehouse. Dragging their wounded with them, the soldiers escaped to their boat and were never seen again, thus ending the story of Roanoke Island's second group of colonists.

The Park Service report listed fragments of "Salt-Glazed stoneware," Spanish majolica, and two shards from a shallow dish or pan "similar to a type of stoneware known as basaltware." This last was worrying because black basalt wares date from the 18th and not the 16th century. "Maybe," I told Audrey, "if we were to go down to the park and take a look at this stuff, we might spot something that our predecessors have missed."

Never one to refuse a trip to the beach or the prospect of a chartered fishing trip, Audrey agreed. Although our request had meant bringing the artifacts back from the Park Service's regional center at Tallahassee, Superintendent Thomas Hartman agreed.

It turned out that the "Salt-Glazed stoneware" wasn't salt-glazed stoneware. The shards were fragments of rough-surfaced metallurgical crucibles. The Spanish majolica proved to be from English or Netherlandish ointment pots used by apothecaries, and the "basaltware" dish pieces came from a globular stoneware bottle made in Normandy in the 16th century. This last was identical to a partially complete example that Harrington had found in his 1965 outwork dig.

As she put the last piece back in its bag, Audrey looked at me and asked, "Are you thinking what I'm thinking?"

"We should take another look at Harrington's finds?"

"I believe so," she replied.

And so we did. The range of his European pottery was virtually identical to the 1983 discoveries—crucibles, ointment pots, plus shards from more than one Normandy flask of a shape used by distillers. And then there were the bricks. Many of the bats were heavily burned at one end, and several had been ground down so that one side was deeply concave. Harrington had speculated that the shaping had resulted from using the soft, sandy bricks for sharpening tools and weapons.

"I wouldn't mind betting," I said, "that they are from the round openings in the furnace."

The pieces of the puzzle were beginning to fit together. The 1585 settlers sent out by Sir Walter Ralegh had included a scientific team headed by Thomas Hariot—astronomer, mathematician, oceanographer, surveyor—in short one of the finest minds of the Elizabethan Age. He was there to assess the commercial potential of the New World, and when he returned with Drake in 1586, he would begin work on the report that still stands at the cornerstone of American natural history. Titled *A briefe and true report of the new found land of Virginia* and illustrated with engravings from drawings by John White, it provided Europeans with their first detailed look at the Native Americans of the new continent's southeast coast.

With Hariot went a crew of miners to search for marketable metals led by "minerall man" Joachim Gans, a Jewish metallurgist from Prague who had gone to England in 1581 to help improve its outmoded copper smelting industry. This was a blue-ribbon team, and like most scientific research efforts today, quality of mind brushed aside barriers of race, religion, or national origin—except for Jesuits and Spaniards who, to the English, were the devil's kin.

That copper was likely to be Virginia's principal mineral had been established in 1584 after Ralegh had sent out two exploratory ships. Their returning captains had reported that the senior Indians wore "red pieces of copper on their heads," and that the king's brother wore "a broade plate of golde, or copper, for being unpolished we knew not what metall it should be." Believing that where there was copper there might well be silver and even gold, Ralegh and his backers made sure that the expedition's scientific component would be the very best.

As Audrey and I examined the bricks and pottery fragments,

When John White returned to the island in 1590, his colonists were gone. The chests he had told them to bury he found broken open and their contents scattered.

Richard Schlecht

107

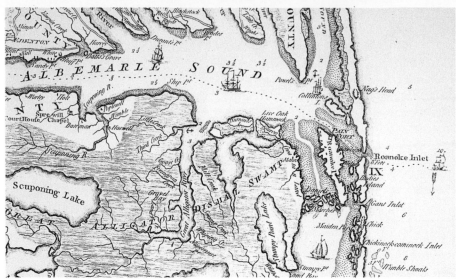

Right: A detail from Henry Mouzon's 1775 map of North Carolina shows a fort at the north end of Roanoke Island and the shipping channel to the tobacco port of Edenton passing close by it. Below: With the reconstructed earthwork no longer a factor and the science center revealed, it was time to rethink the Roanoke story and to begin the search for the village built by Lane in 1585 and reoccupied by White's soon-to-be-lost colonists in 1587.

Courtesy of John Carter Brown Library, Brown University

Ivor Noël Hume

we knew that we were seeing something amazing. These were not trash from Lane's or the Lost Colony's village; they were the relics of America's first scientific evaluation.

The next day, at the end of the promised, but only marginally successful fishing trip, I asked the boat's mate his name.

"I'm Billy Coppersmith," he replied.

Never before having heard of anyone named Coppersmith, I was convinced that here was an omen. "Somehow," I told Audrey, "we've got to find the money and the people to dig again at Fort Raleigh."

Pinky Harrington's impeccable report on his earlier excavations had recorded finding two lumps of smelted copper, one in the silt of the fort's ditch and the other under the remains of its rampart. He correctly deduced that one piece had been deposited *before* Ralph Lane's fort was built and the other *after* it was abandoned. The sequence had to be right. But what about the timing? We know from a letter that Lane wrote on September 3, 1585, that his "New Fort in Virginia" was in existence before Gans and his helpers had any copper to process. That a lump of it lay on the ground before the earthen rampart was piled on top of it had to mean that the earthwork was of later date. But if so, how much later?

Although more digging might prove beyond doubt that the reconstructed earthwork was not Lane's fort, Superintendent Hartman agreed to allow new excavations to be launched by the Virginia Company Foundation and under my direction. Preliminary testing in the spring of 1991 showed what Harrington already well knew: The site had been severely mutilated by a wide variety of disturbances that began when the Civil War soldiers dug their holes. Not only that, when the modern intrusions had been removed, what remained were two extremely friable layers of sandy loam and clay whose testimony could be destroyed by a single misdirected shovel. This was to be surgical work, and only the most experienced surgeons would be good enough to do it.

Rather than following the usual practice of assembling a team of anthropology students and a couple of trained supervisors, I called on the services of most of the good excavators who had worked with me over the years in Williamsburg, people who were now professors and directors elsewhere and used to watching others do the dirty work. They would be the people down on their knees with the trowels and the dustpans. It was to be a remarkable team, and on one day when Pinky Harrington and his archaeologist wife Virginia joined us, we realized that we had four generations of America's foremost historical archaeologists assembled on the site.

But as the spoil heaps grew higher than the earthwork's rampart, I found it increasingly hard to sustain the team's morale. Every area we opened had been disturbed by someone. Trenches for water and electric lines crisscrossed the site. Harrington's excavation trenches were cut by the 1983 digging; the remains of a 1936 road taken up in 1950, and the bed for a still existing walkway, all combined to thwart us. And the weather was getting worse.

A nor'easter had pounded the Outer Banks on the dig's first days, forcing the crew to flee in the dark from their beach house as water rose in their living room. Now, as the last digging day dawned, another storm was approaching—and still we had found nothing we could be sure hadn't been disturbed. And then just before noon, we did.

Because it lay on one of his 1965 survey lines, Harrington had left a narrow strip of ground undisturbed, and by some miracle the 1983 excavators had stopped two inches above it. Pressed into the sandy subsoil were more than a hundred artifacts, broken crucibles, pieces of Normandy flasks, a badly burned Indian bowl that looked as though it had been used in distilling, and pieces of chemical glassware—English glass, the oldest found in the New World.

There were other things too, tiny chips of European flint, a scattering of iron scale perhaps used, as contemporary accounts said, in the making of a high refractory mortar to secure the elements in distilling apparatus. And there were fragments from Indian pipes—doubtless relics of the first English smokers' experience of what they would describe as "drinking" tobacco.

Virginia Company president William Kelso, who found the pipe fragments, recalled that tobacco smoking in England is believed to have started with the 1585 expedition. "Maybe these are the prototypes for all the millions of clay pipes that came after," Bill suggested. And he may well have been right.

There was more to come: a broad scattering of charcoal and one tiny fragment of coal indicative of two different kinds of fuel used in Joachim Gans's mineral assaying furnace, and there were seeds and nuts from long-leaf pine and shagbark hickory that may have been among the plants being distilled by Hariot to test their pharmaceutical and commercial properties. We had found the working floor of what amounted to an interdisciplinary analytical laboratory.

Although Martin Frobisher's earlier expeditions, first in search of the Northwest Passage to the Orient and then for Baffin Island's elusive gold, had included their own German "mineral man," I felt justified in calling what we were finding colonial America's first science center.

But before we could complete the excavation, the threatened nor'easter arrived. The rain came down and so did the overnight tents put up to protect the hallowed ground. The next morning we finished clearing the exposed layer and called for volunteers to return to finish the work in 1992. Two weeks of disappointment were instantly forgotten.

The second season expanded our investigation into the reconstructed fort, where we found more of the same: more crucible fragments, more Normandy flask, and a lead seal bearing its owner's initials—the first letters found on the site since 1590 when John White returned in a vain search for his lost colonists and saw the word CROATOAN carved on a post of their abandoned palisade.

Although the seal is of a type used by clothiers and merchants and so may not bear the initials of one of the first English American colonists, we fervently hoped that it did. Heavily encrusted with sand, the first letter was obscured, but the second appeared to be an L. Immediately we thought of expedition leader Ralph Lane. But when Colonial Williamsburg conservator Carey Howlett was able to remove some of the sand, it was clear that the first initial had to be either a *J* or more possibly and *H*—but not an *R*. Alas, although there are two J. L. candidates, John Linsey in 1585 and James Lasie in 1587, no H. L. is listed on the rosters of either expedition.

In spite of preliminary metallurgical analyses, many questions remain tantalizingly unanswered. Did a lump of smelted copper from the floor come from an American or a European mine? Is a bar of antimony the product of trade with the Indians, or did Joachim Gans bring it with him as a flux to separate silver from copper? And what mineral traces lie hidden in the dross-coated crucible shards?

No matter what the answers may be, it is clear that Sir Walter Ralegh's scientists reached Roanoke Island with state of the art equipment and put it to use in a roughly built lab that was anything but ideal.

And what of the reconstructed fort?

I had hoped to prove that its ditch cut through the science center's work area, and it did. But because no colonists built homes there until the latter years of the 18th century, it followed that the ditch contained only Elizabethan and aboriginal artifacts—all disturbed when the fort was built and later fell back, as the rampart eroded or the ditch was deliberately filled. Finding them there has always been taken as proof that the ditch was open in the 16th century. But if that is not so, the existence of maps of 1770 and 1775 showing a fort at the north end of the island tell a different story. As the fort is absent from two earlier maps, a case can be made that the earthwork was built by local militiamen as an artillery emplacement during the French and Indian War (1754–1763) to defend the admittedly shallow channel into Albemarle Sound and the port of Edenton from the French.

Because the earthwork's entrance faces west, conventional archaeological wisdom has dictated that the 1585–1587 village site must lie beyond it—an assumption bolstered by finding Elizabethan artifacts extending in that direction. But now we know that they were unrelated to the village. If the fort had noting to do with Lane's settlement, with Grenville's garrison, or even with White's Lost Colony, then one is free to look for the village in another direction.

"Yes, but where do we start?" Bill Kelso asked.

"Not we," I replied. Audrey had been adamant that after 43 years I had directed my last excavation. "It's your turn now," I told Bill. "But if I were you, I'd begin over there."

All Ashore at Jamestown

"...one of the great events in the history of the world"

WHEN, ON APRIL 26, 1907, President Theodore Roosevelt opened the Jamestown Exposition at Norfolk, Virginia, he greeted the ambassadors from 14 nations and thanked them for coming "to assist us in celebrating what was in very truth the birthday of this nation." Now, as we approach the 400th anniversary of that 1607 birthday, Jamestown once again becomes a name with which to conjure—and from which to profit.

But times have changed. A hundred years will soon have passed, a fourth of the time since the first squabbling colonists elected to settle on the kind of land they had been told to avoid. Even in 1907 the President hinted at the likelihood that some Americans would feel less rooted to Jamestown than would others. Acknowledging the presence of the British ambassador, he noted that "the fact that so many of our people, of whom as it happens I myself am

one, have but a very small portion of English blood in our veins, in no way alters the fact that this nation was founded by Englishmen."

That this assertion was not nationally applauded even in 1907 is suggested by the fact that only the states in the eastern third of the country chose to participate—with the exception of North Dakota, one of whose private citizens was inspired to build the surviving state cottage and to live in it throughout the exposition.

Although it is still true that the United States owes its language (if not its phraseology) and the foundation of its legal system to England, today the nation's diversity of cultures and national origins threatens Jamestown's cornerstone credentials more legitimately than do promoters of Plymouth and its rock. Nevertheless, there is no denying that had Jamestown succumbed, as did its sister colony in Maine, the history of the United States would have been very different, Spain and France stepping in where Englishmen had ceased to tread.

For the citizens of post-Civil War Williamsburg, neither the present nor the future appeared to hold much promise. It was natural, therefore, that the old families should draw strength from the past, a past that focused first on the gentlemanly fought Revolution and then overleaping the legendary tyranny of several Georges to embrace the no-less legendary heroics of John Smith and the strangely beatified Pocahontas. Just as Monticello stood as the shrine to Jeffersonian enlightenment, so the crumbling, ivy-clad brick church tower at Jamestown recalled the days when stout and loving hearts triumphed over every adversity.

Out of a growing reverence for the past of Tidewater Vir-

hand the association persuaded island landowners Mr. and Mrs. Edward Barney to donate 22 ½ acres that included the ruined church site. Thereafter "Jamestown" became the flagship property of the A.P.V.A., which declared it to be "at once our inspiration and our goal."

The A.P.V.A.'s Norfolk-based co-founder Miss Mary Jeffery Galt took charge of its new property on April 15, 1894, and discovered it to be "a picture of desolation" and a "wilderness of poor deserted farmland." The following year a party of "engineers" with 27 mules and heavy machinery were able to clear much of the wilderness. Posts and old wire netting around the church ruin were replaced with new fencing topped with barbed wire; the brick

On April 26, 1907, President Theodore Roosevelt (opposite) strode up the steps of the just barely completed auditorium to speak the inspiring words and touch the button that opened the Norfolk-sited Jamestown Exposition. Although 50,000 dignitaries and visitors were there to be inspired, many more were to head for the Warpath (above) and its less esoteric attractions.

ginia, in 1884 emerged the Catherine Memorial Society founded by Williamsburg resident Mrs. Cynthia B. T. Coleman in memory of her daughter and dedicated to preserving Bruton Parish Church. She and her associates soon realized that their decaying heritage spread much wider and that they had a duty to preserve "buildings in which stirring deeds have been enacted, and where they have been destroyed to mark the spot on which they stood." Five years later that mandate became the genesis mission of the new, statewide Association for the Preservation of Virginia Antiquities, today the nation's oldest preservation society.

In 1892 the A.P.V.A. appealed to the state legislature to transfer title to its holdings on Jamestown Island, and with that in

tower was cement capped, and in 1897 Miss Galt began to dig:

I dug with my own hands quite deep inside of the south wall of the Church and discovered the little inner wall composed of large bricks and cobble stones. This must have been the foundation of the Argall Church built 1617 or of the earlier one repaired by Lord de la Ware in which our beloved Pocahontas was married.

Opinions about the chronology of churches built on that site have fluctuated over the years, but in this writer's opinion, Miss Galt was close to the mark—if not right on it.

Dave Doody

The success of Miss Galt's lone sortie led to full-scale excavations in 1901, when she returned with a crew of local laborers to uncover the body of the church whose site had by then been stripped of "heaps of debris and vegetation—the growth and accumulation of many years." Helped now by other ladies, her sister Miss Annie Galt and Miss Mary Garrett of Williamsburg, and by government engineer John Tyler, who was officially there to help build a seawall to prevent continuing erosion, the work moved quickly along inside and outside the brick foundations.

Graves were plentiful, but did not deter the Victorian ladies from their digging—nor from dispassionately describing what they found:

One grave that we opened contained the skeleton of a woman—on her breast the scant remains of a tiny little skeleton—the little head by her cheek, and two little skeletons, evidently a previous interment, just under her feet. The tacks that had been on the outside of the coffin partly fastened together had fallen among these bones. Some seemed to be Roman numerals—Others formed the letters E. J.

The Official Blue Book of the Jamestown Ter-centennial Exposition A.D. 1907

Looking at photographs of Miss Galt's excavations in the light of modern archaeological techniques, it is hard not to weep and wish that the A.P.V.A. had been content to fence and preserve the site, which had been described as "hallowed as well as historic." But hindsight is for historians. In truth, the records kept by Miss Galt and her associates were as considered and insightful as those of many a skilled European antiquary of their day. The pioneer ladies of the A.P.V.A. had a date if not with destiny with the developers of the great Jamestown Exposition of 1907. Although the big show would be at Norfolk, the real

Visions of great buildings, avenues, and piers combining history with futuristic modernity (opposite) were lures to convince the other old colonial states to participate. Seas of mud and unfinished buildings photographed barely six weeks before opening date were eventually transformed into the grandeur of Raleigh Square and the equally grand auditorium (above). Nineteen of the 1907 states' buildings still stand on land purchased ten years later for the Norfolk Naval Base (center).

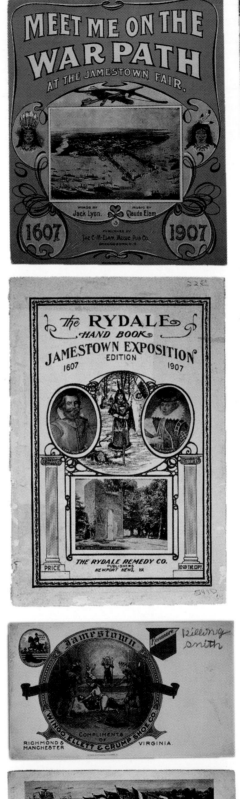

A blizzard of print promoted every conceivable history-hinting product, from sheet music and Rydale's patent tonics for "puny children" and "pale people" to Studebaker's electric automobile. Postcards carried the "noble savage" message far and presumably wide. But, unfortunately, less than half the visitors actually bought tickets, ensuring financial failure for the exposition's Norfolk investors.

Jamestown story could only be told where it happened, and the A.P.V.A. had to be ready.

The body of the church had to be rebuilt while being designed to straddle, protect, and display the foundations of the earlier structure that Miss Galt had discovered in 1897. There was much to be done—and even more at Norfolk.

Due largely to apathy and penny-pinching in Richmond, the City of Norfolk became host to the Jamestown Exposition, and from the start very little went right. Although the first efforts to involve the Commonwealth in planning the exposition had come from ladies of the A.P.V.A., it was not until a delegation from Hampton Roads appeared before the General Assembly and proposed the Norfolk location that the legislature, which reportedly hitherto "had been lethargic in the matter, was aroused to the extent of attempting to delay the proposition."

In 1902 a bill to appropriate $200,000 of state funds to purchase the 340-acre Norfolk site was opposed on the grounds that it could be better spent on restoring the Capitol. Nevertheless, in spite of continuing opposition, the appropriation was eventually passed in April 1903. At that stage, however, state support went no further. The privately managed Jamestown Exposition Company had received a charter from Governor Andrew Jackson Montague in March 1902, but like the fairy queen's requirement that Cinderella be home by midnight, the company had to raise a million dollars before January 1, 1904, or be dissolved. With only nine months left to start fund raising, after the state approved its modest contribution, December 19 found the company a magnum $260,000 short.

Tired and dispirited, the directors met in Norfolk on New Year's Eve to plan their company's dissolution, for, in spite of Herculean efforts, they had missed their target by $30,000. There would be no great exposition, no great naval review, no national jubilation. The story of Jamestown would be told only where it rightly belonged—in and around the little church on Jamestown Island.

But then, as Norfolk's clocks ticked toward midnight, a telegram arrived from Richmond. An anonymous donor would contribute $20,000. For a few minutes the fate of Jamestown's tercentennial exposition hung on a $10,000 thread. But the directors knew what had to be done. Once again they delved into their own pockets—and the exposition was saved.

Today the chosen site is occupied by the Norfolk Naval Base, but in 1903 it was an undeveloped headland west of Willoughby Spit and ten miles from downtown Norfolk. A contemporary described it as having "not a facility in evidence more than one would expect to find on a barren island." There were no roads, no water, no power, no anything. The company was faced with a gigantic task and little more than two years to sell it and build it.

But sell it did, and before long the "dives, dance halls and gambling resorts were going up with greater rapidity and more evidence of backing than the Exposition buildings themselves." When the gates opened on April 26, only a few of the exhibition buildings were complete, and several of those lacked their displays. The Palace of Manufactures and Liberal Arts didn't open until June 15, and the History Building wasn't ready until August 5. As for the landscaping of the show's centerpiece called Raleigh Court that linked the imposing Administration Building to the Susan Constant and Godspeed piers, that wasn't finished until mid-September, nearly five months after the exposition opened and only ten weeks before it closed.

May 13, the focal moment of the exposition, commemorating the 1607 arrival of Christopher Newport's three-ship fleet off Jamestown Island, had come and gone long before the last exhibit case was filled or the last planting hole dug. Nevertheless, the declared "Jamestown Day" was, by all accounts, one to remember—highlighted by the arrival of Field Marshal Baron Kuroki "the hero of the Russo-Japanese war." In Hampton Roads lay one of the greatest international fleets ever assembled, with warships from Japan, Austria, Chile, Brazil, and the largest and finest vessels in the United States Navy. In the evening, illuminated "in a triumph of electrical skill, the masts and funnels were traced in streamers of fire, and for miles the boats afforded a sight that one is not apt to see twice in a lifetime."

Elaborate and brightly lit floats added to the carnival atmosphere that had burgeoned as the day went on. Among them were "Uncle Sam," "Neptune's Chariot," "Leif Ericson's Ship," the "Marriage of John Rolfe and Pocahontas," a "Chinese Junk," and a "Sea Serpent." In contrast to the marching bands, parading U. S. troops and sailors of sundry nations, a

patriotic celebration in the auditorium, and happy hordes munching candy floss along the War Path (the avenue of fun), the celebration at Jamestown was to be markedly modest. But lest excitement should get out of hand, the A.P.V.A. reminded those traveling by steamer that "there is an efficient police force, whose members will give visitors every assistance in their power; but who will rigidly suppress all disorder and arrest any person guilty of disorderly conduct, or of trespass or injuring buildings, tombs, fences, monuments, ruins, etc., or breaking flowers, trees, or shrubs."

Thus reassured and admonished, a patriotic and history-conscious assemblage of the A.P.V.A.'s somber-suited, celluloid-collared, and straw-hatted men and their parasol-protected wives gathered on May 13 to hear Virginia's governor Claude A. Swanson remind them that "with the settlement at Jamestown, the history of America and of modern England really began." He would tell them much else:

Privilege, caste, aristocracy and feudalism were powerless in the wilderness. The needs of the situation were energy and strength to fell forest, cultivate fields, fight savages, build homes, construct roads and bridge rivers. . . . Idle and listless drones, however high their station or gentle their blood, found no suitable place in the primeval forests of America and disappeared in disgrace and despair.

The British ambassador—who had done his bit at Norfolk on opening day—was the island's second speaker. Treading on slightly risky ground, he described Jamestown as the acorn from which the oak of British dominion in America grew. Warming to his theme, he declared that the "landing at Jamestown was one of the great events in the history of the world—an event to be compared for its momentous consequences with the overthrow of the Persian Empire by Alexander"—and even, he added, "one might almost say with the discovery of America by Columbus."

Who in the A.P.V.A. was ready to go that far went unrecorded. But no doubt his excellency's closing observation earned him a patter of applause from many a gloved hand. "In the union of ordered liberty," he declared, "with a law gradually remolded from age to age to suit the changing needs of the people there has lain and there always will lie the progress and peace both of England and of America."

With the great Jamestown Exposition over and remembered primarily through its tacky souvenirs and the 19 surviving state buildings that still grace the Norfolk Navy Base, the cradle of the Republic rocked only for those pilgrims who made trips to the island or who, en route to and from Williamsburg, landed and left there aboard the packet boats that plied the James between Norfolk and Richmond.

The A.P.V.A. had long since put away its shovels and was content to exhibit the products of its digging in the brick building erected in 1911 they called the Relic House. Exhibited, too, was the outline of a major building complex west of the church generally known as the Ludwell Tenement block or the Third and Fourth Statehouses. Those remains had been partially excavated by another amateur, Colonel Samuel H. Yonge, as an archaeological by-product of his serving as director for the government's

On May 23, 1610, William Strachey first set foot on Jamestown Island and "found the Pallisadoes torne downe, the Ports open, and the Gates from off the hinges, and emptie houses rent up and burnt." In such woeful shape was James Fort that the newly arrived Sir Thomas Gates ordered it abandoned. He would ship home anything worth selling but would bury unwanted armor and inter the artillery in trenches outside the fort's river-facing wall.

Jamestown seawall project. Half a century later, with the approach of Jamestown's 350th anniversary, people eager for a new attraction on the A.P.V.A.'s acres proposed reconstructing the row-house building; but, fortunately, wiser heads prevailed. The only erected reconstructions would be those built off the island by the state and named the Jamestown Festival Park.

Before that came about, there had been much more digging—all of it under the direction of the United States National Park Service and virtually none of it on the A.P.V.A.'s 22 ½ acres. The downriver stretch of the island owned by Mr. and Mrs. Barney was purchased by the Department of the Interior in 1934, and that summer it moved excavators from its W.P.A. program at Yorktown to start digging for the first settlement at Jamestown. In charge was an ex-Colonial Williamsburg draftsman and at least one other colleague from Williamsburg's drafting room. They knew little about 17th-century buildings and less about their artifacts, and before long the Park Service brought in a historical architect, Henry Chandlee Forman; and, later, when anthropologists objected, it sent two of their own, J. Summerfield Day and Alonzo Pond.

When the architects and anthropologists failed to get along, and when their procedural differences exploded into shovel-wielding warfare, all were removed and replaced in 1936 with the man destined to become the father of American historical archaeology, Jean Carl Harrington.

Digging continued on a less frenetic scale and ceased with America's entry into World War II. Harrington would return afterwards to excavate the

Louis Luedtke

Jamestown Island today. Seen from the northwest, the foreground isthmus was built by the National Park Service in 1955. The seawall-protected shoreline extending to the right flanks the Association for the Preservation of Virginia Antiquities's 22½ acres. The bushes to the left of the Back River mark the approximate location of an Indian trail that led from the island across the peninsula to the York River. The famed "lone cypress" (opposite, right) that stood more than 80 yards from the seawall was often cited, albeit incorrectly, as evidence of shoreline erosion. It blew down in 1994.

glasshouse and, as the Park Service's regional archaeologist, he would oversee renewed digging across the Park Service's acres in 1955, work supervised by John L. Cotter, a competent and respected archaeologist, whose experience had largely been earned on Native American sites in the Southwest.

Although the public supposed that the Park Service's archaeologists were searching for the palisaded James Fort of John Smith and Pocahontas, Cotter knew very well that he was digging amid the streets and houses of the much later town. Like Harrington before him, he also dug to the east of "New Towne" to test a theory given credence in the 1930s that the original settlement lay in that direction and not in the vicinity of the church. Evidence of occupation to the east by the 1620s was insufficient to make the case, and so Cotter secured permission from the A.P.V.A. to dig a trench through the Confederate Fort that lies

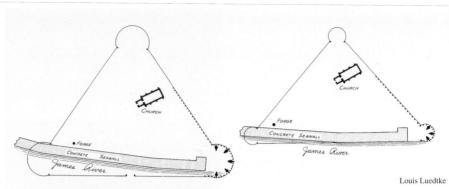

Louis Luedtke

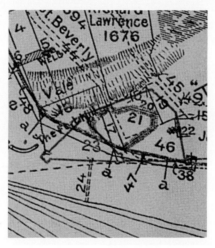

In 1903 Colonel Samuel H. Yonge drew a map (detail, left) that put the present church outside the fort's triangle but inside the first easterly expansion. Above, two interpretations by the author using Strachey's 300-, 300-, and 420-feet curtain wall measurements to place the church inside the fort, and using two versions of the unknown sizes of the bastions to create triangular forts of very different dimensions. That at left contains five saker-sized artillery pieces and that at right, three.

Dave Doody   Ivor Noël Hume

upstream from the church. Again, early artifacts were found but none so obviously early as to date to 1607 or thereabouts.

In 1903, Colonel Yonge (of seawall renown) had devoted careful study to the history and geography of Jamestown Island. In a map he drew at that time, he showed the palisaded triangle of James Fort with its landward corner at the west end of the Confederate earthwork and the rest eroded into the river. Consequently, when the Park Service failed to find any trace of it in the 1930s and '50s, it became convenient to conclude that "in all probability it stood on ground that has been washed into the James River."

A site-orientation panel at Jamestown gives substance to that thought and shows the triangle entirely out in the water. For those who want a pinpointed map reference, Philip Barbour, the editor of the most recent edition of John Smith's Complete Works, pro-

vides it: latitude 37° 12' 30"N., longitude 76° 47' 0"W.

Were it not for the fast approaching 400th anniversary of the Jamestown landing, visitors and historians would be content to leave James Fort out there in the river—out beyond a lone cypress tree. For more than a century the tree stood some 80 yards or more offshore, evidence, one was told, of the land lost to the river since the tree took root. But not so. A late 19th-century photograph shot when the tide was low shows the tree at the end of a long jetty and almost certainly the product of a bird-dropped seed that took root in a rotted pile.

Here, then, was evidence that the erosion had not been as extensive as is popularly supposed. That, coupled with the reinterpretation of the documentary evidence to show that the fortified triangle had been much larger than had previously been supposed, opened the door to a view hinted at by Miss Galt in 1897.

Aerial view shows the A. P. V. A.'s excavations that began in 1994. The statue of John Smith stands to the left, and behind, amid the trees, is the historic church tower. A. P. V. A. archaeological director William Kelso (in white sweater) discusses with assistant Jamie May the contents of a trash deposit containing, along with much else, a telltale quantity of broken window glass. Working to the left is archaeologist William Leigh.

A deliberately (?) buried cabasset helmet of the poorest munition type is shown in course of excavation and after laboratory treatment (opposite, top). Below: The uncovered glass immediately displayed its unusual blue tint. Much of it had been made into wide disks called crowns, seen being spun (right) in an engraving from Denis Diderot's Dictionnaire des Sciences.

Dave Doody

When she dug down with her own hands and found the brick and cobblestone church foundation, she deduced that it may have belonged to the one repaired by Lord De La Warr in 1610. If that were so, then both it and the towered church stood inside the fort—meaning that much of James Fort, indeed, much more than Colonel Yonge suggested—remains on the A.P.V.A.'s land waiting to be revealed.

That exciting prospect has prompted the Association to embark on a ten-year archaeological program it calls Jamestown Rediscovery. It began in 1994 under the direction of Dr. William Kelso and quickly yielded a tantalizing glimpse of things to come.

A test dig located between the seawall and the fenced churchyard revealed several postholes, an as yet unexplained wall of split logs running more or less parallel to the river, a massive ditch running toward the river and filled in the third quarter of the 17th century, and, most important of all, a large pit or cellar hole containing a miscellany of military and domestic artifacts, none of which need date later than about 1610. On the contrary, a coin and two counters are firmly dated to the last years of the previous century.

Dumped into the hole was a thin spread of broken glass—thousands of tiny fragments, many of them coming from large discs or "crowns" of window glass. Rather than being the green color common throughout the 17th century, these were of a rare blue hue, and an early 18th-century builder's dictionary had this to say of crown glass:

That of Ratcliff is the best and clearest Sort. It was at first made at the Bear-garden on the Bank-side; but the Maker removing in 1691, to Ratcliff, it is called Ratcliff Crown-Glass. . . . It is of a light Sky-blue Colour, as appears very distinctly, if it be laid on a Piece of white Paper.

The presence of small glass-coated fragments of crucibles amid the shards was persuasive evidence that this was broken glass from the Bear-garden factory brought over in 1608 to help Jamestown's glassworkers get started but probably left unused in the colony's storehouse.

Resting in the mud on the floor of an adjacent pit sat a common soldier's helmet—a type known as a cabasset or a "pot" helmet—not, it seemed, casually tossed away but placed upright on the floor. Together the 1607–1610 date, the cullet glass, and the helmet could be telling a single story.

Writing in 1613 but describing the abandonment of James Fort on June 7, 1610, the Reverend William Crashawe told how the surviving settlers went aboard the little ships built in Bermuda by interim Governor Sir Thomas Gates and set sail, "their Ordenance and Armour buried, and not an English soule left in James Towne." But first Gates "had caused to be carried aboard all the Armes, and all the best things in the store, which might to the Adventurers make some commodity upon the sale thereof at home."

Broken glass was not worth taking home, but the barrel it was stored in must have been invaluable as a packing crate for arms and other "best things." So here is a possible scenario:

A soldier follows orders and inters his already beat up helmet into a newly dug hole and shovels dirt over it. Meanwhile the partially empty cullet barrel is brought out of the storehouse and its remaining contents dumped into an adjacent and already partially filled hole. The fleet then leaves, meets the arriving Lord De La Warr, and returns. The disappointed soldier, who had thought he was going home, was not inspired to recover his old and uncomfortable helmet and so left it where it lay.

It is even conceivable that the large pit was a storage place actually inside the storehouse, and that when the building was repaired following Lord De La Warr's arrival, the improvements did not call for reexcavating a storage pit beneath the building.

With the A.P.V.A.'s renewed excavations still in their infancy, more questions were raised than answered. But if the cullet and helmet interpretation is correct, one thing is certain: Bill Kelso's team was digging inside the fort that so many have claimed to be out in the river. Furthermore, there survives on land—and waiting to be found—far more than even engineer Yonge suspected when he drew his 1903 map.

Until the excavations discover a row of holes for the palisade posts described by William Strachey in 1610 as "foure foote deepe in the ground, of yong Oakes, Walnuts, &c.," all is speculation. But remembering that Strachey described the ruined chapel as being "in the middest" of the fort and in the vicinity of the market place, and assuming that the reconstructed church occupies the same site, such speculation may not be entirely idle.

We know from Strachey that the curtain walls (the palisades between the artillery flankers) measured 420 feet on the river side, while the triangle's other two extended for only 300 feet. The missing element in the equation is the size and particularly the width of the flankers. If, as one report suggests, they housed as many as five pieces of artillery, the projections could be as much as 80 feet wide at the neck. On the other hand, if there were three or only the "peece of Ordnance or two well mounted" cited by Strachey, the width could be halved—creating a very different triangle and an appreciably smaller James Towne.

There remains the possibility, however, that Colonel Yonge came closer to the truth than even he realized. He knew from the records that by about 1613 James Fort had expanded from its original walled triangle to enclose more houses within a secondary palisade of uncertain character. Yonge showed this area encompassing the surviving church site.

Because it is virtually impossible to distinguish between artifacts of 1610 and those, say, of 1613 or 1615, one cannot yet rule out the possibility that in 1994 the A.P.V.A. began digging not in James Fort but in the suburb that grew from it. If this is so, then the cullet and helmet scenarios are worthless—save as a reminder that in archaeology one scrape with a trowel can transform plausible hypotheses into bad guesswork.

One thing is certain, however: Virginia and the nation owe a debt of gratitude to the A.P.V.A. for its foresight in securing the "hallowed ground" and for having prevented it from being more extensively excavated in the 1950s, when archaeological knowledge and techniques were less developed than they are today.

What, we may well wonder, will be seen and heard by those who will gather at the Jamestown church on May 13, 2007? Will romance have been replaced by revisionist reality, and will the colonists be seen, as did the Reverend Crashawe, as "Murtherers, Theeves, Adulterers, idle persons and what not besides, all of which persons God hateth even from his very soule." Or will John Smith become a born-again hero, and will poets be inspired (as was Anne Cunningham Cole in 1907) to enable Pocahontas to speak for the new century:

I'm a Jamestown maid,
And I'm not afraid
To greet all nations of earth
My home's by the sea,
My flag is liberty,
And I'm proud of the land of my birth.

Ivor Noël Hume

Courtesy of A. P. V. A.

Fig. 2.

Ivor Noël Hume

Remember, remember,
The Fifth of November,
Gunpowder, Treason, and Plot,
There is no reason
Why the gunpowder treason
Should ever be forgot.

Guy Fawkes
and the Gunpowder Plot

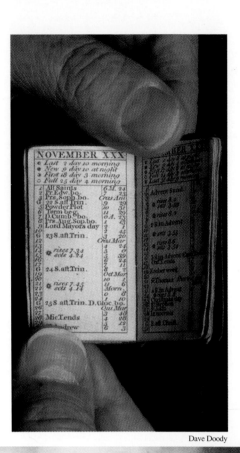

Even ladies were encouraged to remember the 5th of November, as this purse-sized almanac of 1787 attests (right). At Lewes in England the memory boisterously lingers on. Members of the Cliffe Bonfire Society—one of five on the tour—heft barrels of blazing tar to head their annual processions (below).

Dave Doody

Courtesy of Cliffe Bonfire Society

THE YOUNG LADY in an English secondhand bookstore only stopped chewing her gum long enough to ask, "Can I help you?" "Yes, I'm looking for anything relating to the Gunpowder Plot and Guy Fawkes Day," I told her. A vacuous, or maybe it was an incredulous, smile briefly enlivened her face. "Is there like, I mean, is there a connection?" she asked.

I assured her there was and launched into a short lecture on the Catholic attempt to blow up James I and his ministers at the opening of Parliament in 1605. "The King decreed that ever afterwards his lucky escape should be commemorated on the November 5 anniversary," I explained. "Although today the conspirator Guy Fawkes is burned on countless bonfires across the country, at first they burned the pope. Since. . . ."

The assistant's eyes widened, her gum chewing ceased, and her jaw sagged. "You mean they really burned the pope?"

"Not the actual pope," I assured her, "just an effigy."

The lady was visibly relieved. "I thought you meant, I mean, like you know at college, I read that some African tribes elected a king just for one year and then they. . . .

"No, no nothing like that," I told her, though had Pope Leo XI been in London in November 1605, the bookseller's assistant might well have been right.

I mention this exchange as preamble to allowing that it's small wonder that Guy Fawkes Day, or the Gunpowder Treason, is little known in America today. Nevertheless, throughout the colonial centuries that commemoration was listed along with saints' days, the birthday and martyrdom of Charles I, the accession of George III, as well as the beginning and end of summer's dog days that, in case you've forgotten, began on July 3 and ended on August 11.

If nothing else, the story of Guy Fawkes serves as a terrible reminder that making a political or religious statement by blowing up a government building is by no means new. Nor is it unusual for a bomber to risk detection by issuing a warning. One of the 1605 conspirators defeated their plot by advising a Catholic sympathizing relative, Lord Mounteagle, in writing to "retire yourself into your country for though there be no appearance of stirre, yet I say, they shall receive a terrible blow this Parliament, yet they shall not see who hurts them."

Mounteagle, who was as loyal to the crown as he was to his religion, promptly informed the Secretary of State, who passed the information to the Lord Chamberlain, who decided to defer any search of the Parliament buildings until the day before the King's arrival, claiming that by doing so he would avoid "giving suspicion unto the workers of this mischievous mystery."

The mystery's designers, all English Catholics, believed that by blowing up their king and his lords and commons, the way would be clear to restore the old religion. The plotter's leaders were Robert Catesby and Thomas Percy, cousin to the Earl of Northumberland and described by one who knew him as "a subtile flattering daungerous knave." It was Percy who, in November 1604, rented the house abutting part of the Palace of Westminster that accommodated the House of Lords, and there Guy, or Guido, Fawkes spent the best part of three months carrying down as much gunpowder in satchels "as foure or five and thirty barrells, hoggesheads, and firkins could contein." By any reckoning, that was an enormous amount of powder, all manufactured by one Charles Pain, who had no idea how it was to be used. The company he founded remains in business today as Britain's principal fireworks manufacturer and advertises that even Guy Fawkes respected the products "of our Mr. Pain."

The rented house allowed the conspirators to tunnel through the nine-foot-thick stone wall into a cellar adjacent to the House of Lords. While the tunneling was in progress, another cellar directly under the chamber and previously used to store coal became available to rent. Consequently the tunnel was diverted to enable the gunpowder to be transferred into the better placed cellar, where it was concealed behind piles of faggots and coal. By May 1605, all was ready.

On the afternoon of November 4, the day before the scheduled opening of Parliament, the Lord Chamberlain and Lord Mounteagle toured the Parliament building cellars and found a man they described as "a very tall and desperate fellow." Questioned as to who he was and what he was doing there, the man replied that he was a servant of Mr. Percy and was looking after his master's coals. The chamberlain commented that Mr. Percy seemed remarkably well supplied but made no effort to investigate further.

The desperate fellow was Fawkes, the son of respectable Protestant citizens of York but who, like many another convert, had embraced the Jesuit creed with single-minded zeal. As soon as the coast was clear, he left the cellar and hurried to the conspirators' house in Lambeth. Who was there and what instructions, if any, Fawkes received will never be known. Evidently, however, nobody called the plot off, and Fawkes returned to his post in the cellar.

None of this makes much sense, for Parliament was not due to convene until the following day, allowing Fawkes a good night's sleep and a hearty breakfast before returning to the cellar in time to strike the match. Instead, he was there, booted and spurred and with lantern lit (the reputed lantern is now in the Bodleian Library at Oxford) throughout the evening of the 4th. When around midnight he opened the cellar door and looked out, he was easily apprehended by waiting guards led by Westminster magistrate Sir Thomas Knevet.

Searched by his captors, Fawkes's purse (then called a pocket) yielded matches, touchwood, and a watch purchased the day before by Catesby for time-testing the touchwood fuse. A slow burner, it would have allowed Fawkes 15 minutes to escape. Meanwhile, the other conspirators assembled in Warwickshire intending to raise a Catholic army. Sir Everard Digby had been assigned to seize James's daughter, the Princess Elizabeth, and to proclaim her queen. On hearing that the plot had failed, Catesby, Percy, and three others fled to Holbeach House in Staffordshire, where they soon found themselves surrounded.

In a final irony, while trying to dry out their supply of gunpowder in front of a fire, it ignited and "so maimed the faces of some of the principal rebels, and the hands and sides of others, that they opened the gate" and fled into the sights of the invading musketeers. Percy and Catesby reportedly were felled by the same shot. As he lay dying, Catesby insisted that "the plot and practise of this treason was only his, and that all others were but his assistants, chosen by himself for that purpose, and that the

Old England, II, 1845

The gunpowder conspirators were alike both in their hats and in their convictions (top, right). Robert Catesby is second from right and Guy Fawkes third. They met at a Thames-side house at Lambeth (center). The once gunpowder-stacked cellar under the Palace of Westminster (bottom) survived into the mid-19th century.

Guy Fawkes signed his first confession (top) before being "put to the question" and again afterwards. The face of the martyred Henry Garnet appeared in an ear of straw (center, left) that fell from the basket that received his head.

Opposite: The traditional burning of Guy Fawkes continues among pyrotechnically inclined Anglophiles—even in Virginia.

honor thereof only belonged unto himself."

Fawkes would have fared better had he died with his friends at Holbeach. Instead he was first taken to the king's bedchamber at Whitehall, where he insisted that his name was John Johnson and a servant to Mr. Percy. However, he made no pretense of innocence; instead, he told the king that he was sorry the plot had miscarried because "dangerous diseases require desperate remedies." A Scottish courtier who wanted to know why so much gunpowder had been assembled was told by Fawkes that one of the objects had been "to blow Scotchmen back into Scotland."

No matter how appalled even Catholics were at the news of the plan, no one could doubt Guy Fawkes's courage or his religious conviction. He steadfastly refused to name his co-conspirators; and when told that they were either dead or in custody, he replied that in that case they had identified themselves and it "would be superfluous for me to name them." On November 8 Fawkes signed his first deposition in writing bold and clear.

Fawkes was by then imprisoned in the Tower of London, whose keeper was instructed by King James to apply the gentler tortures "et sec per gradus, ad ima tenditur [and thus by degrees we may proceed to extremities] and so God speed you in your good work." After two days of questioning Fawkes signed a second deposition, this time in a hand barely legible. In 1845 the anonymous author of *Old England a Pictorial Museum* commented that "the contrast suggests horrors too appalling for the imagination to dwell upon."

On January 30, 1606, in the wake of public trials, Sir Everard Digby and four others were executed at the west end of St. Paul's Cathedral, and the following day Guy Fawkes and four more died in Westminster's Old Palace Yard. The previously cited 1845 author asserted that "We need not excite the loathing of our readers by a description of the sort of execution that the Christian governors of England in the seventeenth century enforced," to which one can only add "Amen."

The winter of 1605–1606 saw waves of anti-Catholic hysteria sweeping England. People suspected of having aided the conspirators in their flight to Staffordshire or who were suspected of having had knowledge of the plot were summarily convicted. Jesuits were hunted down, particularly Father Henry Garnet, who in the previous century had been arrested for plotting with Philip II of Spain against Queen Elizabeth but who had been pardoned at the time of James's accession. Although away on a pilgrimage in Wales at the time of the intended explosion, Garnet was found and taken to London for questioning and trial. His personal servant, Nicholas Owen, had by then been seized and tortured in the Tower but managed to escape his torment by stabbing himself to death with a dinner knife.

Put in adjoining cells with only a small door between them, Garnet and another Jesuit named Oldcorne were encouraged to talk to each other and thus were trapped into admitting a degree of complicity or at least of prior knowledge. Brought to trial at London's Guildhall, Garnet's pleas were simple: His knowledge stemmed from the confessional and could not be divulged, and that he had done his best to talk Catesby out of the plan. The trial was conducted in such uproar from the citizen spectators that Garnet was unable to testify on his own behalf, and although his dignified bearing was commented on by one of the judges, it did not save

Dave Doody

him. Henry Garnet was executed in front of St. Paul's on May 3.

To the chagrin of Protestants and the delight of Catholics, Father Garnet's death sired a memorable miracle. On being dumped into a straw-lined basket, the dead man's head and quarters propelled an ear of straw into the hands of a spectator. This man, a tailor named Wilkinson, gave the straw to "a Mrs. N., a matron of singular Catholic piety," who put it in a bottle. A few days later she saw in the straw the face of the martyred Garnet. News of the miracle quickly spread to Europe, and soon the wheat ear and its by then crowned face became the printed symbol of hostility toward English Protestantism.

As winter gave way to spring, renewed hysteria surrounding the Garnet trial ensured that anti-Catholic feeling and, more significantly, anti-Catholic legislation ran rampant. In June, Thomas Percy's cousin the Earl of Northumberland was accused of being privy to the plot and imprisoned for life in the Tower. Two other lords, whose crime had been no more than absenting themselves from the fateful Parliament opening, were fined and imprisoned "during the king's pleasure." Lord Mounteagle, on the other hand, received his gratitude, a gift of crown lands and a handsome pension.

What, you might wonder, has any of this to do with Virginia? Well, for a start, the first display of "wildefire woorkes" in English-speaking America took place on Roanoke Island in 1585 or 1586, where amazed Indians concluded that the art "had bin given and taught us of the gods." More lastingly significant, however, was the impact not of fireworks but of the Gunpowder Plot itself.

The autumn of 1606 saw preparations for the first Jamestown settlement, and when the three ships sailed away down the Thames on December 20, anti-Papist fear and suspi-

cion were as virulent as ever. Catholic spies were thought to lurk in every dark corner and families with histories of Catholicism, no matter how professedly loyal to the crown, were suspect. Those same fears and prejudices were built into the Jamestown leadership and contributed in no small measure to the dissension and distrust that was to develop among its members. For example, it could have escaped nobody's attention that colonist George Percy's brother, the Earl of Northumberland, was paying the price for having the Gunpowder Plot's Thomas as his cousin.

On February 10, 1606, the House of Commons had entered November 5 into the official calendar as "a holiday for ever in thankfulness to God for our deliverance and detestation of the Papists." Although there is no evidence that the early Jamestown colonists kept this public holiday, we do know, thanks to the writings of Captain John Smith, that in neighboring Bermuda in 1616, "The fifth of November the damnable plot of the powder treason was solemnized, with praises, Sermons, and a Great Feast." The governor, somewhat tactlessly, perhaps, invited the captain of a recently wrecked Spanish ship to be his guest.

A quick volley of small shot . . . was answered from the Forts with the great Ordnance, and then againe concluded with a second volley of small shot; neither was the afternoone without musick and dancing, and at night many huge bonfires of sweet wood.

Bonfires were then, as still, very much a part of British and colonial life. Across southern England many a town and village has its "bonfire hill," recalling the warning fires lit there in 1588, when Spain's invading Armada was sighted. More often they burned in celebration, of Waterloo, of the 1918 armistice, and in 1995 in commemoration of VE Day. On Tuesday, November 5, 1605, as news of the thwarted plot spread, piles of lumber miraculously accumulated in streets and market places. Wrote perennial correspondent John Chamberlain, "On Tewsday at night we had great ringing [of church bells] and as great store of bonfires as ever I thincke was seene."

It was inevitable that the firing of guns should accompany the bonfires as they had in Bermuda and equally inevitable that, in time, fireworks would substitute for firearms. Thus in 1660, diarist Samuel Pepys noted that "This 5th day of November is observed exceeding well in the City; and at night great bonfires and fireworks." By 1677 children were celebrating at the firecracker level, prompting a *Poor Robin's Almanack* entry for November 5 to offer this:

Now boys with
Squibs and crackers play
And bonfires blaze
Turns night to day.

So important in the English calendar was November 5 that when William III, then only the Prince of Orange, was arriving aboard ship in Torbay on the 4th intending to claim the English throne vacated by James II, his advisors counseled him to wait until the next day. William had wanted to set foot on English soil on the 4th, that being his birthday and the date of his marriage.

Civic bonfires on Guy Fawkes Night, like this one painted by James Wilson Carmichael (above), provided an opportunity to be rid of mountains of combustible trash. Opposite: Although Williamsburg no longer remembers the 5th of November, its Christmas and Fourth of July fireworks, here at the Governor's Palace, still bring gasps from silhouetted and bedazzled crowds.

Recalling an account by William's supporter Bishop Burnet, the *Virginia Gazette* for February 11, 1737, recalled that "the Day following being Gunpowder Treason, our landing that Day, might have a good Effect on the Minds of the English Nation [and due to bad weather on the 4th] were better pleas'd to see that we could land no sooner."

The arrival of Protestant William on November 5th and the ouster of Catholic James II were thenceforth coupled with celebrations giving thanks for James I's and Parliament's escape in 1605. The two events continued to be so linked in America until 1775, whereupon they became an instant irrelevance.

In America the celebration known in New England as Pope's Day went out with the last of the redcoats, and possibly sooner. The *Virginia Gazette* for December 1, 1774, described what may have been in Newport, Rhode Island, the last Guy Fawkes hurrah.

Last Saturday there were two large Popes, &c. carried about this town, in commemoration of the gunpowder Plot. On one of the Stages, besides the Devil and Pope, were exhibited the effigies of Lord North, and that old traitor T. Hutchinson which offered great satisfaction to all Friends of Liberty in the Place. In the evening the Images were burnt, and with them a Pamphlet with the words wrote on the cover: Lord Dartmouth's Pamphlet, in justification of Popery, sent out to the colonies.

Another slightly earlier *Virginia Gazette,* that of September 22, 1774, citing a tongue-in-cheek report from London that "We are informed the Service for the 5th of November is to be entirely new modelled; that celebrated investigator of historical facts, Sir J.D. having undertaken to prove that the horrid Scheme, intended to have been executed on this Day, was not a Catholic, but a Protestant Contrivance." Although intended as a joke, the *Gazette*'s notion has since been seriously proposed by revisionist historians.

In a letter to the editor of the Edinburgh *Evening Courant,* poet Robert Burns prophesied that "the American Congress of 1776, will be allowed to have been as able and as enlightened [as were the English in disposing of James II] and that the fourth of July will be as sacred to their posterity as the fifth of November is to us." However, John Adams had already come to the same conclusion and did so in a letter to Abigail on July 3, 1776. "I am apt to believe," he wrote, that the day "will be celebrated by succeeding generations as the great anniversary festival" with "bonfires and illuminations from one end of the continent to the other."

Just how soon after the war the Fourth of July became fireworks night is a "factoid" that has escaped me, but as pyrotechnics enthusiast George Plimpton has noted, in 1864 a Philadelphia diarist observed that "as a general rule, 30 or 40 houses are set afire every 4th of July."

It may be, however, that for a while, at least, the colonial November tradition had lingered in American memory. In 1789 at Annapolis, according to the *Maryland Gazette* for November 5th, one John Laugien announced that on the following Monday he would mount "a display of FIREWORKS, consisting of an engagement between two men of war of fourteen guns, an Amer-

Colonial Williamsburg

ican and an English, each twelve feet high, the former to be commanded by Captain BARNEY, and each gun to fire seven times; a discharge of 36 rockets of different kinds, three wheels of different kinds, five serpent boxes, six table rockets, two pigeons, &c, &c." The advertisement went on to assure gentlemen and ladies that Mr. Laugien expected to give three times more satisfaction than he did last time.

Because Mr. Laugien's previous offering failed to make it into the Maryland paper, it is anybody's guess whether "last time" meant last year or just a few days or weeks earlier. Indeed, there is no certainty that his show had anything to do with the Guy Fawkes tradition. But if it did, it is reasonable to deduce that Guy Fawkes's place at the firey pinnacle of villainy had been replaced by an English warship. For reasons equally speculative, Annapolis's pyrotechnician let it be known that he wanted ticket buyers to pay up before the show because he "expects to leave town after that."

On the evidence of the 1774 Rhode Island account there can be no doubt that in the colonies any November 5th commemoration remained rooted in religious prejudice, and it continued so in England into the early 19th century, sometimes with the fervor that still colors the annual Orangemen's marches in Northern Ireland.

By 1825, however, English social historian William Hone could write that "It is not to be expected that poor boys should be well informed as to Guy's history, or be particular about his costume. With them 'Guy Fawkes-day,' or, as they as often call it 'Pope-day,' is a holiday, and as they reckon their year by their holidays, this, on account of its festivous enjoyment, is the greatest holiday of the season."

Four years later, archaeologist and author Edward Brayley noted that "The Fifth of November is still one of the principal holydays of London, though of late years it has not been observed by the populace with so much festive diversion as formerly. The burning of Guy Fawkes, a figure made with old clothes, and stuffed with straw or rags, was a ceremony much in vogue with the lower classes, but is now chiefly confined to school-boys. The greater attention given by the police to prevent tumults, and restrain the letting off of fireworks, through which frequent accidents attended the commemoration of the gunpowder plot, are, perhaps, the leading causes of the disuse of ancient custom."

In Victoria's reign, with the religious association largely if not entirely forgotten, Guy Fawkes Night became and would remain an opportunity for young people to have fun with fireworks. Through the preceding week or more, poor children would tour Guy Fawkes effigies through English city streets in push carts and baby carriages crying, "Penny for the guy, sir!" How many pennies went for fireworks and how many for mothers' gin remains anybody's guess. Nevertheless, prodigious quantities of fireworks were ignited and many injuries accrued. Indeed, my own uncle took a rocket in his eye and throughout his life wore a black eye patch. But as he also sported a piratical beard, it didn't seem to matter. Today, like Halloween in America, Guy Fawkes Night in England has come to be marred by ever more dangerous hooliganism, and in many localities exploding fireworks are banned.

Although frowned upon and sometimes harrassed by safety-conscious police, several English towns such as Rye and Bridgewater still take the November celebration very seriously, but none more so than Lewes in Sussex, which supports six bonfire societies. Best organized of them is the Cliffe Society, which marches effigies of Guy Fawkes and the current pope through the town along with blazing barrels of tar. The society's printed program states that "At around half-past nine o'clock effigies of Guy Fawkes and Pope Paul V will be ceremoniously destroyed by means of fireworks. Also giant heads of personages deemed by the Society to be this year's 'Enemies of Bonfire' will be similarly exploded."

Colonial Williamsburg's Fourth of July fireworks and Christmas Grand Illumination displays are so well orchestrated today that they invariably leave crowds eager for more. But, it was not always so. In 1702 Virginia's Governor Francis Nicholson ordered a celebration honoring the accession of Queen Anne, in planning for which "inquiry was made whether anyone knew how to set off fireworks." Although gunners from visiting warships volunteered, the grand event evidently got off to a somewhat apprehensive start, justifiably, as it turned out. Swiss visitor Francis Louis Michel remembered it thusly:

A master [of ceremonies] . . . was considered the most expert and boasted of his skill. But the results showed that he did not succeed in gaining much honor . . . for he blew up everything at once in a great blaze and smoke. As there were all kinds of fireworks, many and large rockets, he like others had to run and he had his clothes burnt. . . .

When it was to begin the governor asked if they were ready. They answered: yes. Then he commanded them to set off the fireworks. This was done with a reversed rocket, which was to pass along a string to an arbor, where prominent ladies were seated, but it got stuck half way and exploded. . . . In short, nothing was successful, the rockets also refused to fly up, but fell down archlike, so that it was not worthwhile seeing. . . . The fireworks were very expensive.

Other 18th-century Williamsburg "illuminations" seem to have fared better. At least there are no reports of memorable disasters. The last big show celebrated the arrival of Lady Dunmore in March 1774, with "an elegant set of fireworks." Waxing poetic, the *Virginia Gazette* reported that "While cannon roar [and] Bonfires blaze, [joy] around every heart exulting plays."

But soon the Dunmores, lady and lord, would be gone, and the volleys and cannonading would be all too real. The Fourth of July and commemorations of victory at Yorktown would erase royal birthdays and any memory of Guy Fawkes from America's official and pyrotechnical calendars.

But not in England. On the night before each opening of Parliament, a detachment of Yeomen of the Guard in their crimson Tudor uniforms are taken to the Parliament building to search its basements, corridors, and every potential powder-concealing nook and cranny. It does not seem to matter that the original building was rebuilt and opened in 1847, following a fire 13 years earlier. Once the Yeoman are satisfied that no Guy Fawkes copycats are lurking, lantern and match in hand, word is sent to the Queen that all is well.

Treasure in a Box

HIDDEN TREASURE—words to quicken the pulse and spark a glitter of avarice in the dullest eye. Tabloid newspapers well versed in human frailty offer countless titillating stories of chimney-repairing workmen being felled by a cascade of gold sovereigns or drowned in a deluge of doubloons. Most such tales are reported from the Old World, very few from the New. But that is not to say either that people in America did not hide their valuables or that such treasures are always centuries old.

Colonial Williamsburg's silver collection proves my point, for it includes a hoard of 18th-century English silver hidden under a piece of slate in a field in nearby Nansemond County, perhaps by a Loyalist family in the early days of the Revolution. No one came back to claim it, and it remained there until, in 1961, a silver mug came up impaled on the blade of a surprised farmer's harrow.

Colonial Williamsburg's research has failed to identify the colonial owners of the Nansemond treasure, and it remains possible that it was buried not by the family but by thieves who stole it.

Before there were bank vaults or home safes to conceal behind the portrait of great-uncle Jed, our ancestors had to find other means of securing their valuables, some of them self-defeating in their ingenuity. Cabinetmakers frequently assisted by building secret drawers and compartments into desks and cabinets. Colonial Williamsburg's furniture collection includes pieces having hiding places where money could be kept from light-fingered servants or love letters concealed from husbands. However, it took only an unexpected death and the heir's decision to sell the furniture to launch dad's assets or mom's secrets on their centuries-long trip into the future. And it can still happen.

Audrey, my first wife, found herself the sole heir to a widowed aunt who, some time before her death in England, sold up most of her possessions and spent her last years in a nursing home. Processing the estate, therefore, was a simple matter for the family lawyer, leaving it only to Audrey to visit the nursing home to go through the few personal things her aunt had left there—mostly letters in an old iron deed box.

When Audrey told me that she planned to junk the box and only bring back to London such letters as seemed to be of family interest, I urged her to reconsider. A 70-year-old deed box was on its way to becoming an antique or at least a "collectible," I claimed.

"It's all very well for you," Audrey countered. "You won't be there to have to carry it." Nevertheless, she did bring it back to our London hotel room. "What did I tell you?" she said. "It's just a very ordinary, somewhat battered box. Everybody had one."

But I rather liked it.

When it came time to return to Williamsburg we had no room for the box in our baggage.

"So let's dump it!"

"No, we'll mail it," I persisted—and proceeded to fill it with

Ivor Noël Hume

The unloved deed box and the contents of its secret drawer.

theater programs, maps, and other standard junk that one accumulates abroad. The box had a removable iron cash tray with lidded compartments on either side of a central block that supported the handle for lifting it out. I packed these compartments with miscellaneous odds and ends, each carefully wrapped in tissue to make sure it didn't rattle about. British post offices don't like parcels that rattle. Satisfied that everything was snugly housed, I wrapped the box up in brown paper and did one of my more spectacular stringing jobs. "That," I said with considerable satisfaction, "is a professional bit of parceling."

"You're sure it doesn't rattle?" asked Audrey.

"Of course it doesn't!"

But it did. Muttering medieval oaths, I untied the parcel, took everything out of the box, and started again. The second parceling looked distinctly less professional than the first. It also rattled.

"Look," said Audrey. "Let's quit on it before you have a stroke. I never wanted the box. I don't like the box. And there are much better ways of passing the morning than wrapping and unwrapping it. So put it in the trash and be done with it!"

"Not on your life!" I replied, fumbling at the knots. "I know what it is, it's that . . . handle. That's what's rattling." With everything again out of the box, I carefully wrapped the tray's handle in tissue, then shook it. But the rattling persisted, even though the flanking compartments were empty.

The sound came from under the handle, and careful investigation revealed that between the two trays there could be a space measuring as much as eight inches long, three wide, and two deep; yet there appeared to be no way of getting to it. Finally, we found it. What looked like welded joints alongside the handle weren't. When out of the box, the tray's handle and entire base could be made to slide sideways to reveal the secret compartment. In it were several pieces of jewelry—including two rings later appraised at more than $12,000.

A Voyage to Virginia

*"... our seamen frequently fell overboard,
without any one regarding the loss of another ..."*

Louis Luedtke

"We then proceeded and went to the 'Change. Advertisements hung as thick round the pillars of each walk as bells about the legs of a morris dancer, and an incessant buzz, like murmers of the distant ocean, made a diapason of our talk."

Ned Ward, *The London Spy*, 1690

After Wenceslas Hollar, 1644

"We grew acquainted on the Royal Exchange with Capt. John Locker, whose bills upon the posts made us know he was master of a good ship—untruly so call'd."

The Month of August, Anno 1649 being the time I engag'd to meet my two comrades, Major Francis Morrison, and Major Richard Fox, at London, in order to a full accomplishment of our purpose to seek our fortunes in Virginia ... all parties very punctually appear'd at the time and place assign'd.

SO BEGAN THE STORY of Colonel Henry Norwood and his terrifying journey to Virginia—surely one of the most graphic accounts of disaster at sea to survive from the 17th century. Today it is so easy to fly to London and back that we tend to as readily dismiss the travel experiences of our forefathers. We allow, of course, that a sea voyage to Virginia took a while, maybe six or eight weeks, but if one was somebody—and Colonel Norwood was somebody, a kinsman of Virginia's Governor Sir William Berkeley—life in the great cabin must have been relatively pleasant, albeit boring.

Norwood had never before been to Virginia, but at least one relative may have preceded him—though he did not say so. He was Richard Norwood, whose fare to the colony, along with those of 39 others, had been paid by a previous governor, Sir Francis Wyatt, and recorded six years earlier. Colonel Henry Norwood had fought for his king in the first English civil war and had allied himself with other royalists in the exiled Charles II's movable court in Holland. His opinions, therefore, of Oliver Cromwell and his Puritan pals were direct and unequivocal. Referring to the execution of Charles I, Norwood declared that "this unparallel'd butchery made the rebels cast away the scabbards of their swords with both hands, in full resolution never to let them meet again."

The colonel's companions were of a like mind. Major Morrison had the exiled king's commission naming him captain of the fort at Jamestown. Norwood carried a letter from the king recommending him to Governor Berkeley's "particular care." And Fox was in it for the money.

On September 1, 1649, the trio made its way to the Royal Exchange, there to scan the notices pinned to the building's promenade posts in search of a Virginia-bound ship in need of passengers and cargo. Captain John Locker's ad caught their attention. His *Virginia Merchant* was, he assured them, a good ship—as sound as any afloat—and large. Her 300-ton burthen made her commodious and her 30 and more guns safe.

After mandatory haggling, Norwood, Morrison, and Fox agreed to take passage for themselves and their servants at six pounds a head, their destination loosely defined as "into James River."

As so often happened, America-bound convoys took on their cargoes at Gravesend and then sailed around the Kentish coast to anchor in the Downs, the relatively hospitable water behind the dreaded "Shippe Swalower," the Goodwin Sands from which protruded, as diarist Samuel Pepys would note a few years later, "many wrecks and masts which are the greatest guide for our ships." There the fleet waited until September 23, when the wind veered to the east. With a fresh gale behind her, the *Virginia Merchant* could clear the English Channel in three bracing days.

Captain Locker was steering the short route. Rather than heading south to the Canary and Cape Verde Islands before crossing to the Caribbean, he set his course for the Western Isles—now the Azores—and reached them in 22 uneventful days. Most of the 340 passengers and crew were unaware the cooper had discovered that the levels in his water barrels were far too low to supply their needs all the way to Virginia. Consequently, rather than bypassing the Portuguese islands, Captain Locker made for the island of Faial and anchored in its harbor on October 14. Faial was both a ready source of water and of wine—as his crew discovered on their first evening ashore.

Drunkenly mishandling the *Virginia Merchant's* longboat, they watched it dashed to pieces on the harbor-side crags. The crewmen, wrote Norwood, "lay up and down dead drunk in all quarters, in a sad pickle."

The pickle persisted. Forced to rent island boats and to buy water, Locker soon realized that his seamen "on shore continued in their debauchery, with very little advance of our dispatch, and so full of delays by drunken contests of ours with the islanders" that he was losing beer faster than he was buying water. In those days beer was the normal shipboard drink, while water was used largely for cooking. So, with the imbalance still uncorrected, the *Virginia Merchant* set out on the next leg of her voyage that was to bring her in sight of Bermuda and its spray-drenched reefs.

Norwood left no hint that he had prior knowledge of the English colony on Bermuda, and therefore it is unlikely that he was kin to Bermuda's surveyor Richard Norwood or to Captain Mathew Norwood, who made several supplying voyages to the islands between 1675 and 1680, his last aboard the doomed *John* being one too many.

The *Virginia Merchant's* crew and perhaps some of the passengers were acquainted with the reputation of the islands that Shakespeare had called the "still-vex'd Bermoothes," and with the wind high and the sea rough, the sight of a waterspout to leeward may have been seen by some as a portent of terror to come. Norwood thought it more interesting than intimidating, but he did allow that had the helm been toward it, the force would have been enough "to hoist our ship out of her proper element, into the air and to have made her do the supersault."

The omen, if such it was, was premature. Eleven years later another *Virginia Merchant* with 179 passengers aboard would drive onto a reef only 250 yards from shore with the loss of all but ten. Captain Locker was luckier. Gale driven, he cleared the islands without incident and headed for Cape Hatteras.

With Bermuda astern, the passengers believed themselves within a very few days of land and leaving what Norwood then termed "a hungry pester'd ship and company." It was now November 8, and he was up before dawn conversing with the ship's mate, whose watch it was. Somewhat nonchalantly, mate Putts said that he would take a look out and see whether in the night there had been a change in the color of the water. No sooner was he on deck than Norwood heard him bellowing to the crew, "All hands aloft! Breaches, breaches on both sides! All hands aloft!"

But the seamen, on seeing the surf breaking over the shoals, lost their nerve and dropped to their knees, commending their souls to heaven. Captain Locker joined them, leaving it to mate Putts to urge the crew into action. "Is there no good fellow that will stand to the helm, and loose a sail?" he demanded. But only two came forward, one taking the helm and the other climbing up to free the fore topsail. As the wind howled about her, the *Virginia Merchant* lurched first one way and then another, as seaman Tom Reasin tried to steer her between the deadly shoals of Cape Hatteras. But luck and skill could not endure forever, and the ship struck bottom "and raised such a wall of water and sand together, which fell on the main chains, that now all hope of safety was laid aside."

Miraculously the ship remained intact and afloat and, better still, found herself driven into a channel along which she escaped into deep water. The crew regained its courage, shook hands as

Louis Luedtke

"His face was clouded with ill news he had to tell us, namely, that we were now residing on an island without any inhabitant [opposite], and that he had seen its whole extent, surrounded with water deeper than his head."

"We were not gone far till the fatigue and tediousness of the journey discovered itself in the many creeks we were forc'd to head, and swamps to pass (like Irish bogs) which made the way at least double what it would have amounted to in a straight line" [below and right].

Louis Luedtke

"About the midst of February, I had an opportunity to cross the bay in a sloop, and with much ado landed in York river."

"men risen from the other world," and returned to work, setting the sails that would carry them to seaward. But worse was in store.

The gale out of the northwest developed into a violent storm that propelled the ship away from Virginia and out into the Atlantic. "The Mountainous towring north-west seas that this storm made, were so unruly," wrote Norwood, "that the seamen knew not how to work the ship about." In the hope of preventing masts from snapping, crewmen climbed aloft to lower the spars that held the sails in place. But it availed them naught. The foremast snapped. Norwood explained that the whole trimming and rigging of the ship depended "much upon stays and tackle fixed to that mast," adding that "we had reason to expect greater ruin to follow." And it did.

Around midnight Norwood "heard and felt a mighty sea break on our fore-ship," but it was not until later that he learned that the whole of the forecastle had been swept away along with six guns, all but one of the ship's anchors, its galley, and its two cooks. The bowsprit, released from its stays and rigging, was swinging wildly back and forth, hammering the ship's bow until carpenters cut it loose. The ever-heroic Tom Reasin, fearing that the main-topmast would soon come down, began to climb up to secure it but was called back just as it and the mainmast itself came crashing down—mercifully into the sea and not on deck, where soaked seamen struggled to clear lines and other debris.

The mainmast now lay alongside the hull, pounding its planks amidships like a mighty door knocker with every wave that struck, until it too could be cut loose. The *Virginia Merchant* had become a powerless hulk, a barely floating wreck adrift at the ocean's mercy. "Tossed up and down without any rigging to keep the ship steady," wrote Norwood, "our seamen frequently fell overboard, without any one regarding the loss of another, every man expecting the same fate, tho' in a different manner."

The storm continued unabated until November 12 and then slowly died away, so that by the 17th, Norwood could note that "The seas were much appeas'd." But there was little else to give encouragement. The storm having swept away the forecastle and the galley, there was nowhere to cook such food as remained. The quantities of water shipped into the hold through the forecastle's gaping hole had ruined much of the bread supply, and the freshwater from Faial was long since gone. Soon passengers and crew would be starving.

Once again, seaman Tom Reasin proved to be the ship's savior. By driving spikes into what was left of the mizzenmast, he could climb high enough to rig tackle to raise a sail. Then, using one of the spars saved when the storm began, he was able to graft it into the stump of the mainmast and thus rig enough sail to hold the shattered vessel to the wind. But to what course? Neither Captain Locker nor his officers had the first idea where they were, but believed that they had been driven south of Cape Hatteras.

Although from time to time land was in sight, mists and day-long blankets of fog rendered it a game of now you see it, now you don't. Putts, who was both mate and pilot, had made the voyage 22 times before; and in one of the land-ho! breaks, he thought he recognized clumps of trees as a point southward of the Virginia Capes. But later in the day the land vanished, and Putts concluded that he was mistaken, that they were farther to the north and abreast of the Chesapeake Bay. With the *Virginia Mer-*

chant's sailing capability no better than that of "a western barge," Putts was unable to correct his course, and so the ship drove northward to who knew where.

For another nine days the ship was carried out into the deep ocean, where the wind ripped her sails to shreds. One of two pumps gave out; and, as Norwood put it, "we were in mortal apprehension, that the guns which were all aloft, would shew us a slippery trick, and some of them break loose, the tackle that held them being grown very rotten." A break in the gale enabled Putts to untie the heavy guns and lower them one by one into the hold, thus "making the ship (as seamen say) more wholesome, by having so great weight removed from her upper works into her centre, where ballast was much wanted."

Some aboard were convinced that they had been blown southeast almost to Bermuda. Others favored trying to ride the western current back to the Azores. But with food down to half a biscuit per person per day and nothing to drink but Malaga sack, which inflamed rather than decreased thirst, the majority voted to try to reach land anywhere on the American continent.

"The famine," wrote Norwood, "grew sharp upon us." Rats that had been a plague earlier in the voyage were now selling for 16 shillings a piece. A pregnant woman offered 20 shillings for one, was refused, and shortly thereafter died. Norwood recalled that his "greatest impatience" was thirst, and that his dreams were all of cellars "and taps running down my throat, which made my waking much the worse by that tantalizing fantasy." Christmas came and went, highlighted in the captain's mess by the creation of a "Christmas pudding" made from Malaga sack, seawater, fruit and spice, fried together in oil.

On the afternoon of January 6, 1650, the *Virginia Merchant* reached within seven miles of land, and the ragged rabble of passengers begged that the ship's only remaining anchor be dropped, and that mate Putts should go ashore and try to find out where they were. The proposal brought opposition from one of the older officers, who warned that if the weather changed and they had to cut and slip, those aboard would have no means of mooring no matter where they wound up. Then, too, the anchor cable was too short for ocean anchorage; and, thirdly, they should not risk the lives "of the rest of the ship's crew, many dead and fallen over board, and the passengers weakened by hunger, dying every day on the decks, or at the pump."

But those who wanted the anchor dropped prevailed. Using the only small boat (described as a wherry), Putts set out, taking with him Norwood's companion Major Morrison and "twelve sickly passengers, who fancied the shore would cure them." Five hours later Putts returned bearing joyful news of fresh water, abundant game for the hunting, and a creek capable of harboring the ship. Morrison had stayed with the invalids, expecting that the entire ship's company would quickly join him.

Captain Locker decided that first he must see for himself before committing everyone to an uncertain fate on land; he, Norwood, and several others landed and found the bounty to be as Putts had described. A bar at the creek's mouth seemed to be no obstacle to bringing the ship safely to shore. So Norwood was surprised when Locker whispered in his ear asking whether he would join him in returning to the ship. Norwood declined but was soon to regret it.

Shortly after dawn, he unwrapped himself from the cloak that had protected him through a bitterly cold night and saw the *Virginia Merchant* under sail, heading south for the Virginia Capes. Astern of it rowed Captain Locker and his seamen, doing their best to catch up with her. Norwood would later learn that mate Putts persuaded the crew to heave to long enough to let his captain get aboard. It seems evident, nevertheless, that Locker had intended to abandon those ashore, and that he had been pre-empted by his mutinous crew.

Before going ashore, Norwood's Dutch servant told him that in the bundle his master was carrying were 30 "bisket cakes" he had saved and hidden from his own portion. These Norwood now shared with his 18 companions—12 of them the sick and nameless passengers of whom three were women, his friend Major Morrison (Major Fox had remained aboard), a blustering and troublesome Major Stephens, a young man named Francis Cary whom Norwood frequently referred to as his cousin, and four other unnamed individuals.

Sent on a reconnoitering mission, Cary returned from the opposite direction to the one in which he had set out—this because he brought bad news. The sandy, piney-groved land that they had thought to be part of the mainland was in fact an island, uninhabited, and surround by water "deeper than his head." The good news was that a rich bank of oysters would keep the marooned company alive for quite some time.

At first, in the cold January weather, migrating geese, ducks, and other birds were plentiful and easily shot, but as the weather warmed, the birds became scarce and finally avoided the island altogether. Spring tides coupled with onshore rain caused the oyster bank to be submerged. Powder was running out, guns were "unfix'd and out of order," and "so hopeless and desperate was our condition, all expectation of human succour being vanished and gone."

In a passage reminiscent of Jamestown in the starving time of 1609—but ever since spared the moral outrage that had erupted from it—Norwood described how one of the three weak women passengers was fortunate to die. "It was my advice to the survivors, who were following her apace," he wrote, "to endeavour their own preservation by converting her dead carcass into food, as they did to good effect. The same counsel was embrac'd by those of our sex," he went on, "the living fed upon the dead." A storm of hail and snow one Sunday night in January hastened the death of four malnourished men, whose passing gave further strength to the living.

On January 14 Cary reported that he had seen Indians on the mainland, but when Norwood reached the place, they were gone. However, he did shoot a goose that he decided to keep to himself on the grounds that its nourishment would prepare him for an attempt to swim to the mainland in search of help. Leaving the goose hung in the notch of a tree, he went in search of the company's cook. But when they returned, only the bird's head remained. The rest had been eaten by wolves—or so Indians would later tell him.

Reports of Indian sightings persisted, but Norwood dismissed them until he learned that one night Indians had come with food to two sick women who were housed apart in their own cabin. The women said that the Indians had repeatedly pointed to the southeast. Several days later they returned—men, women, and children bringing bread and corn. Unlike the tales told by John Smith at Jamestown, who apparently was able to lecture to comprehending Indians on every aspect of the cosmos, communication was awkward, slow, and often unproductive. Norwood noted that he had read Smith's travels and thus learned a single Indian word—weroance, or king—but which "(like a little armour well plac'd) contributed to the saving of our lives."

The Indians provided canoes to carry Norwood and his companions to shore. But Major Stephens resisted the idea, arguing that the weroance was not to be trusted. He proposed instead that the survivors should steal the canoes, head out to sea, and row to the Virginia Capes. Norwood refused, countering that if the Indians had meant them harm, they could as easily have stayed away until death beckoned the last of them.

The surviving women were too ill to travel and remained behind in the hut of an Indian fisherman, while Norwood and his weak but reviving companions were passed from tribe to tribe southward toward Jamestown. His detailed account of the journey and the hospitality he received from the Indians provides an important chapter in our understanding of the Native Americans' character and culture, and it closely parallels the account of Captains Amadas and Barlowe on their first visit to Roanoke Island in 1584. That this degree of compassion and friendship should endure not far to the north of the areas of conflict associated with the massacres of 1622 and 1644 is in itself remarkable.

English fur trader Jenkin Price, visiting one of the Indian villages, provided Norwood with an Indian guide named Jack, who would lead the survivors down to Accomac on the Eastern Shore. It was to be a long walk, but eventually the little party reached Price's Northampton County plantation. Passed from plantation to plantation, Norwood crossed Chesapeake Bay in mid-February aboard a sloop sent by the colony and landed near the home of Ralph Wormeley, where he found the house full of old royalist friends from Holland. The next morning, on a borrowed horse, Norwood set out for Jamestown and Governor Berkeley's seat at Green Spring, where he would remain until May.

Of the three adventurers who had left England with such high hopes in September, all three survived, Major Fox having been among those passengers who had reached Jamestown aboard the *Virginia Merchant*. As for the battered and broken ship, its carcass was beached somewhere along the James River, where its remains may yet be found by future archaeologists.

At Berkeley's bidding, Norwood was sent to England as an emissary to the still-exiled king with the governor's request that he be appointed treasurer of Virginia. And he was, though he never returned to America. Instead, he became a controversial deputy governor of Tangier. Samuel Pepys would record in his diary that on February 4, 1666, he dined with Norwood in London and was surprised by his passion for discussing his meat and drink, which he did "with the curiosity and joy that methinks was below men of worth."

But just as rich men who once were poor may become obsessed with saving, so Henry Norwood's memory of that frozen January day 16 years earlier, when he had urged the living to eat the dead, may have left a taste that could be expunged only by a surfeit of words.

Ghosts at Green Spring

In the gathering darkness amid the ruins something stirred . . .

Dave Doody

A leaning wall of Green Spring's colonial plant nursery (above) reminds us of past glories. In the labeled portrait (opposite), Sir William Berkeley uncharacteristically poses in a dancing master's notion of a martial stance.

COLONEL NORWOOD'S RIDE from Ralph Wormeley's house at the mouth of the York River to Green Spring took him first to Jamestown, where he learned that the almost derelict *Virginia Merchant* had limped into the James without any further loss of life. That he and his sickly band had been deliberately marooned on a Delaware island must have been explained away by a glib Captain Locker, for there is no evidence that Norwood ever attempted to bring him to book.

The colony's governor Sir William Berkeley (then pronounced and sometimes spelled Barkly) greeted Norwood on his arrival at Jamestown and then took him to his mansion house at Green Spring. By mid-17th-century Virginia standards, it was a massive and impressive pile, its principal feature being a five-arched colonnade. Scarcely eight years old when Norwood first entered it, the building was not as large as it appeared, its principal room—described in an undated inventory as a "spacious hall"—measured only about 20-by-26 feet. Nevertheless, it

Sir WILLIAM BERKELEY Brother
to JOHN the first Lord BERKELEY of

was to be the setting for decisions that would shape the politics of Virginia for decades to come and even perhaps of America in its groping toward human rights.

Berkeley was appointed to the governorship by Charles I in 1641, just a year before England's first 17th-century civil war broke out, a war that was to end four years later in a parliamentary victory and two years later still with the king's public execution. Royalist supporter Henry Norwood remembered "the horror and despairs" to which Cavalier minds were reduced "at the bloody and bitter stroke of his assassination." While the rank and file of

the crown's disbanded army went home to make the best of life under the protectorship of Oliver Cromwell and his puritanical Parliament, many of the king's officers fled first to Holland and then to Virginia. Norwood was among them, and he recalled that in Rotterdam a tavern keeper, whose name would later become familiar to Virginians, "kept a victualling house in that town, liv'd good repute, and was the general host of our nation there." That was John Custis—father of John Custis of Arlington in Northampton County—who would become a vigorous supporter of Governor Berkeley when, like his king, he was faced with

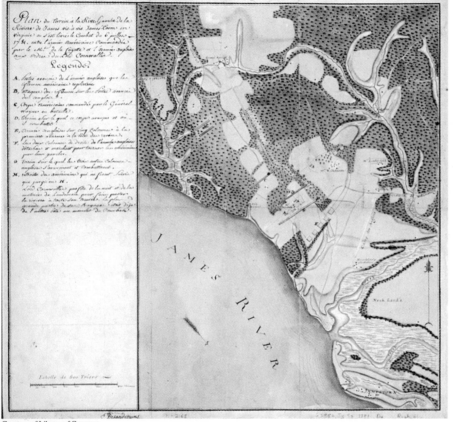

Colonel Desandroüin's 1781 map of the Green Spring battlefield (above) includes at top left the layout of the plantation and its road to Jamestown. The aerial view (right and opposite) looks across the open ground of the 19th- and 17th/18th-century house sites and down the road to Jamestown, seen now as a shadow through the woods. Lady Berkeley watched through a broken window (left), as the king's commissioners departed down that same road.

demands for civil rights that could lead only to civil war.

In England, the first war ended in 1646 and would have remained so had not local committees assumed dictatorial powers that the vanquished could not tolerate. The war broke out again in 1648; and on January 30, 1649, the headsman's ax severed England from her monarchy, two months before Pontefract Castle, the last bastion of the Royalist cause, fell to Cromwell's New Model Army.

After some hesitancy the Scots remained loyal to the monarchy and in August 1650 provided the exiled Charles II with a springboard for invasion. In spite of suffering a shattering defeat in September, the following January Charles was crowned at Scone, the traditional coronation setting for Scottish kings, and in August marched south to claim the English throne. His subsequent defeat and flight at the Battle of Worcester brought to an end nine years of civil war, a victory that republican Cromwell described as "a crowning mercy."

It was against this backdrop of smoke, bloodshed, and uncertainty that Virginia's colonists looked for guidance, their allegiance at risk for nigh on 16 years. Governor Berkeley had no

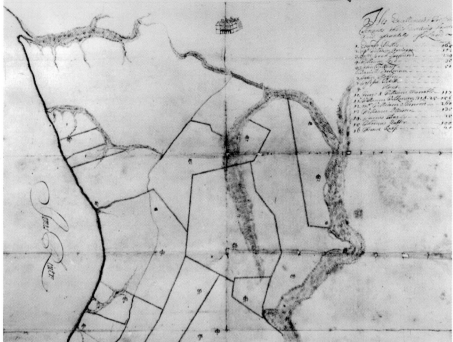

A late 17th-century plat of the parcels south of Green Spring (right) includes the only contemporary rendering of the original manor house, at top center. Its plan is depicted in heavy outline (below) in a drawing that shows it in relation to later Ludwell expansion. Benjamin Latrobe's careful rendering of the decaying mansion and its environs (1796), bears little resemblance to the archaeologically revealed foundations.

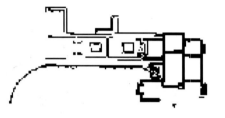

Courtesy of William Salt Library, Stafford, W.S.L., D1716/24

Courtesy of Maryland Historical Society

doubts. He was the king's appointee, and no republican edict would unseat him. As Norwood put it, "he shew'd great respect to all the royal party, who made that colony their refuge. His house and purse were open to all that were so qualify'd."

In May 1650, thinking that the exiled Charles II was in Holland, Berkeley provided Norwood with money to go there to seek the king's appointment as treasurer of the colony, a post "which the governor took to be void by the delinquency" of the incumbent William Claibourne. Two years later Claibourne would be back as secretary of state aboard a fleet loaded with sol-

diers prepared to oust Berkeley. Claibourne and a respected Puritan moderate, Richard Bennett, were two of four commissioners sent out by Parliament (the others drowned on the way) to replace Berkeley and his Royalists with a governor and council appointed by the Cromwellians. Berkeley raised 1,000 men and prepared to defend Jamestown against the parliamentary troops. But after the Assembly had carefully reviewed the terms of surrender and found them far less punitive than expected, Berkeley agreed to step down and to disband his army.

For the next eight years Berkeley retired to Green Spring

The Berkeley-Ludwell mansion complex was revealed for the second time by Dr. Louis Caywood in 1954–1955 (left). He is shown working at his drafting table in the basement of the old manor house. Below is a grim reminder of Governor Berkeley's harsh justice—a human leg and halved pelvis found in a Jamestown well. Today, only a wall of the nursery and, beyond to the right, the ruined jail bear visible witness to the diversity of what once was there (bottom).

Courtesy of National Park Service

Dave Doody

and there continued to receive his Royalist friends. Meanwhile in England, the death of Oliver Cromwell in 1658 and the accession to the status of Lord Protector by his less-than-dynamic son Richard found the republican dream falling apart. Parliaments came and went, and one attempted revolution followed another, until General George Monk, the Commonwealth's most successful tactician, concluded that enough was enough and was instrumental in restoring the monarchy.

Following the death of Virginia's Governor Samuel Mathews in 1658, the Assembly had already turned again to Berkeley,

appointing him provisional governor with instructions to uphold the present parliamentary laws of England—which he did "in the interests of the King in order to save His Majesty's colony from divisions and ruin from within." Once again Green Spring had become the political and social center of Virginia.

Confirmed by the king on July 31, 1660, Berkeley was now "his Majesties Governor" and no longer answerable to the burgesses. For the next 17 years he ruled Virginia with an increasingly autocratic hand. Most Virginians expected that their governor's loyalty to the crown would be rewarded by special

143

favors. Instead, the king followed in his predecessors' footsteps, imposing trade restrictions and ordering a curb on tobacco growing, the colonists' principal source of income. To make matters worse, the summer of 1666 yielded the largest crop ever, so great that half rotted in the barns unable to be shipped, thus causing prices to plunge.

Berkeley's fear that British war with the Dutch would bring an enemy fleet into the Chesapeake prompted him to impose painful taxes to pay for military preparedness. By 1667, therefore, when the Peace of Breda called a five-year halt to hostilities, Virginia's Secretary Philip Ludwell declared that only God had kept the impoverished people "from mutiny and confusion."

By this time the kindness shown by the Indians toward Colonel Norwood and his sickly band had become an event less well remembered than more recent reports of murders and scalpings that led Berkeley to declare war on the Potomac and Doeg Indians. On August 31, 1675, he and his Council met at Green Spring and ordered Colonel John Washington and Major Isaac Allerton to raise the militia and to "attacque and do such execution upon the Indians as shall be found necessary and just."

The war did not go well. The next months found small groups of Indians attacking and slaughtering wherever and whenever the opportunity arose. Berkeley's response was to build forts and other defensive positions, believing that moderation was the best policy in dealing with so elusive an enemy. The colonists, by and large, did not agree.

When residents of Charles City heard that a large war party was heading their way, they sent a deputation to the governor seeking permission to raise a company of volunteers and go against the Indians. But the delegation found Berkeley in no mood to be pressured. He called them "fools and loggerheads" and sent them away, shouting "A pox take you!"

A visit to the already assembled volunteers by planter Nathaniel Bacon, Jr., proved too heady a reception to be ignored; and, before he knew it, Bacon found himself at the head of a rag-tag army drawn largely from the small and impoverished landowners outside the circle of the governor and his grandees. But having taken up arms without the governor's commission, Bacon's followers were embarking on a civil war—the war between the haves and have-nots that for so long had been the legislature's recurring nightmare.

Aged 28 and a resident of the colony for scarcely a year, Berkeley, nevertheless, appointed Bacon to his Council, declaring the young man to be of a quality rare in the colony and therefore deserving of rapid advancement. Now, two years later, the governor was calling this rare young man a rebel and his followers mutineers. Bacon was also an Indian fighter, and when he won, he found himself the colony's hero—much to the frustration of the Lord of Green Spring.

The story of Bacon's Rebellion has oft been told, but it also is the story of Green Spring, where a once-beloved governor and his manipulative wife listened only to the voices of rich, royalist sycophants. At 70 Berkeley wore his years poorly; he was deaf, mercurial, hasty in his judgment, a harborer of grudges, and no longer in control of events. "How miserable," he wrote, "that man is who governs a people wher six parts of seven at least are poore[,] endebted[,] discontented[,] and armed." The fact that the

armed and discontented had grown to see their aged governor as the Indians' protector strengthened their support for the young and decisive Bacon.

Knowing that the rebel army was encamped near modern Richmond, Berkeley and his remaining supporters crossed the York to Gloucester to try to raise an opposing force, but found few if any volunteers. Gloucester, he discovered, was for Bacon. Before returning to Jamestown, Berkeley stripped the fort at Gloucester Point of its arms and ammunition lest it fall into rebel hands—a step that was to light the fuse of the explosion to come.

Late July found Bacon's army encamped at Middle Plantation (destined to become Williamsburg) in the very heart of the colony, where he urged all who cared for the peace and future of "His Majesty's distracted Colony," to meet in convention. Declaring himself "General by Consent of the People" and calling on those present to sign an oath of loyalty to him, Bacon issued a declaration justifying his assumption of supreme power and demanding the surrender or arrest of the governor and 19 of his "wicked and pernicious councellors," declaring them traitors to the king.

Some of Bacon's supporters balked when they learned that he also expected them to subscribe to opposing the king's troops, if they should be sent against them. But while they debated this issue that went beyond ousting a governor to defying their king, word reached the convention that Indians were attacking in Gloucester County. Residents who had fled to the fort pleaded that they were in desperate need of the arms that the governor had capriciously removed. On hearing that news, the last waverers hurriedly put their names to Bacon's Declaration.

Firm in his belief that war with the Indians took precedence over his intent to oust the governor, Bacon led his troops in forays against them. Meanwhile, Berkeley retreated to the still-loyal Eastern Shore, where he set up his headquarters at John Custis's Arlington plantation. There he assembled a fleet and enough not-overly-eager soldiery to oppose Bacon in the field. With this force Berkeley occupied undefended Jamestown and proceeded to fortify it against the expected attack.

By this time Bacon's army had grown from about 136 to some 300 and had chosen Berkeley's Green Spring home as their camp from which to march on Jamestown. After five days of skirmishing and cannonading, Berkeley realized that his Eastern Shore recruits lacked the zeal to die for him, and so he took them home—abandoning Jamestown to Bacon's incendiaries.

Buoyed by their easy victory, Bacon's troops returned to Green Spring, where for several days they amused themselves, no doubt to the ruination of Berkeley's possessions. Thus rested, the army moved to Gloucester County, where three weeks later an already sick Bacon died.

Robbed of their eloquent and charismatic leader, the rebel army broke up into local companies that, one by one, succumbed to Berkeley's forces. The governor retook Green Spring on January 22, 1677, and found it a shambles, its foodstuffs looted and its horses, sheep, and fences gone. Nevertheless, a month later the mansion was in sufficiently good order to host the General Assembly. Green Spring also was an ill-prepared host to 200 of Berkeley's own troops as well as to 30 rebel prisoners (probably the men stationed there at the time of Bacon's death) whose fate the grimly vindictive governor had yet to decide. It was there, too, that Bacon's friend and neighbor Captain James Crewes was court-martialed before being hanged on the road to Jamestown at nearby Glasshouse Point.

In the months following his return to power, Berkeley's minions routed out rebel suspects wherever they could be found or imagined. The public gibbet and the hangman's noose became frighteningly common sights—this regardless of the fact that the king had sent over a pardon to all but the already dead Nathaniel Bacon. The pardon had been carried by two of the three royal commissioners, all charged with investigating the rebellion's causes and finding the means to restore peace and tranquility to a turbulent colony. Lest there should be any doubt of their purpose, the commissioners arrived with 11 ships and 1,000 soldiers.

One of the three commissioners was Colonel Francis Moryson—the same Francis Morrison who had been marooned and near death with Henry Norwood on the Delaware island and who had been appointed by the king to be commander of the fort at Jamestown. He later became speaker of the House of Burgesses and much later deputy governor of Virginia. Now, however, he had returned with the king's warrant to examine the conduct of Governor Berkeley, the man who had given him shelter and friendship in earlier, happier days.

At the Green Spring meeting of the General Assembly, the members proclaimed the king's pardon to the rebels—but not as broadly as he had intended. Hangings continued, and fines and property seizures not only crippled Bacon's supporters but enriched the purses of Berkeley and his Green Spring gentry. Worse, the proclamation refused to pardon "persons or persons whatsoever (although they be not perticularly named . . .) that did beare any command," thus keeping old Baconian supporters in fear for their lives. Even servants who had dutifully followed their masters in Bacon's cause were to be punished—their sentences cruelly deferred until their indentures expired.

The governor's first term of office and the early years of his second, marked by liberal and wise policies, had deteriorated into a reign of terror as much an enemy to tranquillity as an Indian's shout or the muzzle of a rebel musket. Wrote a York County resident: "the Hangman [was] more dredfull to the Baconians, then there Generall was to the Indians; as it is counted more honourable, and less terable, to dye like a Souldier, then to be hang'd like a dogg." When, eventually, Berkeley surrendered his governorship and returned to England, the king is reputed to have observed that the "old fool has hanged more men in that naked country than he had done for the murther of his father."

Berkeley did not go quietly into the twilight of history. Encouraged by a likeminded, vengeful, and much younger wife, he tarried too long in Virginia, and when finally he did go, he let it be known that he intended to return. Thus the dark shadow of Berkeley's vengeance lingered on.

The king's commissioners had treated the volatile governor with gentlemanly restraint and had put up with his frequent tactical delays, obfuscation, and deferred departure. They even acquiesced to some of his hangings and the public humiliation of the king's pardoned rebels; but one event taxed them beyond breaking.

On April 22, 1677, the three commissioners visited Berkeley and several Council members at Green Spring. On taking their leave, Colonel Moryson and his colleagues—who lived aboard the ship *Bristol* moored in the James River—expected to be driven to the landing place by the governor's liveried coachman. Instead, he had been replaced by another of Berkeley's more prominent servants—the public hangman. The commissioners complained that the "public odium and disgrace cast upon us" became the talk of the colony. They also noted that Lady Berkeley had gone into her own chamber to witness their discomfort through a "broken quarrel of the glass," and they blamed her for the insult.

The commissioners' statement is of interest on several counts; first, that Lady Berkeley had a broken window in her bedroom; second, that it may be evidence of damage to the house at the hands of Bacon's soldiers; and third, that the quality of the glass in Green Spring's casement windows was of such poor quality that its color and unevenness rendered it optically useless. That in itself is not surprising, because most 17th-century window glass was of that quality. What is surprising is that in the three cold months since the Berkeley's reoccupied Green Spring, nobody had repaired her ladyship's window.

The house, she said, had become "like one of those the boys pull down at Shrovetide, & was almost as much to repair as if it had beene new to build." Lady Frances Culpeper Berkeley was prone to exaggeration. The widow of Captain Samuel Stephen of Warwick County and kin to Lord Culpeper, who was destined to succeed her second husband, Frances was only 43 when Berkeley sailed for England. She would not see him again. The once respected and finally feared and hated governor died shortly after his arrival. The twice widowed Lady Frances soon married one of Berkeley's closest Green Spring associates, Colonel Philip Ludwell, thus bringing title to the plantation into that family where it would remain for more than a century.

Ludwell continued to play important roles in colonial politics, being elected Speaker of the House of Burgesses, an envoy to England, and in 1693 Governor of North Carolina. What changes, if any, were made to the mansion that Lady Berkeley had described as "the first seat in America & the only tollerable place for a Governour" remains unclear. But many were to come—so many that architectural historians lost track of who did what or when.

Most of the 18th century came and went, leaving Green Spring to pass from one Ludwell to another, with "improvements" large and small reflecting the changing tastes of the times. Then came the second populist war to track its troops across Green Spring's acres. On July 6, 1781, a retreating British army under Lord Cornwallis—he would have called it a redeployment—was preparing to cross the river at Jamestown when an overly eager Anthony Wayne and his 900 cavalry and riflemen under the command of the Marquis de Lafayette ran into the back of it. Realizing too late that Cornwallis had set a trap for them, the Americans were routed in what came to be known as the Battle of Greenspring Farm.

The Green Spring residence that had slipped from mansion house to farmhouse was briefly the marshaling area for Wayne's troops, who reportedly left it in ruinous condition. Farm though it may have been, it covered no small area. French cartographer Colonel Desandroüin's 1781 map shows a central, south-facing,

L-shaped block with three flanking outbuildings to east and west and three more on each side extending southward. Three others are shown in no particular order. Few Tidewater plantations were better arrayed.

In 1796 owner William Ludwell Lee hired the French architect Benjamin Latrobe to propose how the house could be repaired and improved. Although Latrobe's proposals remained just that, he did make a surviving drawing showing how the south elevation might have looked had they been implemented. Latrobe called Green Spring "the oldest inhabited house in North America," and evidently assumed that the L-shaped plan was essentially the same as that adopted by Berkeley in the 1640s. "It is a brick building of great solidity," wrote Latrobe, "but no attempt at grandeur. The lower story was covered by an arcade which is pulled down," he went on. "The porch has some clumsy ornamental brickwork about the style of James the first."

Latrobe evidently learned about the mansion's history as Ludwell family members thought they knew it. "Many of the first Virginian assemblies were held in the very room in which I was plotting the death of Muskitoes," he wrote. It is true, nonetheless, that the house remained the seat of Virginian power for some time after Berkeley's departure. Lady Frances rented it to Governor Culpeper in 1680 and to his successor Lord Howard of Effingham four years later. We know, too, that the General Assembly convened there in 1691. But was the room where Latrobe swatted mosquitoes really the one where all that and more had happened?

In 1929 Jesse Dimmick, an amateur antiquary and owner of the property, undertook an extensive excavation of the house site and came up with a relatively accurate plan of the foundation. Regardless of Dimmick having found the 1781 Desandroüin map's garden wall cutting across—and thus postdating—the easterly foundation, architectural historian Thomas Waterman concluded that the long, three-room ground plan extending westward represented the Berkeley period, adding that "This arrangement was almost certainly unique in seventeenth-century Virginia."

With the approach of Virginia's 350th birthday in 1957 and the establishment of the Virginia 350th Anniversary Commission, its chairman declared that "the preservation of the [Green Spring] site would be one of the most valuable permanent effects of the Jamestown Festival which could possibly be achieved." To that end, the state underwrote another excavation, this time under the direction of National Park Service archeologist Louis R. Caywood. Most of his work involved the thankless task of reexcavating foundations previously dug out by Dimmick, and he did it at the worst possible time of the year and to the detriment of the remains that the excavation was intended to preserve. Wrote Caywood: "The most disheartening development was to see the day-to-day deterioration of the brick and mortar in the foundation as they literally exploded from the constant freezing and thawing conditions to which they were subjected, sometimes for weeks." The weather from January to March, Caywood explained, "was most uncooperative."

That the work was done when it should not have been is explained by the 350th Anniversary Commission's eagerness to have the Berkeley "manor house" reconstructed in time for its 1957 celebration—no matter at what cost to the foundations. The

dollar cost to fully reconstruct the building and its environment was less easily ignored. The price would almost certainly be higher than the commission could afford, and so it looked first to the tobacco industry and then to the man for whom rebuilding another governor's palace was but a drop in his monetary bucket.

On an April day in 1955, John D. Rockefeller, Jr., is said to have been persuaded to visit the site of Louis Caywood's excavations. He saw, he thanked, he departed. The commission's report said only that "the failure to find a sponsor to finance the project" discouraged the state from any attempt at restoration. The report did take credit for providing funds late in 1955 "to back-fill and thus protect the crumbling foundations of the most important plantation house of 17th-century Virginia'"—which, having put them so damagingly at risk, was work that should have been funded and completed much sooner.

With Caywood unable to date accurately any of the changes and additions to the Green Spring complex, and in spite of the discovery in 1957 of a tiny drawing, the appearance of Sir William Berkeley's plantation house remains elusive. Its historical and architectural importance, however, have not diminished, for it still remains, as the state's 1957 commission claimed, "the most important plantation house of 17th-century Virginia." One can but hope, therefore, that sufficient interest can be aroused to enable a third excavation to find the answers that eluded both Dimmick and Caywood.

The house site and the acres immediately around it were purchased by the National Park Service in 1967 for a modest $526.31 an acre, with a view to creating a historic corridor between it and Jamestown along the unspoiled and beautiful Greenspring Road. Now in an era of cut-backs and underfunding, the Park Service has no plans to develop Green Spring. The site lies locked and silent, and the road to Jamestown is no longer unspoiled.

Those who believe in the supernatural will tell you that places once the scene of great emotional or physical stress retain their energy and can release it years, even centuries, later to those of us tuned to the right wave length. Having had two such experiences (albeit 50 years ago), I visited the Green Spring site at dusk on January 22, 1996—319 years to the day since a victorious Governor Berkeley returned to oust its defenders and begin the reign of terror that so horrified the colony.

The trees were still; the ground was hard, cold, and crackled under foot. The headlights of my parked car barely carried to the only still standing ruin—the one known as the jail and believed to have housed Berkeley's doomed prisoners. I listened there for the rattle of fetters of the pleading voices of the weak, the cold, and the hungry.

Standing on the house site, I thought for a moment that I heard a woman's laughter—Lady Frances watching through her broken window? I remembered her husband's propensity for expletives and listened in the gathering dark for his rasping voice as he raged against rogues and traitors, perhaps in the room on whose site I was standing. I heard a snapping twig as the fall of a gavel ending the court martial that sent Captain Crewes stumbling past me down the dirt road to his death at Glasshouse Point. Suddenly a chill wind blew across the open field rustling the dead grass; I pulled my coat tighter around me and was anxious to be gone. At Green Spring there should be, must be, ghosts.

The Ruins of Rosewell

Virginia archaeological jewel finds in its glittering past a new beginning

William K. Geiger

If thou would'st view fair Rosewell aright,
Go visit it by the pale moonlight . . .

THE LINES ARE BORROWED from English poet Sir Walter Scott's evocation of the ruined Melrose Abbey in Roxburghshire, but his advice applies equally well to Virginia's Rosewell. No more romantic ruin survives from the glory days of British America, and in the eyes of many architectural historians no finer house was ever built.

I saw it first in the summer of 1956 —glimpsed is a better word, for a jungle of trees and creepers enshrouded it so tightly that coming upon it was akin to discovering a Mayan ruin in the forests of Guatemala. Hacking one's way with a machete amid the vines, you'd see through the leaves the arched corner of a majestic brick window opening; and later as wind nudged the treetops, a massive stone chimney cap would appear blindingly white in the sunlight, only to vanish as quickly as the green curtain closed again below it. I remember well the steamy summer silence. Only the rustling of wind-stirred leaves intruded. No crickets chirped, no birds sang—save for the occasional rasping cry of a distant crow clearing its throat.

The sense of melancholy that encompassed the ruin is impossible adequately to describe. Suffice it to say that on a boiling summer's day when salt-laden perspiration dripped from one's brow, sudden and inexplicable cold chills coursed down

In ruin Rosewell is perhaps more awesome than its builder intended.

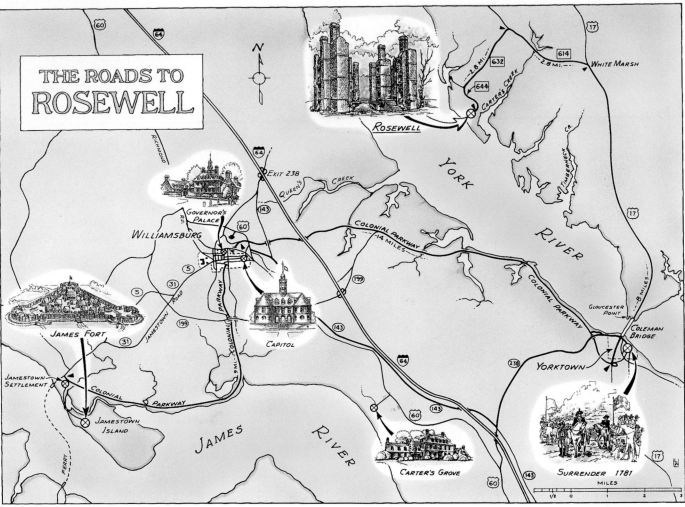

Louis Luedtke

one's spine. Small wonder was it that Rosewell was said to be haunted.

The house burned in 1916, bringing to its close a chronicle which, like that of many another Virginia mansion, had begun in wealth, dignity, power, and optimism, and ended in penury and despair. The history of the property—though not of the house—goes back to 1639, when George Menefie was granted 3,000 acres on the north bank of the York River. The tract was flanked by Jones and Timberneck creeks. Between them intruded the wide bay and creek first known as Rosewell and later as Carter's Creek. There, in the wake of subsequent sales and inheritances, and at the close of the 17th century, Mathew Page and his wife Mary Mann built their home—a home of which, until recently, we knew nothing about.

Mathew Page died in 1703, and his widow, who owned the Rosewell tract through dower right, married his cousin John Page. Two years later Mary Mann Page died. She left the land and the home to her son Mann Page I, who was then in England acquiring the education, taste, and aspirations of an English gentleman.

Short of watching a friend's vacation slides, few experiences are more painful than reading his family's genealogy. But to understand the rise and decline of Rosewell, a few more begats are unavoidable.

By the time Mann Page returned to Virginia in 1712, he was

not only a young man of property but also of presence. And if anybody doubted it, his marriage to Judith, daughter of the colony's secretary, Ralph Wormeley of Rosegill, ensured his place at Virginia's top table. Alas, in 1716, Judith Page and her new-born infant died at Rosewell and were buried in the family graveyard to the east of Mathew Page's old house. If the young widower was inconsolable, he bravely overcame it and within a year had married better still—this time to another Judith, the daughter of Virginia's richest planter, Robert "King" Carter of Corotoman.

Robert Carter's home in Lancaster County became the legendary genesis for the several great mansions built by his progeny and relatives in Tidewater Virginia, among them the mansion begun by Mann Page I in 1726, five years after his grandfather's Rosewell burned down. Before it was complete, Corotoman also burned—without leaving behind any pictorial rendering or description of its supposed grandeur. Only nearby Christ Church testified to King Carter's architectural taste. Built by him in 1732, its gauged and rubbed brick doorways, one with an arched and the other an appexed pediment, were closely paralleled by the north and south entrances to Rosewell. The supposition that Mann Page was earning brownie points with his father-in-law by copying his house seemed to make sense—until the foundations of Corotoman were archaeologically excavated and found to bear no resemblance to Rosewell or to any other Tidewater mansion.

Where woodland now surrounds the mansion ruin, gardens once reached to a boat landing on Carter's Creek (above). Beyond flows the York River on whose opposite side lies the mouth of Queen's Creek, the colonial water route between Williamsburg and the Page plantation. Through a basement arch (left) archaeological committee director Captain George Whiting and the author discuss current consolidation work with Richard Pape, who is responsible for the property's maintenance.

Rosewell was no copy. Instead, it was a structure unique in Virginia's colonial history: three full stories over an English basement, with projecting pavilions at east and west, each pierced by tall, arched windows that cast cathedral-like shafts of light into the stair hall, and the pile grandly topped by stone-capped chimney stacks that in silhouette resembled giant nails anchoring the regal building to the common earth beneath. As the huge stacks of locally made bricks and imported Portland stone nestled into walls that grew ever taller, many an awed Virginian must have compared them to the newly built Governor's Palace in Williamsburg—and some historians have concluded that that was Mann Page's intent. But if so, he did not live to savor the satisfaction. He died in 1730, leaving to his widow "the mansion then building."

At that time, and since the 1721 fire, Mann and Judith Page had been living elsewhere; and consequently, Judith inherited an as-yet-undiscovered "dwelling house" and its associated outbuildings. The brick mansion was still unfinished in 1737 when her son, Mann II, fell heir to the Rosewell estate, and it was he who finally completed the building. He also inherited his father's debts. It would appear that by 1744 he was in financial difficulty, and the Rosewell mansion had received its last enrichment.

As would Nathaniel Burwell of Carter's Grove, Mann Page II decided that the lower Tidewater was no longer to his liking and so set about building a new house in Spotsylvania County. To do so, he had to sell off some of his Rosewell acres, a step that—like Burwell's move to far-off Frederick County and the subsequent neglect of Carter's Grove—began Rosewell's retreat from greatness.

Around 1765, Mann Page II's eldest son John moved into the vacated mansion and learned to his cost that tobacco farming in Gloucester County was an unreliable way to wealth. Writing to his London agent, John Norton, on May 27, 1769, Page explained that

. . . no Body hates the Thoughts of being in Debt more than I do: but the Great Scarcity of Money here, the Shortness of my Crops for four years past, & the necessary Expenses of an increasing Family joined to the Commencement of Housekeeping in a large House, have forced me to submit to it for a while . . .

Ivor Noël Hume

Courtesy of Rosewell Foundation, photo by Alice Hoachlander

Dave Doody

The jungle that surrounded the ruins in 1956 (opposite) was cleared by Rosewell Foundation volunteers in the 1980s, allowing professionals from the James River Institute for Archaeology to begin exploring the mansion's environs (above). Exposed in the foreground are the remains of an earlier building about which nothing was known until the digging began. Left: Fragments of melted window glass spilling from within the unexcavated ruin reminded the author that the mansion's final hours have yet to be archaeologically studied.

Another four years found him no better off and painfully aware that a big house has matching maintenance demands. Writing again to Norton, this time on October 11, 1771, Page admitted that "as my house is very much out of Repair, I have engaged a Man to put it into a saving Condition next Spring." He enclosed a list of paint, nails, and related materials to do the job, among them "A Glaziers Diamond of a 20/ Value." Windows evidently needed replacing, and 186 years later archaeology would provide a clue to which windows those were.

John Page never regained the wealth of his forebears. On the contrary, his financial fortunes declined even as his political star rose. Elected to the House of Burgesses in 1771 and a member of Lord Dunmore's Council, he made his allegiance clear when he joined the Committee of Safety. In the war that followed, Page saw active duty in the campaign against Benedict Arnold. He was elected to Congress in 1789 and held his seat until 1796; six years later he crowned his career by becoming governor of Virginia. He died in 1808, leaving a life interest in Rosewell to his widow Margaret. Being a resident in Williamsburg, Margaret Lowther Page presumably joined many another absentee landlord, either hiring overseers to run the plantation or letting it to tenants. Neither course would have furthered the needs of so maintenance-hungry a house.

Forty years later, Rosewell and its remaining acres were still in the hands of John Page's executors, who doubtless had been loath to spend more on repairs than was absolutely unavoidable. In 1837, therefore, when they received an offer from neighbor Thomas B. Booth, it was one that they had not the slightest desire to refuse.

Thomas Booth's entry into the Rosewell story is sometimes portrayed as one might the black-cloaked villain of a Victorian melodrama. Colonial Williamsburg architectural historians Howard Dearstyne and Lawrence Kocher in their book *Shadows in Silver* described him as one who "should rank high in the annals of vandalism." Although disgruntled descendants have assured me that Booth has been sorely misjudged, he has been charged with selling the lead from the mansion's roof, the marble mantels, the pavers from the central hall, and the paneling from the walls. He is accused, too, of dismantling the wall around the Mann and Page family graveyard and selling its bricks and of felling the stately avenue of cedars that lined the mansion's landward approach. He had bought the property for $12,000, sold the scrap for $35,000, and 10 years later disposed of the mutilated plantation to his cousin John T. Catlett for $22,000, thus earning a nice profit of $45,000—and a nasty reputation.

Catlett, who already owned adjacent land on Carter's Creek, moved into the denuded mansion in or soon after 1847. During Booth's allegedly destructive ownership, Rosewell's taxable value had declined by about a third. But in John Catlett's hands, between 1850 and 1851 it tripled, suggesting that he undertook major improvements needed both to halt its decay and to convert it into a livable, albeit oversized, Virginian-Victorian home.

Opinions differ as to the pleasures of living at Rosewell in the post-Civil War years, but descendants of the Page and Dean families (the Deans of Gloucester bought it from Catlett in 1853) have fond childhood memories of visits and parties there in the years immediately preceding the 1916 fire. In stark contrast, however, is this description written at the end of the 19th century:

Dismantled now and scarcely habitable, with a dismal "flavor of mild decay" pervading its halls and passageways, as if the sickly malarial damp creeping up from the river had bored to the very marrow of its wooden bones, this relic of Colonial Virginia, once the pride of its fair lords, shivers out the last years of the span of life allotted it, neglected and forgotten.

So said Thomas Allen Glenn in his book *Some Colonial Mansions*, published in 1899.

"Nonsense!" cry the friends of Rosewell; but the author was right in prophesying the end of the mansion's allotted span. On March 24, 1916, a fire broke out that could not be contained and, by the time it had run its course, only the four walls remained, their melted and smoldering windows staring like black-ringed, sightless eyes, framing the smoking void within.

Had the devastated Dean family the will, and more importantly the money to do so, they might have erected a temporary roof to protect the walls for future restoration. But in 1916 Virginia, in those pre-Colonial Williamsburg days, there were no preservationists to hurry to the rescue. What was gone was gone. As their rural forebears had from countless charred ruins before them, the family salvaged what little it could and left Rosewell to the beckoning hands of nature. But unlike the blackened skeletons of abandoned wood-built homes, Rosewell proved difficult to absorb. Although trees and underbrush rapidly consumed the once formal gardens, and a few trees sprouted amid the rubble within the walls, the structure remained grandly and defiantly intact. Not until 1955 when the south face collapsed did the process of decay accelerate.

Both the date and the responsibility for the collapse have been debated, one thesis blaming 1955's hurricane Diane and another an oversized explosion at the military testing ground across the river at Camp Peary. Indisputable, though, is the certainty that with the box broken, the stability of the remaining walls was jeopardized. Nevertheless, approaching from the north as I did in the summer of 1956, the damage was obscured, and the walls and chimneys appeared awe-inspiringly intact.

Although the 18th-century steps had been replaced by an ugly concrete platform, one could approach and stand in the splendid doorway that architect Thomas Waterman described as "the finest and most elaborate of the period." Because it is not for an archaeologist to tread on architectural toes by waxing euphoric about details he is incompetent to correctly describe, I must be content to recall that even to the layest of eyes, the rich molding of the architrave frame, the narrow pilasters with their fine rubbed bricks separated and defined by wafer-thin lines of white shell mortar, left one in awe of the builder's skills and evident prior architectural experience.

But just as a poor man may walk a dark street in safety while a wealthy man may not, so the richness of Rosewell's structure proved its ultimate undoing. In the late 1950s and '60s architectural vandals—people who surely should have known better—went with hammers and chisels to chip away the cut and

Bits and pieces tell the story

Digging near the mansion ruin in 1957–1959 yielded a treasure trove of artifacts—among them hundreds of green bottle fragments. The almost-intact pear-shaped bottle was once cased in wicker and came from France; the seal bears the initials of Mann Page II and comes from a bottle of the 1760s. The other bottles date ca. 1729–1730, as does the wine glass. The three glass seals are from Flemish Pyrmont Water bottles. The pewter shoebuckle bears the slogan NO EXCISE and was worn by a supporter of the English radical John Wilkes. To its right are sleeve buttons and a French silver half-écu of King Louis XV dated 1719. At bottom left a saltglaze "house" teapot of about 1745 in the Colonial Williamsburg Collection parallels a fragment from the Rosewell site. At the other end of the social scale are fragments of an Indian bowl (beside trowel) made in a European shape and probably used by Rosewell slaves in the mid-18th century.

Rosewell volunteer leader George Whiting (below) examines a rubble-filled wall trench discovered in 1996 that may be part of the stable.

Hans Lorenz

Ivor Noël Hume

Courtesy of Rosewell Foundation

153

Dave Doody

molded brickwork of the north doorway until eventually nothing remained. More desirable than bricks were the fluted Portland keystones that capped each window, and for many a year one of them would decorate a garden behind a home on Williamsburg's Duke of Gloucester Street. Like the ears of an exhausted and dying bull, these were Rosewell's ultimate trophies. To cut them loose the collectors spent many a barbarous hour hurling bats and rocks at the adjacent brickwork until it eventually fell away and the stones dropped.

How do I know?

Because I watched them at work but did nothing to prevent them—for reasons that I am about to explain.

On my first visit to Rosewell I was accompanied by Colonial Williamsburg's archaeological conservator John Van Ness Dunton. While struggling through the woods in search of the icehouse he came upon a groundhog burrow beneath the roots of a tree. Spoil thrown out at the entrance to the burrow's several tunnels included quantities of oystershells and fragments of 18th-century bottles. The animal had made its home in a Page family trash pit.

The following year, after being invited to return from England to develop a new approach to archaeology in Williamsburg, I realized that I first had to convince the architects' office (of which archaeology was then a mere appendage) that there was more to digging than uncovering old foundations and salvaging builders' hardware. I needed to demonstrate that time capsules provided by abandoned wells and trash-filled pits could yield all manner of tightly datable information about a household's life, possessions, taste, affluence, eating habits—even its politics—at a single moment in history.

So, in the autumn of 1957, with the permission of co-owner Miss Nellie D. Greaves, I returned to Rosewell to evict the groundhog. Fortunately, it had already moved out, leaving, we later discovered, several of the best artifacts assembled in its bed. With the help of my archaeological partner and wife Audrey, John Dunton, and several weekend volunteers, we removed the overlying tree and tried to determine the size of the pit. Most such pits are five or six feet in diameter, four or five feet deep, and take two or three days to excavate. This one turned out to be more than 50 feet long and 21 feet wide, and it kept us busy on and off for 18 months.

Here was no ordinary domestic trash pit but rather, so I concluded, a vast hole dug to extract clay for brickmaking and into which domestic and architectural waste was dumped. Scarcely had we stripped the topsoil on the very first morning of the dig than we discovered a splendidly preserved silver coin that remains to this day the second largest found on a Virginia site—a French half-écu of Louis XV dated 1719. Visions of buried treasure danced like fireflies before our astonished eyes.

That dramatic, never-to-be-forgotten moment would within hours be followed by another when, with my machete, I whacked at a root that turned out to be my thumb. The subsequent flight from the depths of Gloucester County on a Saturday afternoon in search of a doctor equipped with needle and thread added a bloody, coin-rivaling footnote to the latter-day history of Rosewell.

Finding the coin of 1719 at the top of the pit led us to expect that everything buried below would be of similarly early date. But

Opposite: The well-preserved staircase at Tuckahoe plantation (ca. 1712–1730) in Goochland County possesses details closely paralleling the once-grand staircase at Rosewell.

Faded photograph (left) shows the north front of Rosewell around 1910, its basement windows boarded and hinting at the lack of maintenance within. The hall and great staircase (below) were photographed in the 1890s, after paneling had been stripped out. An 18th-century Italian storage jar stands in front of the fireplace; agricultural tools lean in a corner. The once glorious balustrade is marred by straight posts substituting for broken and lost banisters.

Colonial Williamsburg

it wasn't. Instead, the evidence pointed strongly to the pit having been dug and filled no earlier than 1763 and probably in 1772. The first date was provided by a pewter shoe buckle decorated on two sides with hogsheads and at the ends with the slogan NO EXCISE. That cry was loudly proclaimed in England by the radical John Wilkes following passage of the so-called Cyder Act of 1763.

Wilkes became a champion of colonial rights, and his words were avidly read by discontented Virginians. "Pray send me the Newspapers & Magazines & Political Registers regularly," asked Roger Atkinson of Mansfield near Petersburg in 1770, adding that he wanted "Everything that relates to my old friend J. Wilkes, Esq're."

Although John Page's surviving letters do not, to my knowledge, mention Wilkes by name, his disillusioned political views were clear enough—though probably not to Governor Dunmore when the Master of Rosewell was named to his Council. Writing to agent Norton in August 1768, Page had this to say after reading news of pro-Wilkes rioting:

In what an unhappy situation was Great Britain! Unsteadiness in her Councils, Confusion, Riots & Tumults, little short of Rebellion in her very Metropolis; Discontent in all her colonies, each, & every one justly complaining of the Arbitrary Proceedings of Parliament; and many of them provoked at the Severe Restrictions on their Trade, are ready to give a stab almost vital to the Trade of G—t B—n.

How tempting it is to imagine a man in such a mood enjoying the satisfaction of, if not openly wearing his heart on his sleeve, proclaiming it quietly on the top of his shoe!

Fanciful speculation aside, the presence in the pit of a buckle made no earlier than 1763 gave us what archaeologists call a *terminus post quem*—the date after which the pit was filled. However, a more likely and precise terminal date is provided by the presence of architectural debris: worked Portland stone similar to that used to ornament the mansion, builder's hardware, broken paving slabs, plaster, and window glass. The flooring slab fragments were of white Purbeck and black Belgian marble reminiscent of the floor in the hall of the Governor's Palace in Williamsburg. Shell mortar attached to them left no doubt that they had served a similar purpose at Rosewell and were not discarded unused during the construction period. Because the surviving photograph of the hall taken shortly before the fire shows no marble floor, historians had been led to suppose that the slabs had been removed during the 19th-century stripping blamed on Thomas Booth. But now the archeological evidence was saying that the floor may well have been removed or extensively repaired during John Page's renovations in 1771-1772.

No less revealing were the window glass fragments, several of them clearly marked with a glazier's diamond. Was this the tool that John Page ordered from London in 1771? In all probability it was. Another glass fragment recalled the 18th-century practice of scratching inscriptions on windows. That tantalizingly incomplete pane read ". . . orn A . . . ." Was it a mere coincidence that John Page was b[orn A]pril 1743? That clearly was old glass stripped from a broken window, but the pit also yielded new glass in the shape of the central bull's-eye from one of the great discs

called crowns and from which quality window panes were cut.

Most unexpected among the window-glass fragments were pieces from sheets molded in relief with diamond-shaped patterning and designed to admit light while confounding prying eyes. Although an attribute pertinent in crime-ridden cities, it seemed less than essential in the sparsely inhabited depths of colonial Gloucester County. While such glass is recorded as being used to glaze the windows of basements, in more than 20 years of digging in Williamsburg and on Virginia plantations, I have not seen its like again. But I had once before, for I found it in London in a trash deposit dating from the second quarter of the 18th century—glass used and discarded at the time that Mann Page II was completing Rosewell.

Is it not reasonable to conclude, therefore, that a house intended to be the best in Virginia should have its basement windows fitted with the latest thing in window glass? But just as modern novelties are rarely as useful as advertised, so it is likely that John Page's servants, being less concerned about squirrels watching them at work than letting more light into their basement rooms, persuaded him in 1772 to replace the thick molded glass with regular crown panes.

In addition to two brick advance buildings similarly placed to those at the Governor's Palace, Rosewell also possessed a large brick-walled stable that stood to the west of the mansion and was described in an 1802 insurance policy as being 120 feet long and 24 wide. Although in our 1950s digging we failed positively to locate it, we did find buried in the underbrush a short section of brick wall with cobbles—perhaps the stable yard—abutting it. Nearby lay several pieces of worked Portland stone, one of them perhaps the base of a column, suggesting that the stable may have matched the mansion in the grandeur of its design.

From the excavated pit came evidence—scrap iron, cut waste, and unfinished tools—to suggest that the stable unit included a blacksmith's shop. The unexpected discovery of a lump of unprocessed copper ore became less so when we discovered that in 1728 Mann Page I had joined Robert "King" Carter as a partner in the Frying Pan Company to mine copper on the borders of Fairfax and Loudoun counties. Although mining there in 1728 was far in time from a lump of ore discarded at Rosewell in 1772, there may be relevance in a *Virginia Gazette* notice of January 13, 1767, reporting that the ship *Sally* had been cleared out of the York River bound for London and carrying in her cargo five casks of copper ore.

Archaeologists and anthropologists have a penchant for coining imprecise words, and "foodways" is one of them. It is not, contrary to popular belief, the name of a grocery store but a blanket term embracing all things relating to food preparation and consumption. The Rosewell pit provided its share of animal, bird, and fish bones—70 pounds in all (archaeologists like to weigh things) but a meaningless figure, when a few beef bones weigh much more than a lot of fish bits. Nevertheless, the pit revealed that John Page's household ate beef, pig, chicken, turkey, oysters, unidentified fish, perhaps even Carolina box tortoises, but probably not the cat whose bones were found at the bottom.

The ceramics proved even more diverse and ranged from delftware chamber pots and wash bowls to Chinese porcelain plates, bowls, cups, and saucers. Strongly represented were good quality tankards, cups, saucers, and teapots in English white salt-glazed stoneware, among them a single fragment from a relief-molded "house" teapot with the English royal arms over its door. Tradition has it—probably coined by an imaginative antique dealer—that such teapots were popular gifts to the mistresses of newly built houses. Dating from the 1740s, when Mann Page II finished the mansion and married Alice Grymes, it may be no coincidence that some surviving house teapots look remarkably like Rosewell.

Although fragments of at least 351 wine bottles represented two-thirds of all the domestic vessels recovered, only one was adorned with a Page seal, that bearing the simple M:P initials Mann Page II also used as his tobacco mark. That the bottles ranged in date from around 1700 to the 1760s suggested that John Page's improvements to the basement had included clearing out an ill-kept wine cellar.

King Carter is known to have had a taste for Belgian mineral waters and, even if his Corotoman home did not inspire Mann Page I to copy its design, the family may have aped its father-in-law by developing a taste for Pyrmont Water. The seals from three different varieties of these spa water containers were found among the broken bottles.

It is not my purpose to list everything we found in the astonishingly rich Rosewell pit. Suffice it to say that the catalog runs from cuff links and cutlery to weights and wine glasses—all of it now in the collections of the Smithsonian Institution. I had gone to Rosewell to try to demonstrate to a skeptical Colonial Williamsburg that archaeology could contribute to a far wider understanding of colonial life than had hitherto been supposed. And this we did—at no cost to anybody beyond the price of the gas to get us back and forth from Williamsburg. And that, too, is a lesson taught but, alas, rarely learned.

The Rosewell project had absorbed 360 man hours of digging followed by an unrecorded number for processing, researching, and writing, but it was all freely given by people eager to learn. Today, such projects are rarely even contemplated unless backed up by grants and budgets of coffer-emptying dimensions. Meanwhile, legions of would-be volunteers wait in vain for the trained and welcoming leadership that can enable them to emulate what three eager young people accomplished all those years ago.

But even as we dug, the vandalous destruction of the Rosewell mansion went on. From our site hidden in the jungle about 190 feet from the house, we could hear the voices and the thud of brickbats hurled against its walls; yet we dared not reveal our presence. Instead, as long as the robbers were there, we spoke not a word and even used canvas instead of metal buckets to deaden the sound of dumped dirt, for had the brick-throwers known what we were doing, the excavation would have been looted before we returned. Often when the voices seemed dangerously close, work would halt altogether and, in consequence, much time was wasted. Nevertheless, Rosewell's buried treasure remained unmolested to the end.

Unfortunately, the same could not be said of the mansion. Into the 1960s the vandals continued in their assaults until most of the keystones had been knocked out. And with those gone, the brickwork between the successive window openings crumbled,

so weakening the west and north walls that both collapsed, leaving little but the corners and their stone-capped chimney stacks pointing like skeletal fingers to the sky. Nature, too, played its part, the jungle encroaching to within touching distance of the walls, and ivy swaddling the brickwork and leaching the strength from its mortar. Meanwhile architectural historians and assorted preservationists debated the question of "what to do about Rosewell" and even assigned the topic to several generations of summer students.

In 1979 Miss Nellie Deans Greaves and her brother Lieutenant Colonel Fielding Lewis Greaves deeded the ruins and the few acres surrounding it to the Gloucester Historical Society, which, 10 years later, created the Rosewell Foundation to preserve, study, and present the site to visitors. Under the vigorous leadership of the builder's descendant, Colonel Cecil Wray Page of nearby Shelly, and Gloucester resident Captain George Whiting, local volunteers devoted more than 3,000 hours to clearing the trees and underbrush so that today the red ruin rises clean and stately out of a greensward.

Advice, first from Colonial Williamsburg's renowned architectural historian, the late Paul Buchanan, and subsequently from his successor Edward Chappell, enabled the Foundation to relatively discreetly reinforce the standing masonry while embarking on a more thorough analysis of the structure than had previously been attempted. And in 1989, almost exactly 30 years after our first Rosewell excavation ended, digging resumed—using anxious-to-learn historical society volunteers under the supervision of Colonial Williamsburg's John Hamant.

Limited to test cuts close to the ruin, they soon became aware that wherever they dug, a jigsaw of rubble-strewn layers and foundations came to light, all of them significant—but significant of what? Clearly, more time was needed than John could donate, and to that end the Foundation invited Nicholas Luccketti and his James River Institute for Archaeology to take over.

In August 1990 the new team, still with local help, made the most important discovery that the site, perhaps *any* site, has yielded in recent years. Rubble thought to have come from changes to the mansion itself proved to belong to other foundations that passed at an entirely different angle beneath it. In short, Mann Page I had built his great house atop what are almost certainly the remains of Mathew Page's original Rosewell plantation—the residence reported by Robert "King" Carter on March 8, 1721, as "Colonel Cage's [sic] house" and which along with its barn "had burned to the ground."

Further archaeological testing in 1991 by University of Virginia students, seeking information about landscape and gardens that once surrounded the mansion, discovered (as had John Hamant and Nicholas Luccketti) that foundations were appearing wherever they dug—several of them oriented not to the mansion but to the plantation complex that had preceded it. Inch by inch Rosewell was revealing itself as the most complex and arguably the most important colonial archaeological site in Virginia if not in America.

The team of local enthusiasts who had rallied to assist the professionals in 1990 matured in the capable hands of Captain Whiting into a competent archaeological unit in its own right. With their help, and at the close of the American archaeological

Dave Doody

Stars streak the sky over the ruin in this moonlight time exposure. The overly large chimney caps are to preserve the crumbling stone and brickwork.

career that had begun at Rosewell (and relegated to unpaid and therefore amateur status), I returned to try to find the site of the brick-walled stable whose scattered traces we had seen 36 years earlier. This time there could be little doubt of this important building's location, although as I write in the spring of 1996, only one robbed wall line has been uncovered.

Were it not that the Rosewell Foundation desperately needs a permanent visitor center and museum building, and my belief that it can best be located behind and within the reconstructed shell of the stables, digging would have been halted until a master plan and the necessary funding can be secured to undertake a long-range research program that can thoroughly examine not only the site's archaeological history—beginning now in the late 17th century—but also carefully to reveal such charred traces of the mansion's last years that almost certainly lie under the rubble that still fills much of the interior.

Tremendous credit and gratitude is due to the dedicated preservation-conscious citizens of Gloucester County; for while experts talked, they acted, and through their intervention the mansion's future may prove as impressive as its past. Or as H. G. Wells put it: "The past is but the beginning of a beginning, and all that is and has been is but the twilight of the dawn."

On Passing the Test

by John Hamant

Audrey Baines Noël Hume, wife and colleague of Ivor Noël Hume, died August 21, 1993, in Williamsburg. She was born in Wimbledon, England. Colonial Williamsburg Director of Special Events John Hamant, a sometime associate and long-time friend, affectionately shares his memories of her.

THE FIRST time I encountered Audrey was the occasion of THE TEST. I was being considered for employment in the Colonial Williamsburg Archaeology Department. Aside from a burning desire to learn the secrets of this mystic art, my entire archaeological experience consisted of having read most of Noël's books.

Having been ushered by the secretary into a long room in which every horizontal surface was crammed with small containers in which rested the treasures of Martin's Hundred, I was told, "Sit here, and don't touch anything. Mrs. Noël Hume will be here to give you THE TEST."

Alone with my thoughts, I didn't dare imagine what THE TEST might entail. Was it written? Oral? Historical? Artifactual? What was Mrs. Noël Hume going to be like? Would she like me? Did it matter? Within moments my mind conjured up visions of every Dickensonian scene ever filmed. There was the creaking door, the forbidding presence of Edna May Oliver, who, with haughty voice inquires, "Have you come for THE TEST?" Able simply to nod, I am ushered into a dim chamber wherein capers the redoubtable Mr. Dick, skewered through and through with office pens, and bound hand and foot with red tape. . . .

The door at the end of the room opened, and in charged a small animated lady who looked for all the world like my image of Miss Marple. Rosy-cheeked with eyes full of life and humor, she approached with a small box containing about a dozen ceramic shards. "You must put these together," she said, "and I'll warn you, there is a trick. By the way, I shall be timing you." With that she presented me with the box, engaged

the stopwatch, and bustled off through another door.

I suppose Audrey didn't have much confidence in my ability to discover that the shards were from two very similar pieces, for I finished the test in short order, and after waiting several minutes, took off in search of my "monitor." Combing the labyrinth of the archaeology lab, I found her in the midst of high drama—the removal of the first Wolstenholme helmet from its plaster shroud. Suddenly noting my presence,

Ivor Noël Hume

Audrey at Rosewell with Churchy (who preceded Willie and Tail) in the summer of 1957.

she glanced at the stop watch, raised her eyebrows to an amazing height, and said, "You have done very well."

For the next 16 years I had the tremendous good fortune of having Audrey in my life as teacher and friend. She was, after all, a private person who seldom took the time to suffer fools gladly. Looking back, I realize how

lucky I was to have been given the gift of her friendship.

Audrey had an incredible enthusiasm for everything in life. She never simply read, researched, cataloged, gardened, or even shopped—she took on each of those tasks with a will. Over the years I would bring her artifacts for identification. Whether it was on the site or through her partly open office door (with Willie, and later Tail, attempting to gnaw at my leg), her response was always, "Oh, isn't that a nice piece," after which she would tell me at length about the whole object, where and how it was made, and its importance to the interpretation of the site.

She was one of the most selfless and giving people I have, thus far, encountered. Audrey never sought the limelight. Her joy came from working quietly behind the scenes to unearth some new fact, improve the management of the collections, and track the millions of bits of information that brought color to our images of the past. There are many of us who have played major roles in the sweeping drama of bringing the past to life; trodding the boards to present our story to the public. None can deny that our efforts have met with fruition, but most of our success hinged on one important fact—we had Audrey as our stage manager.

She managed, somehow, to keep us on track with her razorlike wit, boundless generosity, and insistence upon attention to detail. She encouraged us by her enthusiasm and gave us comfort through her devotion and commitment to those she loved. She gave us guidance through her belief that one's value is measured in what is given, not in what is received.

I learned much from Audrey. Certainly I learned enough about material culture to develop from inexperienced excavator to senior archaeologist, but the lessons she taught about life were of much greater value toward the making of a decent and civilized person.

I pray that, with Audrey's help, I will pass the test.